D0081506

Unionism in baseball and player-management showdowns are not new phenomena introduced to the world in the 1960's by Marvin Miller and the Major League Baseball Players Association. James B. Dworkin describes the origins of baseball's labor-management confrontation in the late 19th century when players, rebelling against increasingly stringent reserve clauses and maximum salary rules, formed their own league in direct competition with the National League. The result of that struggle is just one of the many fascinating developments chronicled in this colorful study of baseball unionism. Others include:

- rebel and rival leagues;
- walkouts and blacklists;
- grievances and arbitration;
- pensions and pay;
- court decisions, appeals, and reversals; and
- the landmark cases of Curt Flood and Messersmith/McNally.

From the reserve clause of 1879 to the free agency of 1981, James B. Dworkin covers all the events and people that have impacted today's owner-player relations. In clear, everyday language he explains and analyzes the Major League Baseball Rules, Uniform Player Contracts, and landmark Court Decisions so that the reader can understand and appreciate the complexities underlying player-owner discord today.

OWNERS VERSUS PLAYERS

OWNERS
VERSUS
PLAYERS

Baseball and Collective Bargaining

JAMES B. DWORKIN
Purdue University

 Auburn House Publishing Company
Boston, Massachusetts

Library of Congress Cataloging in Publication Data
Dworkin, James B. 1948–.
    Owners versus players.

    Includes Index.
    1. Trade-unions—Baseball players—United States—
History. I. Title.
GV880.2.D86   331.89′041796357′0973   81-3472
ISBN 0-86569-072-3   AACR2

Printed in the United States of America

To my wife Nancy,
who is *my* best friend.

PREFACE

In the latter part of the nineteenth century, it was customary for professional baseball players to engage in a process called "revolving" at the termination of each season. In simplest terms, this involved signing a contract to play baseball for the upcoming season with the highest bidding club. Of course, this might be the player's current club, but often players could earn more money by signing with another team in their league.

The players were quite happy with this competitive labor market situation, which allowed them to realize the highest possible wages for their admittedly short careers. The owners, on the other hand, became increasingly wary of this system because it led to higher salaries, more player bargaining power, and often the loss of a particularly popular player to another team.

Thus, around 1880, the owners collectively decided that they had to take corrective action for the good of the game and the fans. The action they took was the implementation of the now famous "reserve clause" which later became a part of every player's standard contractual agreement. This clause gave the player's current club a perpetual option on the player's services. A player could no longer revolve to a team wishing to pay him a higher salary. The reserve clause essentially meant that players were owned by the team they had signed their original contract with for as long as they remained in baseball. Of course, there was nothing to prevent a dissatisfied player from pursuing another career if he so chose. Also, teams could choose to trade or release players, but even in these cases the player would then become bound to whatever new team he eventually signed with.

The abolishment of "revolving" (what we now term "free agency") was undoubtedly the most important catalyst in turning the thoughts of the players to unionization and collective bargaining in an attempt to preserve, codify, or regain some of their former freedom. This book is about these unionization attempts on the part of the players, their failures and successes, and their impacts on the game of baseball as we know it today.

The initial chapter examines the various predecessors to the modern-day players union, the Major League Baseball Players Association (MLBPA). It is important to understand the motivation behind ballplayers' early attempts at organizing and the extent to which they have affected the development of modern unionism in baseball. A key issue in this and later chapters is a thorough exploration of the "whys" of unionism: Why do workers join unions? And, in particular, why do professional baseball players join unions?

While the first chapter deals with associations that are now extinct, Chapter 2 is devoted to the union that has represented professional baseball players since 1954, the MLBPA. After four previous failures, why did this fifth attempt prove so robust and successful? An extensive examination of the differences between the MLBPA and its forerunners is presented to convey an understanding of the various internal and environmental factors that determined this union's success.

In Chapters 3 through 5, the major impacts of collective bargaining on the game of baseball are reviewed. Entire chapters are reserved for two crucial areas—the elimination of the perpetual reserve clause and the increase in player bargaining power brought on by the adoption of final-offer salary arbitration beginning with the 1974 championship season. In each of these chapters, I have relied heavily on my previous theoretical and empirical research to add a different dimension to the typical legal and descriptive treatments of these subjects. For the interested reader, more technical material is reserved for appendices at the conclusion of each of these chapters. I have tried to write the body of the text in non-technical language so that the main thrust of the arguments can be readily understood by someone who does not wish to delve into the more technical material. Chapter 5 contains a descriptive treatment of the many other changes in the employment relationship that have been brought about by the advent of collective bargaining, including increases in the minimum wage, improved pensions, and fairer scheduling.

The book would not be complete without some treatment of the other major sports that have witnessed transitions to unionism similar to baseball's. In Chapter 6, I compare and contrast the developments in baseball with those in basketball, football, and hockey in several key areas of player concern. Additionally, the upsurge of unionism and strikes that we have recently witnessed among sports officials in baseball and basketball is reviewed, and its significance for the future of professional sports is considered. An explanation of why baseball and basketball officials are unionized, while their counterparts in football and hockey are not, is developed.

The concluding chapter deals with several larger issues such as the overall impacts of player unionism and the future of the game of baseball itself. Several predictions for baseball and unionized ballplayers are culled out of the analyses presented in the earlier chapters.

It is my hope that the readers of this book will develop an appreciation for and understanding of the workings of industrial and labor-management relations in a unique industry in the American economy—professional baseball. And if that interest can manifest itself in a renewed effort aimed at serious, scientific research concerned with any of a number of the key issues raised in this book, my modest goals will certainly have been exceeded. The application of science and the scientific method of research to foster improved labor-management relations in all sectors of our economy must certainly be one of the most important tasks we face in the remaining two decades of the twentieth century.

JAMES B. DWORKIN
West Lafayette, Indiana

CONTENTS

Chapter 1

UNIONIZATION OF PROFESSIONAL BASEBALL PLAYERS, 1885–1954

In baseball as well as in any other industry, the study of labor relations entails a careful, analytical treatment of the employment relationship. Several sets of questions must be answered before we can truly understand the development of organized labor in general, or in a particular case, such as baseball. As former Secretary of Labor John Dunlop has noted: "The facts do not tell their own story; they must be cross-examined. They must be carefully analyzed, systematized, compared and interpreted."[1] All too frequently, scholars have chosen to separate descriptive, historical treatments of the labor movement from theoretical work. But history and theory need not be so distant. Indeed, collections and sequences of facts can be more meaningful when treated in a theoretical context. Thus, it is one goal of this text to blend historical, theoretical, and empirical analyses in order to present a more complete treatment of the development of unionization in baseball.

Development of the U.S. Labor Movement

Four questions have been at the forefront of concern in the literature seeking to explain the development of the labor movement in the United States. These same four questions are crucial in examining any particular industrial relations setting such as baseball.[2]

1. How is one to account for the origin or emergence of labor organizations? What conditions are necessary and what circumstances

1

stimulate the precipitation of labor organization? Why have some workers organized and others not?

2. What explains the patterns of growth and development of labor organizations? What factors are responsible for the sequence and form in which organizations have emerged in various countries, industries, crafts, and companies? Since there is great diversity in the patterns of development, any theory of the labor movement must account for these differences.

3. What are the ultimate goals of the labor movement? What is the relationship to the future of capitalism? What is its role in the socialist and communist state?

4. Why do individual workers join labor organizations? What system of social psychology accounts for this behavior of the employee?

While it is obvious that all of the above queries do not apply directly to the unionization of professional baseball players, the major thrust of each question is an important one for our analysis. Thus, in this and in succeeding chapters, such fundamental questions as:

1. Why did unions of baseball players emerge in the first place?
2. How did these unions grow and develop? What were their patterns of success and failure?
3. What were the goals of these unions in baseball?
4. Why do individual ballplayers choose to form and join unions?

will be answered using the blend of historical, theoretical and empirical analyses alluded to earlier.

A recent review article by Thomas Kochan echoes the above sentiment where he states that[3] "A comprehensive model of the behavior of unions as organizations must therefore address at least the following questions or issues: (1) Why do individuals join unions? (2) What factors influence trade union growth? (3) What influences the goals of trade unions? (4) What influences the internal structure of unions? (5) What influences the internal democracy of unions? (6) What influences the organizational effectiveness of unions?"

Thus, industrial and labor relations is concerned with the study of employment relations in industry, that is, the study of people at work. Translated to the baseball setting, it is the study of the employment relationship that has developed between club owners and individual ballplayers and their unions. In the preceding paragraphs, I have described the major questions that must be answered if we are to have a better understanding of industrial relations in the baseball industry. It is to an examination of these issues from the middle 1880s through 1954 that we now turn our attention.

Conditions Leading to Unionization

Perhaps the most crucial of the Dunlop and Kochan questions regarding the development of labor organizations in the United States and in the world is why individual workers choose to join unions. Theory suggests that people join unions when they perceive a need for this type of collective action to protect their individual and group interests. It also suggests that the intention to unionize is strongly related to the actions of management, or the "institutional response" as it has been termed by Freeman and Medoff, among others.[4]

Before we delve specifically into the baseball industry, let's take a look at what we know about the theory of why workers join unions. These insights will prove useful in guiding our discussion of the various attempts to unionize professional baseball players that will be described later in this chapter.

Early Views of Labor

The role of work itself has undergone major changes throughout the history of civilized societies. The early Greeks viewed work as an extreme form of drudgery to be reserved for the very lowest of social classes.[5] Leisure was viewed as the way to a fulfilled life and was usually reserved for the upper classes. Of course, any attempt at unionization among the lower classes was likely to be met with the harshest of consequences. These attitudes changed considerably with the advent of Christianity. Various religious scholars described the virtues of work for the soul and indeed, for the accomplishment of a "full life."[6]

At the same time that religious scholars were extolling the virtues of work, the rise of the industrial revolution led many classical economists to analyze the functions that labor serves in a modern society. These writers viewed labor as a factor of production (a commodity) to be treated just like any other factor in the production process. Natural laws of economics tended to shape the conditions under which labor and management interacted.[7] Since labor was subject to these natural forces of supply and demand much as were capital and land, these economists felt little need for the development of a special branch of their discipline to study the role of people at work. Indeed, the forces of the market were available to shape the best interests of the largest numbers of workers in society. Workers who were unsatisfied with their current conditions were free to use the power of their *exit voice*,[8] that is, to move on to another job where they could find conditions more to their liking. These economists felt that the "invisible hand" of the competitive market would work in the best interests of all in society and that unions were unnecessary evils that just served to obstruct the smooth and efficient operation of the competitive system.

However, over time other groups of writers challenged the deductive, theoretical notions of the classical economists. Their most pressing criticism of this former group of writers was their inability to see that labor as a *commodity* could not be separated out from the labor of a *human being* with all of the normal human wants, needs, and desires. Writers like Karl Marx[9] emphasized the role of trade unions as serving in the vanguard of the movement toward the eventual overthrow of the capitalistic system. He stressed that workers would not remain passive under onerous conditions but would rise up in mass to form unions to represent the "proletariat" in their dealings with management and the government. These unions would exist only so long as was necessary to achieve their desired social reforms. They would then fade away as they would serve no further useful purpose in a socialistic (Marxist) society.

Additionally, some economists finally began to challenge the writings of their predecessors.[10] A new branch of the discipline known as *institutional economics* was developed around the beginning of the twentieth century in which the classical notion of viewing labor as a commodity was simply rejected. Institutional writers such as the Webbs, Richard Ely, and John R. Commons[11] shifted their emphasis in the study of labor from ". . . commodities, individuals and exchanges to transactions and the working rules of collective action."[12] They were highly critical of the deductive reasoning of the classicists. Instead, they favored an inductive look at the facts in their attempts to explain the relationship(s) among sets of observed phenomena in the real world. They believed strongly in the principles of free trade unionism and collective bargaining. It was this *normative* framework that was to a good deal responsible for later changes in attitudes of the public, courts, and legislatures towards the rights of workers to form free trade unions. Additionally, they strongly favored empirical analyses to go along with their inductive lines of reasoning, in spite of the popular misconception equating institutionalism with "thick" description, devoid of much analysis.[13] Of course, the institutionalists were hampered in their efforts to quantify things by the lack of modern computational facilities.

Why Workers Join Unions

The successors to the institutional economists developed clear theoretical notions as to why workers join unions. In a now famous article on this subject, E. Wright Bakke succinctly summarizes why some workers join unions while others do not.[14]

> *The worker reacts favorably to union membership in proportion to the strength of his belief that this step will reduce his frustrations and anxieties and will further his opportunities relevant to the achievement of his standards of successful living. He reacts unfavorably in proportion to the strength of his belief that this step will increase his frustrations and anxieties and will reduce his opportunities relevant to the achievement of such standards.*

Based on extensive interviews with both workers who joined and those who refused to join unions during a number of organizational campaigns, Bakke identified five worker *goals* which were related to his hypothesis about workers' propensities to join unions. These five goals were:[15]

1. *The society and respect of others.*
2. *The degree of creature comforts and economic security possessed by the most favored of his customary associates.*
3. *Independence in and control over his own affairs.*
4. *Understanding of the forces and factors at work in his world.*
5. *Integrity.*

In essence, what Bakke told us nearly forty years ago was that workers join unions for several reasons, which can be summarized by the following hypotheses:

1. Workers who feel deprived, downtrodden, and inferior socially will be more likely to join unions.
2. Workers who have lower wages and less pleasant working conditions than their counterparts or "comparative others" will be more likely to join unions.
3. Workers in jobs which are mundane, boring, nonchallenging, and heavily supervised will be more likely to join unions.
4. Workers who feel that they lack both an understanding of the

forces that shape their employment relationship and a means
to communicate their desires to management will be more
likely to join unions.
5. Workers who feel that they lack self-respect, fairness in the
   employment relationship, and a sense of justice in what hap-
   pens to them in their world of work will be more likely to join
   unions.

These important findings of Bakke have been fortified by a
number of other theorists in the field. For instance, Seidman, London, and Karsh[16] concluded after an intensive series of interviews
with the leadership and active and inactive members of one large,
militant Steelworker's local that there are ". . . a wide variety of
reasons why workers become union members . . . may join a local
when they are enthusiastic about unionism, when they are moderately interested, wholly indifferent, or even opposed."[17] Among the
independent factors cited in workers' decision processes regarding
whether to join a union or not were family union background, work
and/or union experience, experiences within the plant, informal
group pressure, and being forced to join.

In another but similar study, William F. Whyte spent five months
as a participant observer in an oil company during the time of a
C.I.O. organizing drive during the early 1940s. His goal was to
identify the factors that led to the development of three groups of
worker attitudes toward the union, which he classified as:[18]

1. Strong anti-union.
2. Fence-sitters.
3. Strong pro-union.

It is interesting to note that the factors identified in his study very
closely resemble those mentioned above in the Bakke and Seidman *et al.* works. While the union lost in a very close election,
one of Whyte's conclusions seems especially relevant today. He
found that most workers make up their minds early in an election
campaign and that only a relatively small percentage of the workers
are fence-sitters. In other words, because of the various factors mentioned earlier, most workers have already made up their minds as to
whether to vote for a union or not. All of the campaigning that goes
on prior to an election is aimed at a very small group of employees,
the fence-sitters, the only ones who might possibly be influenced by

union or management rhetoric. The close resemblance between Whyte's findings in the early 1940s and those of Getman, Goldberg, and Herman[19] in the 1970s is indeed testimony to the fact that we are beginning to understand the motivating factors behind the decision to unionize or not.

In recent years, theoreticians from several disciplines have attempted to extend the basic case study/interview methodologies of earlier writers in an attempt to test their theories using more modern analytical techniques. Examples of such studies include the works of Schriescheim,[20] Hamner and Smith,[21] and Farber and Saks.[22] While their analyses and interpretations are based on widely disparate academic origins, all of these newer theoretical/empirical studies conclude that the institutional writers such as Bakke were *correct*. That is, workers do join unions in those instances where the perceived benefits from organization exceed the perceived costs. While one could develop a lengthy list of factors that enter into these benefit/cost calculations, it seems that a simple three-way classification, as used by Farber and Saks, is most efficient. These authors summarize the causal factors in the go/no go decision as being:[23]

1. Wage-related.
2. Nonwage-related.
3. Individual.

In other words, some workers join unions because unions can secure higher wages[24] and a fringe benefit package more in line with their desires and needs.[25] Other workers may join because of poor supervisory subordinate relationships, feelings of unfair or inequitable treatment, or feelings that they have no chances to be promoted. And even after considering all of these very important *wage* and *nonwage* factors related to the decision to unionize, there are still *individual difference* variables such as age, sex, race, education, and the like, which may have independent and statistically significant impacts on the decision to unionize or not.

Thus, the question of why workers unionize does not lend itself to a simple, unicausal explanation. Instead, the decision to unionize or not is often based on a whole host of factors that may act independently or combine interactively in the individual's decision-making process. With this mixture of simple truths and complexities in mind, we now turn our attention to applying some of the above analyses to the setting of professional baseball.

Unionism and Baseball

Why would a baseball player, one who *plays a game* to earn his living, ever feel the need to join forces with his fellow players to bargain collectively? After all, baseball players have the easy life. They are well paid, have great working conditions, are adored by the fans and admired by the public at large, and most importantly, they are doing something they love. They are, after all, *playing a game!* They must be the most contented and well satisfied of all workers, not to mention all athletes. Or are they?

Why *did* baseball players turn to unions and collective bargaining? What factors, either individual or environmental, led them to decide to try group pressure rather than to continue the individual bargaining between player and team that had been a hallmark from the past? What aspects of the *adversarial relationship*[26] between player and club were highlighted in the drives to unionize? How did this begin?

The average man on the street, if queried, would probably guess that the roots of unionism in professional baseball were rather short. In fact, the vision of unionism in baseball beginning with Marvin Miller and the Major League Baseball Players Association is not an uncommon one. And certainly, the MLBPA has been by far the most successful of the reported unionization moves.

But the MLBPA actually represents the *fifth* organization that has developed over time to represent the collective interests of the professional ballplayer. Each of the prior four associations will be discussed in turn with emphasis placed on why each organization emerged, the successes and failures of the organization, and the reasons for the eventual demise of each of these unions.

The National Brotherhood of Professional Baseball Players, 1885–1890

Early in the history of professional baseball, when there was just one league (the National League), it was quite customary for players to switch teams at will. Of course, once signed for a particular season a player had to honor his contract unless he was traded or given an outright release. Multi-year pacts were uncommon, and at the termination of each season, the open competitive market operated at its best. Players were completely free to sign with whatever team they wished, assuming that this team was also interested in the players' services. In the terminology of today, the players enjoyed the perfect freedom of *free agency* and, in fact, this system of the mid-1800s was much more competitive than the system that exists today. While today's ballplayer must wait for six years before becoming a free agent, the stars and no-names of yesteryear were eligible to sign with any team in the league after the completion of *each* and *every* season.

Naturally, given the economic nature of humans to rise to the highest possible level, this system was much to the players' liking, as it allowed them to increase their salaries either with their previous team or by signing with a new team. Players realized that performance was crucial and that they could get more if they had a good season and held out for what they thought they were worth. Whatever the undesirable consequences of being a ballplayer might have been during these early years (including such things as poor playing and travel conditions), they were undoubtedly outweighed by this system of free agency that existed at the time.

However, the revolving that went on during each off season was not without its own undesirable consequences for the team owners. First and foremost, revolving was responsible for higher and higher salaries in baseball. Teams were afraid of losing star players to their competitors and thus, bidding wars ensued. These bidding wars exemplified the favorable bargaining power position the players were in due to the competitive free agent market. In addition to salaries, owners were worried about fan interest and enthusiasm. Fans purchasing tickets constituted the major source of revenue for clubs, and the thought of their becoming disenchanted with the home team because one or more favorites had been bid away by another franchise was enough to make the owners very nervous. If they couldn't let a player go, this meant they had to at least match the price offered by other teams. But the other teams also had the incentive to keep bidding prices up in order to sign the star ballplayers. And a player's worth to one team might far exceed his value to another team in a much smaller city. In general, management in professional baseball began to view this system of revolving as inimical to their control and operation of the sport. Just as management in other industries fights to retain unilateral control over such employment decisions as who to hire, what to pay, and what type of product to produce (the doctrine of managerial rights or prerogatives), the club owners in baseball feared the loss of control over their operations to the players. The loss of unilateral decision-making power in the area of player salaries, if extended to other areas of day-to-day operations, could prove financially crushing to the owners.

The Reserve Rule.   The stage was set for the owners to take some drastic action to curtail revolving. This action took place on September 30, 1879, at a secret meeting of a high-ranking group of National League officials. As first adopted to begin in 1880, the *reserve rule* allowed each club to protect five players from raiding by the other teams. Now five players may not seem like a lot out of a complete baseball team roster, but just consider how many teams today have five bona fide star players who would be hot prospects on the open market. Couple this with the fact that in the early days of baseball, rosters were nowhere near the twenty-five player limits that we see today, and it becomes apparent that the owners had put a significant impediment on the free operation of the baseball player's labor market into place. It was clearly hoped that this reserve rule would have the effect of holding down player salaries by preventing the reserved players from accepting higher offers from other teams. Even if other teams would be willing to pay a reserved player a higher wage, there was clearly no necessity for the current team to do so. For other teams to contact a reserved player was a violation known as tampering. The only thing the current team had to consider in deciding to pay a reserved player less than he was worth on the open market was the effect that this lower wage might have on the player's overall performance on the field. Thus, this morale factor might suggest that owners would pay players some higher wage rate but still less than that they could have obtained under the former free market system.

The reserve rule was amended in 1883 to increase the number of reserved players to eleven, again in 1887 to increase the number of reserved players to 14, and soon after, the reserve rule applied to every player on every team.[27] In essence, each year when a player signed his standard player contract, the terms included the so-called "reserve rule," which bound him to that team for the next season as well. And when next season's contract was signed, a similar clause applied to the following season. It is easy to see how the owners felt that they owned each of their ballplayers into perpetuity, a subject which will be discussed in much more depth in Chapter 3.[28]

Understandably, the players reacted to this important change in the conditions of their employment with some hostility. Used to freedom of movement among teams, the players did not accept lightly being the property of any one team for life. The first union of professional ballplayers, the National Brotherhood of Professional Ball Players, was formed in 1885 in order to air some of the players' dissatisfactions with their employment conditions. Under the leadership of Billy Voltz, this association at first existed, as many unions do, for fraternal purposes. No attempts at collective bargaining were made until the reserve rule changes came into effect along with a rule setting a *maximum* salary of $2,000 per season.[29] John Montgomery Ward, the first ballplayer president of this union, stated the goals of the association to be "To protect and benefit ourselves collectively and individually. To promote a high standard of professional conduct. To foster and encourage the interests of . . . Base Ball."[30]

The association was a secret one until 1886 when Ward allowed the news of the union's existence and goals to be leaked to a leading sports newspaper of that era. Along with their dissatisfaction over the maximum salary and reserve rules, the players also disliked being sold from one team to another when they did not get a share of the purchase price and the blacklisting of ballplayers who were termed troublemakers (often strong union sympathizers) by the League.

The Players League. Over the next couple of years the battle lines were drawn for what was to be the big showdown of the season of 1890, when the rebellious players decided that they would form their own League (The Players League) in direct competition to the National League. The players chose to establish teams in the same cities with similar home schedules so as to force the fans to make the ultimate choice of which was the preferred league. In this way the players hoped to force the National League into some sort of a compromise arrangement with them by which all parties could prosper.

Unfortunately for the players, the National League was not about to buckle under due to this new threat. They passed a resolution calling for the prosecution of all players who had jumped leagues in violation of the reserve rule in their contracts. The new league's leaders were denounced as "hot headed anarchists . . . long chance capitalists whose only possible interest . . . is the amount of money they hope to realize out of it."[31] Such propaganda was focused on the fans, who were after all to be the ultimate arbiter of the dispute. The National League bribed several star players to return and these

individuals were quickly branded as "scabs" to the union movement
in baseball.

Neither league fared well financially during the 1890 season. Estimates of their losses hovered around $300,000 for the season.[32] In
the final analysis, the Players League outdrew the National League
for the season by well over 150,000 fans, 980,887 to 813,678.[33]

Despite this apparent victory, the existence of the Players League
was in extreme jeopardy. Financiers of the operations were convinced that baseball could not exist with two leagues. Therefore,
some sort of a compromise solution had to be reached. A meeting
between officials of both leagues followed the completion of the
regular season, signaling the end of both the Players League and the
National Brotherhood as the National League assured players of no
reprisals and fairer employment conditions, including a revision in
the reserve clause to change it into an "option to renew" clause.

The two leagues compromised on a proposal that would merge the
better of their teams and establish fairer employment practices.
However, the latter condition was to prove quite elusive. John
Montgomery Ward had tried and failed, yet both he and the National League officials knew that other attempts at unionization to
increase player power would probably follow. As theory would
suggest, players had organized because of their dissatisfaction with
salary and nonsalary components of their employment conditions.
This is a pattern that we shall see time and time again. And we have
also seen how the owners unified in a solid front to combat effectively the players' attempt to wrest power from their grasp. It is clear
that Ward had learned that "baseball is a business, not merely a
sport."[34] It is instructive to keep this quotation in mind and see how
differently the Supreme Court of the United States would feel on
the very same issue some thirty years later when ruling on the
applicability of our nation's antitrust laws to the game of baseball.

The League Protective Players' Association, 1900–1902

The second experiment with the unionization of professional
ballplayers occurred some ten seasons later, in the year 1900. The
League Protective Players' Association was to be the second
shortest-lived of all the unionization attempts, lasting but a brief two
years. In order to understand the motivation behind this union, it is
important to review both the employment conditions within the

National League and the role played by the "rebel" American League around the turn of the century.

As far as working conditions were concerned, things had not changed much since the previous unionization drive some ten years earlier. Maximum salaries were now at $2,400 per season; clubs were free to pay players whatever minimum figure they could. Additionally, players were forced to purchase their own uniforms, suffer through poor travel conditions and hotel accommodations, and dress in poorly lighted and ventilated clubhouses. Finally, the reserve rule applied to every player on every team in the National League. Despite these conditions, there was little that the professional ballplayer could do on an individual basis to improve his lot. Once again, the ballplayers turned to unionization in an attempt to redress some of their grievances. And once again, it was the presence of a rival league which proved to be a most important catalyst to the players' efforts.

The American League.   This rival league, known as the American League, was organized by Clark Griffith, who was later to become the owner of the Washington Senators. At the time of the new league's formation, Griffith was a pitcher for the Chicago Cubs of the National League, as well as being an officer in the Players' Association.

After the 1900 season, several leaders of the American League tried to persuade Griffith and other players to "jump" to their league, stressing the fact that they would no longer have to play under the oppressive conditions that existed in the National League. It is important to remember that while the reserve rule and other employment conditions such as maximum salary schedules were enforceable among all National League teams, these rules had *no bearing* on the conduct of teams in the upstart American League. Higher salaries could be paid, and most importantly, players were not bound to the reserve clause terms. If they desired to remain in the National League, they were, of course, bound to the team which currently held their contract. However, these National League rules *could not* prevent them from jumping to the rival American League for better salaries and working conditions, and many of the best ballplayers did just that.

In essence, the new league breathed life into the players' union, as it provided them with some bargaining clout that they previously has not possessed. Put very simply, the National League owners were susceptible to being whipsawed by the union in order to try to stop players from jumping leagues. The stage was set for one of two events to occur. First, the union stood to achieve some real gains from the National League owners if it could guarantee that players would remain with their teams *in the National League*. This tradeoff was likely to provide benefits to both sides. Alternatively, if the union could not prevent league-jumping, there was the strong possibility of another rival league "shoot-out" like that witnessed during the 1890 season, with a high probability of some type of compromise solution being reached shortly thereafter.

Late in the summer of 1900, the union called a meeting at which terms were drawn up to present to officials of the National League regarding improved employment conditions. The major demands included a $3,000 *minimum* salary and free uniforms. When presented with these demands, Arthur Soden, then president of the Boston National League team, replied, "Gentlemen, we will file your demands and consider them before this meeting is finished."[35]

But these demands were never discussed. Angered by this rebuke, the players' union, headed by Griffith, recruited a long list of established players to play with the rival American League during the playing season of 1901. Seeing that the union indeed was serious, the National League finally did make several concessions to the union in an exchange for the promise of no league jumping. However, the union could not prevent players from being enticed by the decidedly higher salaries being offered by the American League. The failure to prevent players from jumping leagues was to be the death knell for the League Protective Players' Association. Had they been able to solve this one complex problem, their union may have prospered and, indeed, may have existed to this date. Additionally, if the union had succeeded in halting league-jumping, it could be argued that the American League would have soon faltered and never risen to the level of prominence it enjoys today.

Since the union could not enforce the reserve clause in individual player's contracts, the National League had no choice but to recognize the junior circuit, which they did in the year 1903. By this time, there was no longer a need for the players' union and indeed, the players ignored their association to the extent that it soon disappeared from the baseball scene.

Baseball had returned to a period of relative tranquillity. Management again was in complete command, not in one league, but in two, operating side by side. The executives of these two leagues realized the importance of preserving their unilateral decision making powers in all areas of the game's operation, including employment conditions offered to the players. While some minor concessions were made to the players, the hallmarks of the previous era—the now infamous reserve clause and the low salaries it brought about—remained intact. The period of tranquillity was to be short-lived, as players soon united again, rallying around the same basic set of issues.

The Baseball Players' Fraternity, 1912–1918

After another lapse of ten years, baseball players again turned to unionism in the year 1912. This new union was organized by a former ballplayer, David Fultz, who was a practicing attorney at the time of the union's formation.

The "Ty Cobb" Strike. One reason for the development of the *Baseball Players' Fraternity* was no doubt the so-called "Ty Cobb" strike, which occurred in the spring of 1912. The incident revolved around Cobb and a New York reporter by the name of Claude Lueker, who continuously and unmercifully heckled Cobb whenever the visiting Detroit Tigers played in New York. At one point, Cobb reportedly heard Lueker yell; "Hey Cobb, you're nothin' but a yellow-bellied bastard!"[36]

As the story goes, Cobb was infuriated by these continuing insults. After the Detroit side had been put out, instead of returning to his outfield position, Cobb jumped into the stands, advanced on Lueker, and proceeded to punch the daylights out of him. Lueker later told police: "He hit me in the face with his fists, knocked me down, jumped on me and kicked me in the ear."[37]

> *The New York fans were so amazed and startled that nobody moved a muscle until Cobb had finished with Lueker. Nobody could believe what they had just seen. No ballplayer had ever dared hop into the stands that way. As Cobb finished, they began to rise in rage. Ty had to fight his way back down to the playing field. All his teammates, led by Wahoo Sam Crawford, stood along the field brandishing bats. They were certain the fans would storm on the field and mob Cobb. They almost did.*[38]

For his actions, Cobb was indefinitely suspended by the American League President Ban Johnson. The Detroit players rallied around Cobb, not so much because they loved and admired him, but because to a man they realized the importance of his presence to the fortunes of their club. The Detroit teammates of Cobb called a strike for May 18, 1912, in sympathy to Cobb: The first baseball strike was broken by a bunch of hastily recruited strike-breakers from the Philadelphia area (where the Tigers were scheduled to play). These "scab" Tigers lost to the Philadelphia team by the score of 24–2. A second game was called off by the League President, who also threatened the striking players with huge fines and banishment from the game if they would not return to work. Cobb appealed to his teammates to resume play. They did, and Cobb was reinstated following a ten-day suspension and the payment of a small fine. Each ballplayer who had engaged in the strike action of May 18 was also fined for his behavior.

Given this sequence of events, it wasn't difficult for the leading players of the day to convince their peers that some form of a player association was indeed a necessity. As in the past, working conditions were particularly bad, and of course the owners were still using the reserve rule to their benefit.

The players' union even applied to Samuel Gompers, founder and first President of the American Federation of Labor, for affiliation and chartered status in the formal American labor movement. Gompers, however, denied their request saying that the baseball players as a group did not have the same interests and goals as did the bulk of craft-worker organizations in America. It is interesting to note that the modern-day successor of this union is affiliated with the AFL-CIO, as are several other unions that represent professional athletes.

The Federal League.   While the new union received little attention from the owners or fans at first, except for in a few cases like the much-publicized Ty Cobb strike of 1912 and his contract negotiations and eventual holdout for part of the 1913 season, the formation of a third league in 1914 changed this situation drastically.

Just as had been the case in two earlier unionization attempts, this rival Federal League forced the owners to think seriously about the players' union and the players' collective demands. The players once again had an important bargaining chip which could be either used wisely or foolishly gambled away.

Immediately, the National and American Leagues agreed to recognize the players' union, in the hopes of enticing players to honor their reserve clauses and refrain from jumping to the Federal League, whose teams were offering substantially better salaries and working conditions. But as had occurred ten years earlier, this union was also unable to force players to remain within their current leagues. Thus, the union took no position either way in the Federal League war.

The one major reform the Baseball Players' Fraternity was able to extract from the league owners dealt with limiting the assignment of major league players with 10 years or more experience to a minor league club without their consent. This idea later evolved into the "waiver rule," which states that no player could be sent to a club of lower classification until clubs of the same classification as his old club were first given an opportunity to acquire the player's services. Of course, this rule still is in existence today in a modified form.

The Federal League died out late in 1915, returning baseball to its former two-league status. Feeling that the union no longer served any useful purpose, individual players neglected to pay their dues and completely lost interest in the union. Several attempts were made to salvage this union, but none was successful, and the Baseball Players' Fraternity faded into history in 1918.

As we have seen with two previous unionization attempts, the aftermath of this third union again produced no radical changes in the game's employment conditions. The reserve clause was to live on for many, many more years. And by now, it is fair to guess that this clause and other equally distasteful employment conditions would again cause players to unite to form unions and attempt to bargain collectively with the club owners. The only uncertainty was *when* this would occur.

The American Baseball Guild, 1946

Twenty-eight years were to pass before baseball players again would form a union and seek to force management to bargain collectively with them over such issues as minimum salaries and conditions of employment. But before speaking specifically about the American Baseball Guild, it is instructive to review briefly the major events of this interim period, which, of course, included two major world wars.

From the players' standpoint, no major improvements in conditions of employment were enacted. During the First World War, with attendance poor and ticket prices slashed, the players threatened to strike the 1918 World Series in a dispute over the distribution of the pool of money. But this strike never materialized, and the fall classic went on as usual. During the reign of Commissioner Judge Kenesaw Mountain Landis, organized baseball thrived during the period between the two world wars. There were two attempts at unionizing ballplayers (one in the 1920s and the other in the late 1930s), but both failed for lack of interest on the part of the players and due to the iron rule of Judge Landis. Ray Cannon, the man who led both of these aborted unionization drives, is also credited with initiating legislation (as a Congressman from Wisconsin) that would have led to an antitrust examination of organized baseball as a monopoly in violation of the Sherman Act of 1890.[39] In this aborted legislative attempt, Cannon was, of course, referring to the famous Supreme Court case of *Federal Baseball Club* v. *National League*,[40] in which organized baseball was declared to be a game and not a business, thereby granting this industry total immunity from our nation's antitrust laws. This immunity still is in effect today, as even in recent court cases, judges have based their rulings on this critical Supreme Court decision. Since this decision would affect the legality of baseball's reserve rule, a complete treatment of the case and its impact will be reserved for Chapter 3. Suffice it for now to note that this position of immunity from the nation's antitrust laws has had a major impact on the game of baseball and indeed, on the labor-management relationship that has evolved ever since.

Birth of the Guild.   With the added leverage granted them by this Supreme Court decision, baseball's magnates were in a more enviable and powerful position than ever. In fact, it wasn't until April 16, 1946 that baseball's fourth union was born in Boston.[41] Organized by a lawyer named Robert Murphy, the Guild was supposed to be attractive to all ballplayers in that it would be able to redress their major grievances of the past fifty years. Among the items high on the Guild's list for collective negotiations were:

1. Putting an end to the hated reserve clause.
2. Arbitration over salaries and all other player-owner disputes.
3. Guaranteeing players a share in their purchase price.
4. The institution of Spring Training pay.
5. A minimum salary of $7,500 per season.[42]
6. A more equitable contractual arrangement than the one used currently, where owners could cancel contracts on ten days' notice while dissatisfied players had no similar mechanism that they could employ.[43]

Spurred on by increasing player interest and the passage of the pro-labor National Labor Relations Act of 1935, Murphy decided to choose the strong labor town of Pittsburgh in which to take action. It is also important to note that again, at the time of the formation of the Guild, organized baseball was being threatened by a rival league, the so-called Mexican League. Although there were no formal ties between this rival league and the players' union, as in situations described earlier in the chapter, the fact that the magnates of baseball were facing two serious and simultaneous challenges to the basic fiber of their sport is significant.

Murphy, commenting on the significance of the passage of the National Labor Relations Act for his union's potential success, noted that, "Back in the old days, there was no National Labor Relations Act. Today we have the law behind us, and if ballplayers continue to be as interested in the Guild as they have been up to now, there is no question in my mind that it will be accepted."[44] It should also be noted, for whatever it is worth, that Murphy was a former field examiner for the National Labor Relations Board, the administrative agency that oversees the intent and purpose of the aforementioned piece of legislation. As such, he was thoroughly grounded in the practice of collective bargaining under this law.

Confrontation. The club owners regarded Murphy's organization with some suspicion but, until the night of June 7, 1946, had little reason to be overly alarmed. After all, ballplayers had tried to unionize before and in each case, the owners had prevailed on them to forget about collective bargaining and concentrate again on the playing of the game. What had been accomplished in the past could easily be attained again. Or could it?

Murphy presented the Pittsburgh management with his demands for union recognition and collective bargaining rights on the evening of the game, boldly announcing that a failure on the owner's part to acquiesce would most surely lead to a player strike. But Murphy had made one big mistake. He threatened a strike before being absolutely certain that the Pirate players were solidly behind him in his endeavors. In a two-hour-plus meeting, the ballplayers voted in favor of the strike by the slim margin of 20 to 16. However, a previous arrangement had set at two-thirds the number of tallies needed for the strike vote to pass. Thus, for the lack of four votes, Murphy's effort fizzled in a tense locker room scene while the crowd in the stands awaited the players' decision.[45]

Management was quick to act in order to preserve some semblance of player satisfaction with the game's working conditions. Where Murphy had failed because of his tactical blunder and his being viewed as a one-man union devoid of player participation, constitution, and by-laws, the club owners were instrumental in preempting the union's claim to have improved working conditions.[46] For instance, they allowed Commissioner A. B. (Happy) Chandler to choose a player representative from each club to discuss working conditions jointly with the owners. These player representatives were able to meet with league officials in July 1946 to present and discuss their proposals, which included improvements in travel arrangements and money, exhibition game pay, and a pension plan. The owners did concede on several of these issues as they instituted a pension plan and modified the old waiver rule.[47] And to this day, players refer to their "Murphy money" when speaking of spring training pay, in remembrance of their former union boss.

Thus, the owners countered this latest threat by resorting to a policy of meeting and conferring with designated player representatives, a system many in the labor movement would refer to as "company unionism" in baseball clothing. But just as Gould stated in his remarkably accurate article in 1946:[48]

> *Eventually the newer generation of intelligent, non-subservient players will tire of company unionism. Just as they responded once to the Guild, so they will turn to it, or another version, once the more important demands are denied. But it will take recognized stars to take over and succeed where pioneer Murphy valiantly, though foolishly, failed, and it will take players who recognize that their greatest weapon is the strike and who will not hesitate to employ it if they must.*
>
> *Regardless of what succeeds, Murphy has made a definite contribution toward bettering the ballplayers' lot. The union bug has bitten baseball and is certain to infiltrate into other sports in America.*

Summary

Initially, baseball players were completely free to switch teams at will following each season and this free agency outweighed a number of undesirable factors in their employment relationships with their individual teams. After the owners acted collectively to prevent further revolving and to hold salaries down, this host of other factors, including the now-hated reserve clause, caused the players to look to unionism as a possible way to help them solve their employment problems. Their reasons for forming and joining unions have been shown to be entirely consistent with the theoretical framework presented in the initial part of this chapter. In other words, players joined unions because of wage-related, nonwage-related, and individual difference factors.

The four major attempts at unionization from 1885 through 1946 have been described and placed in the economic and environmental contexts that the game itself faced during each period. In each case, a rival league was on the scene, in some instances playing a major role in the successes and failures of the unions. Additionally, while the players had many gripes about working conditions, including management's use of substitutes to sell peanuts and hot dogs in the stands while they were not actually involved on the playing field, the major concern over time was the players' insistence that management abolish or liberalize the reservation system. In each unionization attempt, this issue was discussed, but no changes were forthcoming. Along the way, club owners made several minor concessions that served temporarily to satisfy the players and their union bosses. But just as the waves in the ocean can be counted on to roll in over and over again, the reserve clause issue was far from dead. Unionization was at low tide for the moment, but that moment did not last long.

Endnotes

1. John Dunlop, "The Development of Labor Organization: A Theoretical Framework," in Richard Rowan (ed.), *Readings in Labor Economics and Labor Relations* (Homewood, Illinois: Richard D. Irwin, 1968), p. 42.
2. *Ibid.*, pp. 43–44.
3. Thomas Kochan, "Collective Bargaining and Organizational Behavior Research," in B. M. Staw and L. L. Cummings (eds.), *Research in Organizational Behavior*, vol. 2, 1980 (Greenwich, Conn.: JAI Press, 1980), p. 166.
4. Richard Freeman and James Medoff, "The Two Faces of Unionism," *The Public Interest* 57 (Fall 1979), pp. 69–93.
5. Thomas Kochan, *Collective Bargaining and Industrial Relations* (Homewood, Illinois: Richard D. Irwin, 1980), p. 2.
6. *Ibid.*, pp. 2–3.
7. *Ibid.*, p. 3.
8. Freeman and Medoff, *op. cit.*, p. 70.
9. Kochan, *op. cit.*, pp. 3–5.
10. *Ibid.*, p. 3.
11. *Ibid.*, p. 5.
12. *Ibid.*, p. 5.
13. Brian Becker, "On the Institutional Method and Industrial Relations Research," paper prepared at the School of Management, SUNY, Buffalo (October 1979).
14. E. Wright Bakke, "Why Workers Join Unions," *Personnel* 22 (July 1945), p. 37.
15. *Ibid.*, p. 38.
16. Joel Seidman, Jack London, and Bernard Karsh, "Why Workers Join Unions,"

Annals of the American Academy of Political and Social Science (March 1951), pp. 75–84.

17. *Ibid.*, p. 83.
18. William Whyte, "Who Goes Union and Why," *Personnel Journal* 23 (December 1944), pp. 215–230.
19. Julius Getman, Stephen Goldberg, and Jeanne Herman, *Union Representation Elections: Law and Reality* (New York: Russell Sage Foundation, 1976).
20. See Chester Schriescheim, "Job Satisfaction, Attitudes Towards Unions and Voting in Union Representation Elections," *Journal of Applied Psychology* 65 (1978), pp. 548–552.
21. W. Clay Hamner and Frank Smith, "Work Attitudes as Predictors of Unionization Activity," *Journal of Applied Psychology* 65 (1978), pp. 415–421.
22. Henry Farber and Daniel Saks, "Why Workers Want Unions: The Role of Relative Wages and Job Characteristics," *Journal of Political Economy* 88 (April 1980), pp. 349–369.
23. *Ibid.*, pp. 361–367.
24. H. Gregg Lewis, *Unionism and Relative Wages in the United States* (Chicago: University of Chicago Press, 1963).
25. Richard Freeman, "The Effects of Trade Unionism on Fringe Benefits," National Bureau of Economic Research Working Paper No. 292, October 1978.
26. Jack Barbash, "Values in Industrial Relations—The Case of the Adversarial Principle," Industrial Relations Research Association Presidential Address, September 1980.
27. Mark Goldstein, "Arbitration of Grievance and Salary Disputes in Professional Baseball: Evolution of a System of Private Law," *Cornell Law Review* 60 (August 1975), pp. 1049–1074. Also see Paul Gregory, *The Baseball Player: An Economic Study* (Washington, D.C.: Public Affairs Press, 1956).
28. See James Dworkin and Thomas Bergmann, "Collective Bargaining and the Player Reservation/Compensation System in Professional Sports," *Employee Relations Law Journal* 4 (Autumn 1978), pp. 241–256.
29. Gregory, *op. cit.*, p. 182.
30. William Holley and Kenneth Jennings, *The Labor Relations Process* (Hinsdale, Illinois: The Dryden Press, 1980), pp. 521–564. Also see David Voigt, *American Baseball: From Gentleman's Sport to the Commissioner System* (Norman, Oklahoma: University of Oklahoma Press, 1966), p. 167.
31. Voigt, *ibid.*, p. 161.
32. *Ibid.*, p. 166.
33. *Ibid.*, p. 166.
34. *Ibid.*, p. 169.
35. Gregory, *op. cit.*, p. 189.
36. John McCallum, *Ty Cobb* (New York: Praeger, 1975), p. 83.
37. *Ibid.*
38. *Ibid.*, p. 86.
39. Gregory, *op. cit.*, p. 191.
40. *Federal Baseball Club* v. *National League*, 259 U.S. 200, 208 (1922).
41. Gregory, *op. cit.*, p. 192.
42. "Minimum of $7,500 in Majors Sought," *New York Times*, May 3, 1946, p. 16.

43. Gregory, *op. cit.*, p. 192. Also see Paul Gould, "Unionism's Bid in Baseball," *The New Republic* 115 (1946), pp. 134–136.
44. Gould, *ibid.*, p. 135.
45. *Ibid.*, p. 136.
46. Erwin Krasnow and Herman Levy, "Unionization and Professional Sports," *Georgetown Law Review* 51 (1963), pp. 762–764.
47. "Minimum Salaries, Other Reforms Gained by Major League Players," *New York Times*, September 17, 1946, p. 4.
48. Gould, *op. cit.*, p. 136.

Chapter 2

THE FORMATION AND DEVELOPMENT OF THE MLBPA

An old adage about unions goes something like this: Any management that gets a union deserves it! The best way to remain nonunion is to treat employees well, in fact, well enough that they are satisfied with all facets of their employment contract. As this saying and the theory in the previous chapter note, these satisfied employees will then react by choosing to remain nonunionized. If management can take care of them this well, why do they need a union? What could a union possibly provide them that they do not already have? In baseball, the owners began to realize that if they did not act quickly, the players would soon forget about the minor gains they had achieved and once again turn to unionism. Thus it was that the owners took swift action to try to end permanently the threat of unionization in baseball. The action they took has been labeled the "representation plan."

Management Fights Back: The Representation Plan

As briefly described in the previous chapter, after the demise of Robert Murphy's American Baseball Guild, the owners soon set up a steering committee to study the state of employment relations in the game. This committee produced a document referred to as the MacPhail Report, in which the owners admitted that[1]

> . . . attempts to organize players represented our most pressing problem. If we were to frustrate Murphy and protect ourselves against raids on players from the outside, we deemed it necessary that the uniform players' contract be revised, and our players satisfied, at least

25

to such extent as is feasible and practical. A healthier relationship
between club and player will be effective in resisting attempts at
unionization—or raids by outsiders.

Thus, intent on preventing unionization, the owners implemented the player representation system in 1946. Under this system, two kinds of player representatives were called for. One type
was a player chosen from each team (there were sixteen teams
at the time of the representation plan's inauguration) by the League
Commissioner to present grievances and make requests directly to
his own club's management. These players were concerned only
with issues germane to their particular club. Secondly, provision was
made for two players (one from each league) to be elected by their
respective leagues' players to sit on baseball's ruling body, the
Executive Council. At the time of the representation plan's implementation, the players had two *nonvoting* seats on this seven-
person council. Since the council met several times per year, the
players did have some opportunities at least to present their grievances to club and league officials. All they needed to do to get an
item on the agenda was to file the particular issue with the Commissioner well in advance of the official meetings. As suggested above,
these items would then be *discussed* at the Executive Council sessions.

This representation system was clearly better than no representation at all. In fact, one could document several examples of teams
acting affirmatively on players' requests and of the Executive Council doing likewise. And this is exactly what management wanted to
happen, that is, demonstrate the ability to give in on some minor
issues and make the impression on the players and fans alike that
they were listening to player gripes and that they were willing to
take corrective actions where they proved to be necessary. But an
important point needs to be made here concerning the difference
between the so-called representation plan and what I will refer to as
"genuine" collective bargaining. The representation plan was not
anything even akin to collective bargaining as we know it today in
both the private and public sectors of our economy. In fact, it was
really just a "meet and confer" plan, that is, a situation where management promises to discuss issues, yet reserves the right to cut off
discussion and, most importantly, to implement its own procedures
in the event of any lasting disagreement. Thus, by the standards of
modern day labor-management relations, the representation plan
had two big flaws:

1. Players were elected to the Executive Council but *were not allowed* to vote on any issues.
2. Management *always* made the final decision on *every* issue.

Gradually, the players became dissatisfied with the owners' system of representation and took two major steps toward unionization. First, they decided to hire legal counsel in the person of J. Norman Lewis in 1953. As might be expected, most of the owners vehemently opposed the hiring of Lewis. Their opposition ranged from the naive bewilderment of a few owners who could not understand why players who already had such a fine representation system would ever feel the need to hire a lawyer, to the much more prevalent and astute speculation of others that this action probably was in the vanguard of a new movement to unionize the players. For their part, most of the player representatives avowed that the hiring of Lewis was not a veiled attempt to unionize but rather, that a lawyer was hired simply for legal advice in the areas of most pressing concern to the ballplayer. To Lewis' credit, he was able to help the players in several areas, the most important of which was in the development of a revised pension plan.

Then in 1954, at a meeting held on July 12 during the All-Star game break in Cleveland, the 16 player representatives voted to form a new association, which they named the Major League Baseball Players' Association (MLBPA). Players involved in the formation of the new association insisted that it was not *now* a union nor would it *ever* become one. The association was described as a players' social or fraternal organization, although many of the owners felt uneasy about this description.

It is interesting to note that most writers at the time did not refer to the MLBPA as a union, and indeed, many felt that the existing representation plan could efficiently handle any and all employment disputes that might arise between the owners and the players. One writer summed it all up by noting that "The four ill-fated unions began the democratic process in baseball; the modern representation system, which replaced them, is evolving into a workable procedure, and the revolt of the players has given way to player-management cooperation. The players now have a voice in the baseball industry and their voice will be heard."[2] Unfortunately for the owners, this prediction of stable employer-employee relations due to the representation plan was not to be proven true. In fact, the most spectacular upheaval in the history of the game's employer-employee relations was just around the corner. And the catalysts in this process were to be none other than the MLBPA and its newly elected executive director, Marvin Miller.

The Major League Baseball Players' Association, 1954

Although players and team owners alike continued to promote the idea that the MLBPA was *not* to be a union, controversies arising during the 1950s led to more and more speculation about just when collective bargaining would become a reality. While the representation plan did have some positive features, the infrequent and short meetings did not allow the two sides to discuss meaningfully and/or agree on the crucial differences of opinion between them at the time. Additionally, disputes arose over the distribution and allocation of post-season and All-Star game revenues as well as the continuing debate over the pension system. Despite these problems, when star pitcher Bob Feller was elected the MLBPA's first president in 1956, he clearly stated his opinion (and, presumably that of most of the players) that "You cannot carry collective bargaining into baseball."[3] And clearly, Feller was not alone in these sentiments. Bob Friend, a National League player representative, expressed the same theme several years later when he noted that:[4]

> *I firmly believe a union, in the fullest sense of the word, simply would not fit the situation in baseball . . . Baseball is different than the ordinary business or industry. Players and management work closely together. If we begin operating a union, we immediately will begin antagonizing the owners. If union negotiators don't have something to argue about, they'll create something. They're always looking for trouble.*
> *. . . If the structure of our players' association was changed to a union, I believe it would result in ill will for the players. It would tend to destroy the image of the baseball star for the youngsters because of the haggling between the players and the owners. . . . We have made tremendous strides with our organization. We have improved the lot of the players financially with a minimum salary, $10 daily for meals, moving expenses when traded, etc. We have improved his working conditions with finer clubhouses, better batting backgrounds, etc. And is there a union that has as lucrative a pension plan as ours?*

Thus, despite being faced with continuing problems in labor relations, the MLBPA was content to remain just an association. It wasn't that the association was completely inactive, it was just inactive on the collective bargaining front. Most of the player representatives felt that they had already gained an enormous amount through the representation plan (remember that these representatives were chosen by the Commissioner, an employee of the two leagues) and that collective bargaining and unionization were simply unnecessary at the time. What more could a union get for them, anyway? Wouldn't a union be harmful to the game? These questions and many similar ones were to be answered when, after twelve years, the MLBPA's relative inactivity ended as the players took another major step forward into the realm of unionization. For on July 1, 1966, Marvin Julian Miller took over as the first executive director of the MLBPA.

From Association to Union

The Influence of Marvin Miller

Before we plunge headlong into a description of the significant gains that have been recorded by the MLBPA in the 15 years Miller has been at the helm, it will be instructive to know something about the background and development of this very important person in the history of baseball unionization. What is it about Miller that has led him to be described as "the commissioner of the players"or "the Ralph Nader of professional sports"? Why has he been able to record such significant gains through collective bargaining where so many others before him had failed to achieve even a modicum of similar success?

Miller was born in 1917 in New York City, the son of immigrant parents from eastern Europe. His formal education included undergraduate work both in education and economics, which led to his bachelor of science degree from New York University in 1938. He subsequently took graduate courses at the New School for Social Research. From the start, he had a keen interest in economics, perhaps kindled by an excellent introductory course with a fine economics teacher during his high school days.

His first experience with labor-management relations came during World War II when he was employed as an economist and disputes hearing officer at the Wage Stabilization Division of the War Labor Board. It was an experience that was to have a significant impact on Miller's career. Miller later moved on to the United

States Conciliation Service for a tour of duty training new personnel. He left government permanently in 1947 to begin his long and impressive career in the labor movement.

The first stop was with the International Association of Machinists, followed three years later by the beginning of his long association with the United Steelworkers' Union. He began as an associate research director of the union and was later promoted to an assistant of president David MacDonald. While serving under MacDonald, Miller was credited with establishing several imaginative labor-management experiments such as the Kaiser Aluminum productivity sharing plan and the industry-wide human relations committee in steel, which was geared toward preventing strikes and increasing productivity. This committee and its ideas can be thought of as forerunners of the current Experimental Negotiating Agreement (ENA) in steel. The ENA is a pledge by both labor and management to avoid strikes in the steel industry by requiring the submission of all unresolved future terms disputes to final and binding interest arbitration. This plan was adopted in the face of the severe problems the domestic steel industry faced due to the hedge-buying cycle that had been created over time in anticipation of lengthy strikes every three years. And in essence, the strike threat became a self-fulfilling prophecy. As firms stockpiled in the anticipation of a long walkout, workers could be certain of being off their jobs one way or another. Either they struck or they faced probable long layoffs due to the slack demand for steel during the first few months after the settlement as firms slowly worked off their huge stockpiles. Miller was able to recognize these problems and others like the threat of Japanese inroads during strike periods and was one of the first to try to attack these issues directly. Even at this early stage in his career, his brilliance in labor matters in general and bargaining in particular was quite evident.

One of the members of the Kaiser committee was Professor George Taylor of the Wharton School at the University of Pennsylvania. It was to be through Taylor that Miller was able to assume his role of leadership with the MLBPA.

Around the beginning of 1966, there was some sentiment for the players to become more active in their association and to advocate the ideals of free collective bargaining. Robin Roberts, a veteran pitcher and association member, felt that the passive role of the MLBPA had to be corrected. Other players, like star outfielder Curt Flood, were much more vocal in their description of their association's shortcomings. Flood was quick to condemn the MLBPA as a company union which did nothing whatsoever for the players.[5] When this was added to the players' growing dissatisfaction with their part-time legal help, Judge Robert Cannon, it was apparent that the stage was set for some action to be taken.

Robin Roberts asked Professor Taylor for his suggestions on a full-time executive director for the MLBPA. Taylor strongly recommended Miller, based on his dealings with and respect for him during their steel industry contacts. Miller was active in campaigning for the job, which he eventually began during the middle of the 1966 championship season. Of course, the owners opposed the appointment of Miller on several grounds that are typical of management concerns across a variety of industries. First, they favored Judge Cannon as the players' representative as they knew him well and felt he could be dealt with effectively through the representation plan. Furthermore, Judge Cannon was no advocate of a players' union. Additionally, the owners realized that the hiring of Miller marked the end of the era of the representation plan. If the players' intentions were unclear up to now, even the most naive observer would have to agree that Miller's hiring signaled the interest of the players in turning the MLBPA into a functioning labor union. And the club owners opposed unionism as they felt it would threaten their unilateral decision making powers—their *managerial prerogatives*. This in fact proved to be very true. Finally, Miller was an experienced labor negotiator for whom organized baseball had no readily obvious counterpart. Who would be able to deal effectively with Miller and the players? What types of demands would be forthcoming? Would the owners have to bargain collectively with the players over a variety of issues heretofore reserved as exclusive managerial prerogatives? They were soon to learn the answers to these and many other similar questions.

Developments After 1966

Chapters 3 through 5 discuss the major gains attained through collective bargaining for professional baseball players from the years 1966 through the present. However, it is useful here to highlight the major events in the history of the MLBPA under Marvin Miller's direction in order to provide the reader with a comprehensive framework from which to analyze and judge the individual accomplishments referred to later.

Miller and the MLBPA wasted little time in pushing for changes in several areas of the employment relationship. As in the past, major concerns were in both the wage and nonwage areas of the employment contract. By the year 1968, when the first collective bargaining agreement had been signed, players had won higher minimum salaries and increases in pension, disability, and health insurance benefits. What could be termed a "good faith" collective bargaining relationship was established on both sides of the table as the parties codified player rights and agreed to a grievance procedure for the resolution of unresolved disputes. Previously, while grievances could be filed, final disposition of all such issues had been reserved to the commissioner of baseball, an employee of the owners. Miller succeeded in convincing the baseball bosses of the incompatibility of this type of an arrangement with genuine collective bargaining. Thereafter, the Commissioner was replaced as the final arbiter by an impartial person selected by both sides. Thus, in this very important area, Miller had succeeded in moving the players' union into the mainstream of American industrial relations. And as we shall see later, this newly won grievance procedure was to play a major role in the demise of baseball's golden egg—the reserve clause.

While several rights were won, players were still concerned about the reserve clause and a further improved pension package which they wanted funded out of lucrative broadcast revenues. A test of strength over this latter issue occurred in 1969 when player representatives urged their teammates to refuse to sign contracts for the upcoming season until the matter of the pension fund was settled. Strong player sentiment in this area prompted the owners to reach a compromise pension agreement with the players just prior to the start of spring training.

The MLBPA took a swipe at the reserve clause with the Curt Flood case of 1970, but, as we will see later, the Supreme Court ruled in favor of the owners. This court decision not withstanding, it is important to recognize here that an early and high priority goal of the MLBPA was the elimination or modification of the existing system. In this respect, the MLBPA was no different from its four predecessor unions. However, in one important respect it did differ from earlier unions in that through a carefully planned, calculated, and executed strategy, it was able to bring about the demise of the reserve clause following the 1975 championship season.

The 1972 Strike

The next collective agreement was a three-year pact ratified in May 1970. This contract provided for further minimum salary increases, better expense money, and an extension of the grievance arbitration principles established earlier. Things seemed to be moving along rather smoothly until the start of the 1972 season, when angered by the pension issue again (determination and amount), the players began spring training by announcing their intention to strike. The player vote was nearly unanimous and should have been a signal to management of the seriousness of the players' concerns. However, management seemed to react with a mixture of anger and surprise, and this general players' strike indeed became a reality. The strike was a short one by many standards, lasting thirteen days and forcing the cancellation of 86 games at the beginning of the regular season schedule. But even a short strike may have long-term effects. Pete Rose has been known to remark that this strike, though a short one, cost him a chance at a 200-hit season. Rose played 154 games that year (eight being cancelled due to the strike) and had 198 hits. Had he played the additional eight games and had the necessary two hits, Rose by now would have broken Ty Cobb's record for the most 200-hit seasons in a career.

These minor quibbles aside, the settlement of the strike that year hinged on two issues—pensions and payment for games missed due to the strike. Agreement was finally reached on a new contract with the owners giving in on the pension issue and the players agreeing to forfeit the portion of their annual salaries that would have been paid had they played during the strike. As is true in most effective collective bargaining situations, both sides had to compromise to reach agreement and sign the final accord on February 28, 1973.

A major gain for players in these negotiations was the addition of the option of final-offer salary arbitration to resolve pay impasses where negotiations between the player and club broke down. Even though the players advocated collective bargaining, the long and strong tradition of *individual* bargaining over salaries was retained intact. Only minimum salary levels were collectively bargained. And indeed, the superstar players, who were often quite active in the union, would have it no other way; a salary schedule implies discrimination against the more talented ballplayers. In fact, collective bargaining over salaries by position, age, or tenure has never been very popular with any group of professional athletes. Compare this notion with the idea of *standardized rates* that is a hallmark of unionism in the private sector, and it will become apparent that this association is a different kind of union. The salary arbitration procedure became functional with the 1974 season and exists intact today, with a few minor modifications.

The 1976 Lockout

The next round of negotiations in 1976 also featured a stoppage of play before a settlement was reached. The owners locked out the players during spring training in the hopes of forcing them to reach a quick agreement. After seventeen days, Commissioner Kuhn reopened the camps, negotiations proceeded, and a settlement eventually was announced in July. This settlement was preceded by strike and boycott threats on the part of the players. The agreement contained many improvements for the players, in areas such as the minimum wage and pension plan. Similarly, management made some gains by reducing the roster limit to twenty-four players from the previous level of twenty-five. These issues aside, the crucial event of the 1976 negotiations revolved around the *reserve clause issue*. While this is the subject of an entire chapter to come (Chapter 3), enough of an overview of what happened will be provided here in order to whet the reader's appetite.

Buoyed by a favorable arbitration decision in the Messersmith/ McNally case following the conclusion of the 1975 season, the players were gunning for major changes in the system. Arbitrator Peter Seitz had ruled that players were not the perpetual property of their clubs as the owners had argued but were bound by the terms of their reserve clause for *only* one additional season after their contract had expired. Thus, players could become free agents and revolve to the highest bidding team, much like what occurred in the 1800s. But both players and club owners alike were against complete abolition of the system that had been at the heart of the games' operation for nearly one hundred years. Thus, the 1976 negotiations featured the hammering-out of a compromise six-year reserve system that would allow free agency after that period of service with a particular team. Rules were set up to guide the process of bidding for free agents and the selection of negotiating rights for free agent players. Unlike negotiators in other sports facing these issues, baseball negotiators chose to pay little attention to the notion of *compensa-*

tion for teams losing free agent players. The agreement specified only that teams losing a free agent would receive one draft choice in the amateur phase of the player draft from the team signing the free agent. Thus, when Philadelphia signed Pete Rose, the Cincinnati Reds received a draft choice (usually a high-school or college player) in exchange. The language of the contract was worded such that the free agency agreement was to be viewed as an experiment, and as such, subject to renegotiation in future bargaining sessions. However, the experimental nature of this agreement should not be taken too seriously as, in effect, all clauses in all collective bargaining contracts are always subject to be reopened for further discussion during future bargaining sessions. Experience, however, has proven that once an item is included in a collective agreement, it is very difficult to have it removed and in fact, even to try to reach some sort of a minor compromise on previously agreed-to language can be exceedingly painful.

The results of this experiment were eagerly awaited by the fans, players and owners alike. And spectacular results they were! Free agency was a real plus for the players, and teams acquiring free agents would *not* be penalized by excessive compensation as was often the case in football and basketball. (In a recent court case, one of NBA Commissioner Larry O'Brien's compensation rulings has been overturned.) (A complete list of the players using the free agency route and their new teams and salaries in those cases where data is available is presented in Appendix II of Chapter 3.) During the years preceding the next negotiations, perceived problems surrounding this free agency system were building up to a crescendo and were to again be the featured aspects of the tumultuous 1980 negotiations.

The 1980 Negotiations

Both sides came to the bargaining table intent on changing the free agency system. Miller and the MLBPA sought a liberalization of the system under which so many players had become rich quickly. The basic idea was to reduce the number of years in the league required before a player could become a free agent from the current language which specified six years. The owners had, as their major concern, compensation for teams losing free agents. They devised a plan whereby teams who lost free agents would be able to select a player from the acquiring team's roster. This proposal, of course, was designed to stop the influx of players using the free agent system by discouraging bidding. The theory was that teams would be more wary of choosing to hire free agents where a crucial member of their own team could potentially be lost in the deal. This proposal was totally unacceptable to the players and an impasse ensued.

It is interesting to note that another major issue involved in the 1980 negotiations was the owners' proposal to revamp the salary arbitration procedure. Thus, the owners were engaging in what would be called "buy-back" bargaining, in that they were seriously concerned with removing or radically changing provisions that they had agreed to in earlier rounds of bargaining. And just as the name suggests, it becomes rather expensive to buy back these types of rights, usually entailing a heavy cost or some type of strike action. Thus, the 1980 negotiations revolved around salary arbitration and free agency.

The outcome of these negotiations is recent history in some instances, and in others is yet to be played out fully in the future. The owners dropped their demand for a revised salary arbitration plan, and thus it remains essentially unchanged from the 1974 procedure. The free agent compensation issue, however, was another matter. The players felt so strongly on this issue that they engaged in one actual and one threatened job action during the months following the expiration of the old collective bargaining agreement on December 31, 1979. The first action was a one-week exhibition season strike, which was followed by a promise for one last-ditch good faith bargaining effort to resolve this complicated issue. The players set a target regular season strike deadline of May 22, 1980. Negotiations seemed to be hopelessly bogged down with neither side willing to compromise. It looked like a regular season strike was inevitable.

But at the final hour, in a drama which is befitting of the process of collective bargaining, an agreement not to strike was reached and the regular season escaped unscathed. Notice that the agreement was denoted as a promise not to strike, and not a mutually agreeable solution to the problem of compensation for teams losing free agents. No workable solution could be reached, so both sides decided to put the issue before a joint labor-management committee for further discussion so as to salvage the season. The exact nature and role of this committee and its progress in negotiations are subjects reserved for the next chapter. But it is instructive to note that it has again been a dispute over player reservation which is at the bottom of the current negotiating problems between players and clubs. And it is probably safe to guess that no matter how it is settled, differences of opinion over this vital issue will not soon fade away.

The MLBPA—Reasons for Survival

After having reviewed the history of five separate experiments with the unionization of professional baseball players, we can profitably take a moment to reflect on why only the last of these unions, the MLBPA, was to prove viable enough to survive the dual forces of time and managerial opposition in such a way as to significantly alter employment conditions of baseball players. A whole host of reasons can be summoned up, but for purposes of brevity and succinctness, all of these factors can be collapsed into *four* items:

1. *The players' readiness for unionization in 1966.* It was apparent to the players by then that the representation plan was just another name for company unionism and that the owners were not yet ready to sit at the bargaining table unless they were legally forced to do so.
2. *The imitation factor.* By 1966, many players were well aware of the benefits unions had provided millions of workers in American industry. Furthermore, the beginnings of unionism in the public sector and the potential gains to be won there left players thinking about "me-tooism." If unions could be so successful in providing other workers with decent wages, hours, and working conditions, why could not this also occur in baseball? Well, by now, most players were convinced that unionism in baseball could work. Player gripes over the reserve system, minimum salaries, pensions, and grievance procedures had festered for too long. As the theory of the previous chapter would predict, the benefits of unionization now far exceeded its potential costs. Thus, players turned to unions in droves in order to enable collective bargaining to allow them to fulfill their needs and goals with respect to the employment relationship. It has done just that.
3. *The hiring of Marvin Miller.* A major turnaround in the philosophy of the players toward unionization occurred when they chose to employ Marvin Miller as their executive director in 1966. Two important aspects of this decision need to be mentioned. First, the players realized that instead of a part-time

company-oriented leader, what they needed was a *full-time* executive director whose total efforts could be devoted toward improving employment conditions in the profession. Secondly, and equally as crucial, the players chose a leader from a *strong union, collective bargaining background.* This was to give them a decided advantage in their dealings with the club owners who did not come to the bargaining table equally well prepared.

4. *The favorability of environmental factors.* It is important to remember that the previous unionization attempts (except one, the Guild) were carried out in an environment very hostile to unions in general, and to baseball unions in particular. Thus, the fact that the MLBPA enjoyed the protection of the National Labor Relations Act of 1935 in its dealings with club owners cannot be lightly dismissed. No matter how any person or club felt individually about a baseball players' union, the right of this union to exist and promote the interests of its members through collective bargaining could not be denied. Thus it was that the MLBPA became the first baseball union to be granted "exclusive representation" status. From that day forth, management was obligated to bargain in good faith with the ballplayers' union or risk being held in violation of our nation's basic labor relations law.

Summary

This chapter describes the history of the fifth and final baseball union, the Major League Baseball Players Association. The emphasis has been on its evolution from a supposedly fair and unbeatable "representation plan" instituted and controlled by the owners for the sake of preserving their own interests. The hiring of Marvin Miller in 1966 represented the turning point in the development of a pure labor union out of what was earlier a loose-knit fraternal club. Many of the achievements of several rounds of collective bargaining have been highlighted, along with a description of some of the major rough spots along the way. The reasons have been presented why this union has persevered while others before it did not. All in all, the picture that has been painted is that of a highly successful, thriving union.

Many of the spectacular accomplishments of the MLBPA have been glossed over in this chapter so as to provide a broad-brush overview. In the next three chapters, a much more thorough and detailed analysis of the major gains won through the collective bargaining process in the past fifteen years will be presented.

Endnotes

1. Paul Gregory, *The Baseball Player: An Economic Study* (Washington, D.C.: Public Affairs Press, 1956) p. 194.
2. *Ibid.*, p. 207.
3. "Players Ask Joint Meeting," *The New York Times*, December 11, 1956, p. 52.
4. "Player Rep Friend Raps Proposal That Athletes Form Labor Union," *The Sporting News*, August 3, 1963, p. 4.
5. Curt Flood, *The Way It Is* (New York: Pocket Books, 1972).

Chapter 3

THE IMPACTS OF COLLECTIVE BARGAINING: THE RESERVE CLAUSE AND FREE AGENCY

In the previous two chapters, we have reviewed the history of unionization attempts among professional baseball players during the past one hundred years. As we have observed, only the Major League Baseball Players' Association, the last of the five unions, was able to survive the dual tests of time and managerial resistance. Our attention must now be turned to a description and analysis of the major impacts that this union has had on the game of baseball in general and its employment rules in particular since the year 1954.

The History of Player Reservation in Baseball

In the early days of baseball, a completely free labor market existed for the players. At the conclusion of each and every season, players were free to sign contracts with whatever team they desired, typically the team that was willing to pay them the highest salary for the upcoming season. This process of changing teams from season to season was known as revolving. Today we refer to this phenomenon as free agency. No compensation was provided for teams losing players through these revolving doors. In these early days of baseball, there existed no professional leagues as we know them today. In fact, all teams were amateur in nature, the first being formed around 1845.[1] But even in the early days there existed a lot of competitive rivalry among the various amateur teams, invariably

41

leading to revolving as teams tried to lure players away from other clubs through promises of higher salaries and better jobs.

The National Association of Baseball Players

In the year 1857, fifteen of these amateur clubs banded together to form the first baseball league, known as the National Association of Baseball Players. This Association grew in size to number sixty teams by the year 1860, and to over 400 clubs by 1870.[2]

This Association tried to curb the practice of revolving as early as the year 1859, when they instituted a rule banning a player from participating in a game unless he had been a member of his new club for at least 30 days. Thus, the origins of player reservation in baseball can be traced back to over 120 years ago.

It turned out that by the year 1870 this amateur league had split into two major factions, one representing the amateur clubs and the other representing those clubs that were more professional in terms of playing ability. This split was finalized in 1870 when the professional clubs withdrew and formed the first professional league, The National Association of Professional Baseball Players.[3] This League maintained the rule on revolving mentioned earlier, but now the time limit was increased to sixty days. Thus, a player could revolve to another team, but he would have to wait 60 days before playing in his first game. If the revolving took place in the off season, as it most often did, obviously the 60 days would run out prior to the commencement of the next official season. Thus, this type of a rule against revolving was essentially meaningless. The new league ran upon very hard times as most of the teams proved to be financial disasters. Commenting upon the reason for this lack of success after the league's demise, A. G. Mills, then president of the National League, put the blame squarely on the revolving process. In a speech given on March 7, 1914, Mills noted that[4]

> As now, each summer's campaign was planned during the preceding winter and the habit was general on the part of the clubs to take on obligations in the way of players' salaries that were not justified, as the spring games would inevitably demonstrate that the majority of such clubs could have no hope of winning even a respectable number of games. Moreover, this condition was greatly aggravated by the general practice on the part of the richer clubs, of stripping the weaker ones of their best playing talent. Then would follow the collapse of a number of these clubs in mid-season, leaving their players unpaid, while the winning clubs, owing to the disbandment of the weaker ones,

would also frequently fail from inability to arrange a paying number of games.

This statement is an early argument for some type of reserve rule to enable the league or leagues to maintain competitive balance. This argument continues to be used today.

Just as the league was about to die, William A. Hulbert, president of the Chicago White Stockings, signed four star players from Boston and two from Philadelphia to play for his team during the 1876 season. This signing had occurred during the regular 1875 season while these players were still under contract to their former teams,[5] in direct violation of the National Association's rules, and so Hulbert, rather than face the music in the almost-defunct league, decided to form his own eight-team league. Thus it was that the National League of Professional Baseball Clubs was founded. This is the National League, still in existence today.

The National League of Professional Baseball Clubs

The new league began with no sanctions whatsoever against revolving during off seasons. As had occurred in the past, the free market for player services led to bidding wars and ever higher player salaries as teams tried to increase their chances of winning a pennant. The owners realized that some action would have to be taken if player salaries were to come down or even just stay put. An official statement from the owners around this time reflected their concerns in this area:[6]

> *The financial results of the past season prove that salaries must come down. We believe that players in insisting on exorbitant prices are injuring their own interests by forcing out of existence clubs which cannot be run and pay large salaries except at a large personal loss. The season financially has been a little better than 1878; but the expenses of many of the clubs have far exceeded their receipts, attributable wholly to large salaries. In view of these facts, measures have been taken by this league to remedy the evil to some extent in 1880.*

The club owners began to question the propriety of revolving. Nobody seems to know exactly when this doubt first crept into the minds of the club owners, but it is clear that it was before the turn of the century. There were several things about revolving that were extremely distasteful to the club owners. First, they did not like the fact that they were apt to lose one or more of their star players and receive nothing in exchange for them. The fans were expected to rebel and stay away from the ballparks due to their disappointment over having lost one or more of their summer heroes to some other team. The owners also complained that the richer clubs would buy up all of the better talent and thus upset the competitive balance in the league. And finally, the most importantly to be sure, the owners realized that revolving meant higher player salaries. Players could switch teams to receive a higher salary, and if the original clubs wished to retain these players' services, they too would have to cough up higher salary payments.

Adoption of the First Reserve Rule

Mounting concern over revolving finally led the owners to take action in the form of a secret meeting of National League officials in Buffalo in September 1879. At this time, the owners adopted the *very first formal reserve rule* in professional baseball.[7] As Gregory points out very clearly, the adoption of this first reserve rule on September 30, 1879, was to a large extent due to the numerous player desertions that occurred in the preceding five seasons. Most prominent among these episodes was the desertion of Boston's four best players after the 1875 season to the Chicago team, as described earlier.

This first reserve rule, proposed by A. H. Soden, specified that each team could reserve five ballplayers for the 1880 season. Other teams were permitted to sign any other players from a team's roster except these five protected persons. It was hoped that in this manner player salaries would be held down as teams would reserve for themselves the best players in the league. This rule proved to be only as good as the word of the club owners that they would not tamper with the reserved players from other clubs. Evidence indicates that salaries decreased, profits increased, and things went rather smoothly.[8] The number of reserved players was gradually increased to 11 in 1883, 14 in 1887, and finally to include the entire roster of every team a few years later.[9]

In the early years, the reserve rule was not a formal part of the player's contract as it is today. Rather, teams would simply list the names of all players that they wished to reserve for the following season and this list would be circulated to all teams in the league. By agreement, no team would tamper with the reserved players from any other team. In abiding by the above rule, each team could be more or less certain that their own reserved players would not be tampered with by the other clubs. In short order all players were reserved in this manner to the teams they had played for in the previous season. Indeed, this reservation system was to prove to be a powerful tool for the owners, enabling them to stop revolving altogether and to halt the spiraling of player salaries.

The Reserve Rule in Individual Player Contracts. The formal incorporation of the reserve rule into individual player contracts in baseball occurred as a result of a meeting between player and owner representatives in 1887. Angered by this process, by which clubs were able to restrict their freedom of movement from team to team, the players decided that they desired to have some say in the wording of any contractual language impacting upon their playing careers. The result was the negotiation of a reserve clause in 1887 to replace the former secret agreement. When the rival American Association challenged the National League in the 1880s, a bidding war ensued for the better players. Naturally, the National League owners were concerned over this spiraling of salaries, and so they agreed to a settlement referred to as the "National Agreement" in which clubs in both leagues could reserve a number of players whom no other team in *either* league would hire. Player contracts of the time noted that players had agreed to be bound by all of the terms of the National Agreement and thereby the players were bound by the reserve rule included in the peace treaty. As noted above, up to this time individual contracts had not contained reservation clauses.[10]

All of this changed as a result of the player-owner meeting held in 1887. The first players' union, the National Brotherhood of Professional Baseball Players, had been formed a few years earlier by player John Montgomery Ward. While this union was initiated for several reasons discussed in Chapter 1, one of its primary purposes was to negotiate over the reserve rule which Ward referred to as[11]

> . . . *a fugitive slave law which denied the player a harbor or a livelihood and carried him back, bound and shackled to the club from which he attempted to escape. Once a player's name is attached to a contract, his professional liberty is gone forever.*

Despite his hatred for the reserve clause, Ward and his fellow players early on recognized the need for some type of a reservation system in organized baseball. Thus, this meeting between club owners and player representatives was set up to negotiate an amicable and workable solution to the player reservation issue. At this meeting, the two sides agreed to replace the National Agreement with a formal reserve clause in player contracts. The first such formal reserve clause read as follows:[12]

> *It is further understood and agreed that the party of the first part shall have the right to "reserve" the said party of the second part for the season next ensuing the term mentioned in paragraph 2, herein provided, and that said right and privilege is hereby accorded to said party of the first part upon the following conditions, which are to be taken and construed as conditions precedent to the exercise of such extraordinary rights or privileges, viz.: (1) That the said party of the second part shall not be reserved at a salary less than that mentioned in the 20th paragraph herein, except by the consent of the party of the second part; (2) that the said party of the second part, if he be reserved by the said party of the first part for the next ensuing season, shall not be one of more than 14 players then under contract—that is, that the right of reservation shall be limited to that number of players and no more.*

The rule limited each club to a maximum of fourteen players who could be reserved in the manner described above. Note also that no cuts in salaries were permitted for any players who were reserved under this contractual clause. Along with this reserve rule, the National League owners also agreed to repeal the salary limits that they had set. The clubs were not to keep their promises in many of these areas, and thus a revolt was in the making.

Effects of the Reserve Rule

As noted earlier, the reserve rule employed by the National League in 1879 quickly led to higher team profits and lower player salaries. The earliest five-player reserve rule was soon expanded to cover all players on every team in the National League. In the year 1879, the National League had formally adopted the usage of a uniform player contract for the first time.[13] The stated purpose of this uniform contract, which contained no reserve rule at this time, was to enable clubs to enforce rules against players found guilty of being drunk or otherwise engaging in conduct reprehensible to baseball. Given the rules of the new uniform contract, players guilty of such transgressions could be suspended and become ineligible to play for any other club in the league. As the reader might expect, this provision for suspending players gave the owners quite a bit of power, and that power was in some cases abused. It was just such abuses of this power that had led to the formation of the first players' union under John Montgomery Ward. These abuses aside, the reserve rule did allow the National League to prosper, and both this rule and the uniform player contract survive to this day in slightly altered forms.

Just as economic theory would predict, the financial successes of these eight National League Clubs during the 1880s led to much interest in rival leagues. Interested investors were able to form a six-club rival professional league known as the American Association in November of 1881,[14] which raided the National League in search of playing talent. Many players jumped to the rival American Association and were able to receive higher salaries by doing so. Several court proceedings had ensued where teams from one league attempted to stop players from jumping to the other league in violation of their contracts or their reserve clauses. The National League owners soon realized that this bidding war for player services had to stop, and the 1883 National Agreement thus was signed by the National League, the American Association, and the Northwestern League, a minor league organization. Also known as the tripartite pact, this agreement was modified several times and by 1889 contained both no tampering and reserve clauses. The reserve clause read as follows:[15]

> *On the 10th day of October in each year the secretary of each association shall transmit to the secretary of the other association a reserve list of players, not exceeding 14 in number, then under contract . . . and of all ineligible players, and such players, together with all others thereafter to be regularly contracted with by such club members are and shall be ineligible to contract with any other club member of either association party hereto . . . .*

Thus, all teams were bound not to tamper with players under contract with clubs in either league, and each club had to respect the reserved players of every other club in both leagues. The signing of this National Agreement is usually referred to as the birth of "organized baseball" in the United States and the man who wrote the agreement, then National League President A. G. Mills, is popularly referred to as the father of the reserve clause in organized baseball.[16]

The Union Association

Shortly after the signing of the National Agreement of 1883, a new league known as the Union Association was formed and attempted to challenge the now established reserve rule. The Union Association attempted to sign players from both the National League and the

American Association in an effort to become competitive. In these attempts, reserved players as well as players already under contract were solicited. It was at this time that the distinction between a reserve jumper and a contract jumper was first brought to the forefront. The former was a player who jumped leagues in violation of the reserve rule in his previous contract. However, this player had not yet signed a contract for the ensuing season. On the other hand, a contract jumper was a player who had already signed a contract to play for one team in a particular league for the upcoming season. This player was then contacted by a team from another league, which offered him a more lucrative contract. The player was enticed by this sweeter contract to jump to the rival league despite the binding nature of his former contract. While all league-jumping was generally despised by the owners, it was pretty much agreed that contract-jumping was the worst of the two evils described above.

The National League and the American Association decided to fight fire with fire and passed the so-called Day Resolution in an attempt to crush the Union Association.[17] Under this resolution, any player jumping to the Union Association in violation of his contract or reserve clause was to be banned for life from playing in either the National League or the American Association. This threatened blacklisting of defecting players worked very well as few established ballplayers were willing to risk permanent banishment from organized baseball to gain a little extra money in the short run. The Union Association could not survive without hiring some of the star players away from the more established leagues. Their failure in these efforts essentially spelled their doom after only one season of operation.

As noted above, the National League and American Association both prospered under the terms of the National Agreement which allowed them to exercise complete control over their player resources. In 1885, the owners' implementation of a salary limit of $2000 had led to John Montgomery Ward's attempt to form a union of professional ballplayers for the first time in history. Besides the salary limit alluded to above, the players were annoyed with several abuses inherent in the reserve clause such as (1) the reservation of players who refused to sign a contract; (2) the buying and selling of players; (3) the transfer of players by sale or trade without the players' consent; (4) the blacklisting of reserved players for failure to sign a contract upon the terms offered by the club; and (5) the practice of farming, or loaning players out, to another club.[18] As we have already seen, the owners agreed to meet with representatives of the first union and together they agreed to the 14-player reserve rule. The clubs also agreed not to reduce the salary of any reserved player and to repeal the salary limits referred to above.

The Players League

However, the problems did not end with these minor concessions. Shortly thereafter, the owners adopted a new salary schedule for players based upon their seniority levels. This breach of a promise, combined with other grievances, led the players to strike out on their own against the National League and the American Association in 1889. This the players did by secretly forming their own Players League in open competition with the older leagues. The National Brotherhood of Professional Baseball Players was successful in coaxing many star players from the more established leagues to jump to the Players League.

A major question arose as to whether the reserve clause in player contracts in the National League and the American Association could be used to prevent players from jumping to the new league. The position of the National League that the reserve clause should restrain players from leaving organized baseball was rejected in several court cases at the time.[19] Thus, players were ruled to be free to jump to the new Players League and jump they did. Most of the players in the new league were recruited either from the National League or the American Association.

The inability to restrain their players from league-jumping led the National League to employ several other tactics in an attempt to gain back some of their star players. Thus, National League clubs offered their former stars huge salaries if they would return, and some did. Also, games were scheduled in direct conflict with Players League games so as to make the fans choose between the two leagues. (Much of this has already been discussed in Chapter 1.) The players had won a symbolic battle, and both sides were ready for the peace treaty that was signed after the financially disastrous 1890 season. The leagues merged and the Players League was officially dissolved.

The National League

However, problems arose almost immediately after the signing of the merger agreement, as the National League and the American

Association disagreed over the distribution of players who had jumped to the now-defunct Players League. This dispute led both leagues to repudiate the National Agreement they had signed some years prior, and thus the 1891 season was to be no better from the standpoint of the clubs than the previous year had been. Again, the players were the beneficiaries of this dispute, as neither league respected the reserve rule they had signed some seven years before. Hence, players jumped leagues at will, salaries skyrocketed, and team financial statements remained in a dismal state. It was estimated that three-quarters of the 16 teams in the two leagues were financial failures during 1891.[20] As the season ended, both sides were in a mood to compromise, and the two leagues merged into a single 12-club National League. The American Association was defunct, but four of its former clubs were invited to join the newly expanded National League.

Being the only league in existence, the National League was guaranteed a virtual monopoly until such a time as a new rival would appear on the scene. The clubs took advantage of their positions of power during the 1890s and were able to force players to sign contracts on their terms or retire from professional baseball. Players who refused to go along with their club's salary terms had very few options to pursue. One player, Tony Mullane, quit professional baseball rather than accept a salary cut after he had performed ably in the previous season. Another player named Amos Rusie sat out the entire 1896 season rather than accept a salary cut of $100 after he had led his New York team in strikeouts and had won twenty-four games in 1895. He believed that after sitting out this one year, his team would no longer be able to reserve him and thus, he would be a free agent able to make the best possible deal for himself on the open baseball market. However, his New York team reserved him again for the 1897 season, and because of the no-tampering and reservation rules that the National League had adopted in their new National Agreement of 1892, no other team was free to deal with Rusie. The player then filed suit for damages and sought to obtain an unconditional release. Unfortunately for the student of baseball law, this case was never decided, as the parties agreed to an out-of-court settlement. Perhaps the New York Giants settled out of court with Rusie to avoid an adverse legal judgment in favor of the player, which would have impact on all teams for all times. In any event, the eventual outcome of the argument over whether or not the reservation clause in the Uniform Player's Contract was perpetual was not to be decided until some 78 years later in the Seitz arbitration decision (to be discussed in a later portion of this chapter).

The American League

Throughout the decade of the 1890s, the National League existed alone; yet it failed ever to achieve true financial success. Many reasons were advanced for this lack of success including too many teams, too many weak teams, rowdyism, interlocking directorates among the various clubs, and a lack of fan interest due to a decline in the perceived integrity of the game.[21] Whatever the exact nature of the National League's financial problems, it was soon to face a far more severe challenge than it had met in many years: a new rival, the Western League.

The Western League officially changed its name in 1900 to become the American League, a name familiar to all baseball fans. As in past interleague wars, the American League sought to entice National League stars to jump to their league by dangling offers of higher salaries in front of them. As had previously been established in several court cases, the National League's reserve rule could not prevent players from signing with a club in a different league. It was only enforceable within a single league, at this time the National League. Thus, the creation of this new league presented players with the opportunity to achieve higher salaries by jumping to the American League, where their reserve rule was not binding.

As reported in Chapter 1, the National League made several concessions to players who had formed baseball's second union, The League Players Protective Association, in exchange for a promise from the union that it would attempt to prevent players from jumping to the American League. However, the new union could not force players to honor their reserve clauses, and it died out in 1902.

Many players did jump to the new American League, which made tremendous strides forward in its first few years. The National League again attempted to restrain its players from league-jumping both by offering them competitive salaries and through legal actions. In essence, the National League again tried to argue that the reserve clause in the Uniform Player's Contract should restrain players from jumping to the American League. The most famous of these cases involved a player by the name of Nap Lajoie, who jumped from the Philadelphia Phillies of the National League to the Philadelphia Athletics of the American League after the 1900 season, in violation of the reserve clause in his contract with the Phillies. In a now-famous decision, the Pennsylvania Supreme Court held that Lajoie was bound to play with the Phillies because of the terms of the reserve clause in his individual contract.[22] While this was a victory for the National League, it should be noted that Lajoie's reserve clause differed from those in most contracts in that its exercise was limited to a fixed period of three years and his salary was fixed at $2400 per season if these options were used. Thus, in effect, Lajoie had signed a three-year contract with the Phillies, and it is doubtful that other players with the standard perpetual reserve clause in their contracts, who had not yet signed with their National League clubs for the upcoming season, would be similarly prevented from jumping to the American League. When Lajoie's case was finalized, his contract was transferred to another American League club (Cleveland) where he played for ten years and was later to be elected to the Hall of Fame. However, whenever his Cleveland team played in Philadelphia, Lajoie did not come with the team for fear of being arrested in Pennsylvania. The Philadelphia Phillies attempted unsuccessfully to have the injunction of the Pennsylvania Supreme Court enforced in Ohio. Thus Lajoie, though technically losing his case, nevertheless succeeded in jumping to the rival American League, and there he enjoyed a very successful career. In essence, there was nothing that the National League could do to prevent their players from jumping to the rival American League in search of higher salaries and better playing conditions.

The so-called American League War lasted for more than two years before both sides decided to call it quits. In January of 1903, the two leagues signed the "Cincinnati Peace Compact," the major element of which was the agreement for mutual recognition of reserved players from both leagues. Thus, teams were bound to honor the reserve clauses of players both in their own league as well as in the other. The formal two-league structure of organized baseball established with the signing of the Cincinnati Peace Compact remains intact today.

One other important change that came about after the Cincinnati treaty was the adoption of a central governing body for organized baseball, the national commission. In a sense, this national commission was the forerunner of the current commissioner system which exists in baseball today. One important rule established by this commission was to require all players to sign a uniform player's contract, which included a reserve clause as one of its provisions. No nonreserve contracts were to be permitted. Of course, this tradition of requiring every player to sign a uniform contract with a reserve clause in it was to be the subject of much heated debate in the years to follow.

The Federal League War and Baseball's Antitrust Exemption

Buoyed by spiraling attendance, the inception of the World Series, new stadiums, and the like, the National and American Leagues prospered in the ten-year period from 1903 to 1913. But once again, when team profits rose due to the factors listed above and the inequities of the reserve rule, which kept player salaries down, new investors sought to get into the act. Thus, in the year 1913, a group of such investors formed the Federal League in direct competition to organized baseball. This new league, as had all of its predecessors, attempted to sign established National and American League stars by offering them higher salaries than they were presently receiving. In effect, the Federal League refused to recognize the reserve clauses in individual player contracts in the National and American Leagues and treated all players as if they were free agents. As was the case in the past, the players again became the beneficiaries of this new league's attitude as salaries did increase greatly. Some players received higher salaries by reserve-jumping to the Federal League, an action that no court of law would prevent. But other players, fearful of being blacklisted for life from organized baseball should the Federal League fold, contented themselves with the higher salary offers they could receive from their respective clubs in the National and American Leagues as these clubs sought to prevent their stars from jumping leagues.

Even though the National and American League clubs raised salaries and threatened ballplayers who jumped leagues with banishment for life, the Federal League was able to attract many, many players away from organized baseball. In an attempt to hold on to their players, they changed the reserve clause in player contracts in 1914 to read as follows:[23]

> 1. *The club agrees to pay the player for the season of 1914 . . . a salary at the rate of _____ for such season; and an additional sum at the rate of _____ for such season, said additional sum being in consideration of the option herein reserved to the club in clause 10 hereof; said*

additional sum to be paid whether said option is exercised or not,
making the total compensation to the player for the season herein
contracted for _____ . . .

   10. *The player will, at the option of the club, enter into a contract*
for the succeeding season upon all the terms and conditions of this
contract, save as to clauses 1 and 10, and the salary to be paid the
player in the event of such renewal shall be the same as the total
compensation provided for the player in clause 1 hereto, unless it be
increased or decreased by mutual agreement.

Thus, the notion of part of a player's salary in exchange for his acceptance of the reserve rule was introduced at this time. Also, players could be reserved, but salaries would not be cut or increased except by mutual consent.

Organized baseball also went to court to stop several of their star players from contract-jumping. These actions met with varied success, with several decisions favoring the players[24] while others actually favored the National and American League Clubs.[25] Even with these few minor successes, the older leagues were simply unable to prevent players from either contract- or reserve-jumping to the Federal League.

During the next few seasons, none of the three leagues was financially successful. In January of 1915, the Federal League filed a suit against organized baseball under the Sherman Antitrust Act of 1890 claiming that the National and American Leagues were an illegal combination in restraint of trade. Therefore, the Federal League hoped to have the national agreement, the decisions of the national commission, and the reserve clauses in all player contracts ruled to be illegal. The presiding judge was Kenesaw Mountain Landis, later to become the first commissioner of baseball. Judge Landis never made a ruling on the Federal League's antitrust suit as the whole matter was settled out of court by yet another peace agreement signed in Cincinnati in December of 1915. Under this treaty, the Federal League was dissolved in exchange for payments of some $600,000 to its backers. Additionally, two Federal League teams, the Chicago Federals and the St. Louis Federals, were permitted to buy out the Chicago Cubs and the St. Louis Browns. Finally, all ineligible players were reinstated and Federal League owners were allowed to sell their players to any major league clubs. Players who were not purchased through this route had their contracts revert back to their original team in either the American or the National League.[26]

The Antitrust Exemption

While on the surface it seemed that all was well after this peace treaty had been signed, there was one very dissatisfied party, the Baltimore Federals of the Federal League. The owners of this club had demanded as a part of the peace pact the right to purchase the St. Louis Cardinals baseball club and move the club to Baltimore. Such a request was denied and was not made a part of the eventual peace treaty. Officials of the Baltimore club then filed a treble damage antitrust suit under the Sherman Act, claiming that the activities of organized baseball constituted an attempt to monopolize the business of baseball, a clear violation of the law. After several years of legal maneuvering, a district court judge for the District of Columbia finally ruled in 1919 that baseball was in violation of the antitrust laws and damages of $240,000 were awarded to the backers of the Baltimore club.

This decision was appealed and reversed by the Court of Appeals for the District of Columbia a short while later. And then, on appeal to the Supreme Court of the United States, Justice Holmes, speaking for a unanimous court, reaffirmed the decision of the Court of Appeals.[27] Thus it was that baseball received its exemption from the federal antitrust laws way back in the year 1922, an exemption that has stood ever since. The court ruled that baseball was a "game" and not trade or commerce. Additionally, it was ruled that baseball games were intrastate affairs and therefore not subject to the provisions of the Sherman Act. The transportation of players across state lines to participate in these baseball games was purely incidental to the playing of these games. Finally, it was ruled that the reserve clause and other baseball rules did not have a direct effect on the interstate features of the baseball business. And thus, for all of these reasons, the Federal club of Baltimore lost its case, but more importantly, professional baseball was to gain a position unique in professional sports even up until the present day, an exemption from prosecution under our nation's antitrust laws. As we will soon see, this important exemption in the Federal Baseball Club case was to be successfully employed many times by professional baseball in the years to come as a defense against legal actions aimed at overthrowing the reserve clause in individual player contracts. This defense has proven to be so powerful that eventually the players had to turn to other means, collective bargaining, in their attempts to revise the reservation system. All of these attempts will be described shortly.

For now, it is interesting to speculate on how differently things might have turned out in the game of baseball had the National and American League owners allowed the Baltimore Federal club to buy out the St. Louis Cardinals and move the team to Baltimore. If this action had been allowed, and it certainly did seem to be quite a reasonable request on its face, as the St. Louis area was having a hard time supporting two teams, it is most likely that no lawsuit would have ever been filed and that baseball would have never achieved its exempt status from the antitrust laws. Perhaps all of the players' dissatisfactions with the reserve system would have been settled through the courts, and the player unions and collective bargaining would have never reached their present level of prominence. But all of this is speculation because the fact of the matter is that the Supreme Court did exempt baseball from antitrust prosecution in 1922 and this ruling has stood ever since. Thus, we must now turn our attention to more recent attempts by the players to abolish the reserve rule.

The Commissioner System and the Mexican War

Even before the Federal Baseball Club decision, the owners of the 16 major league teams had gathered in Chicago in 1920 to place supreme control over the game of baseball into the hands of one man, the commissioner of baseball. As noted earlier, the first person chosen by the owners to occupy this position was none other than Judge Kenesaw Mountain Landis. This decision on the part of the owners was partly for practical reasons and also with an eye toward better financial days ahead. The old governing body in baseball, the National Commission, was essentially defunct by 1920. Every owner realized the need for new, decisive leadership. Additionally, fan loyalty and confidence in the game of baseball was at an all time low due to the fixing of the 1919 World Series, the "Black Sox" scandal. The owners felt that in order to restore integrity and financial stability to the game, they must have a new, strong leader.

For our purposes, the most important powers granted to the commissioner were the authority to investigate and take punitive measures against any players or club owners whose actions were deemed to be "detrimental to the best interests of the national game of baseball." It was based on these powers that Landis suspended eight members of the Chicago White Sox team for life for their participation in the World Series fixing of 1919. Also included under the rubric of detrimental to the best interests of the national game of baseball were contract- and reservation-jumping. Several players who did so were banned from organized baseball for a period of one year, a rather lenient penalty compared with what was to occur in later years.

The years following the appointment of Landis as commissioner were prosperous ones indeed for professional baseball. Of course, the reserve rule was in effect during these years, and the lack of competition from any sources allowed the 16 professional clubs to enjoy a favorable bargaining power position during salary negotiations with their players. As we have seen before, salary bargaining was pretty much on a take-it-or-leave-it basis. A player could either play for his club at the salary offered to him or pursue another occupation. No negotiations with any other team in either league were permitted.

As compared with the decade of the twenties, the thirties and the war years brought hard times to baseball as they did to most other industries in the United States. The popularity of the game and its financial status did not really pick up again until the conclusion of World War II. The years immediately after the war featured record attendance levels and a pretty bright profit picture for the clubs.

Formation of the Mexican League

But everything was not as bright as the club owners might have liked, because for the first time in over thirty years, they were again to be faced with a rival league. This time, the rival league was the Mexican League, and the ensuing battle has become known as the Mexican League War. It all began in 1946 when Don Jorge Pasquel, the president of the Mexican League, challenged the National and American Leagues by seeking to raid players from the north. Of course, those players who were lured to Mexico went with the promise of higher salaries, a situation very similar to that which we have examined previously.

And as previously was the case, organized baseball fought back hard. Then commissioner of baseball, A. B. (Happy) Chandler, announced that any player fleeing to Mexico in violation of either his reserve clause or a signed contract in organized baseball would be suspended for a period of five years. The record shows that despite this threat, 18 ballplayers did jump to the Mexican League. Organized baseball, as in the past, was unsuccessful in legal actions in which they attempted to prevent ballplayers from jumping to this rival league.

Most professional ballplayers in 1946 decided to stay with their clubs in organized baseball rather than risk a trip to the Mexican League. And in fact, the record indicates that of those 18 players who did play in Mexico, many soon became disillusioned and desired to return to their former teams in the National and American Leagues. The commissioner steadfastly refused to admit them back until after their five-year suspensions had been served. When these players sought to organize their own teams for the purpose of playing exhibition games, they found that they could not play as all of the ballparks were run by organized baseball. Chandler further threatened to suspend or fine any National or American League players found to be participating in exhibition contests with these blacklisted players. The commissioner was effectively preventing these players from pursuing their livelihood for five full years due to the fact that they had either jumped their contracts or failed to abide by the reserve clauses in their previous contracts.

Because of his inability to attract star players and retain those players that had been raided from organized baseball, Mexican League president Pasquel decided to get out of the raiding business; he retired and was replaced as president by Dr. Eduardo Pitman. Pitman and Commissioner Chandler then negotiated a nonraiding pact in which both leagues promised not to go after players in the other league. The finalization of the oral understanding really brought the Mexican League War to an end. Since 1946, organized baseball has never been seriously challenged by a rival league and the prospects for any such challenges in the future seem dim at best.

But the end of the Mexican League War did not mean that the contract and reserve jumpers would be automatically reinstated with their former teams. Quite to the contrary, although many of these players pleaded with Chandler for leniency, he was bound and determined to stick by his original penalty of a five-year suspension for each player. Failing to persuade Chandler to change his mind on humanitarian grounds, several players including Danny Gardella brought antitrust litigation against organized baseball in order to attain reinstatement in the game. In each of the cases filed evolving out of the Mexican League War, the courts refused to reinstate the players, basing their decisions on the earlier Federal Baseball Club decision, which exempted baseball from antitrust prosecution. Even though the times had changed quite a bit since this 1922 decision, organized baseball was able to retain its exempt status, and thus the player actions to sue baseball under the antitrust laws were all dismissed.[28] It was only after the courts had refused to reinstate Gardella and the other league jumpers that Chandler finally offered to reinstate all the blacklisted players. Having won the cases in court, Chandler was willing, as he put it, "to temper justice with mercy."[29] Of all the cases described above, Gardella's is of the most interest because he was a reserve jumper and *not* a contract jumper, as were the other players. But Gardella did win a victory of sorts when a Court of Appeals reversed the earlier dismissal of his case and sent it back to the District Court Judge for a trial to ascertain whether the allegations that Gardella had made were true.[30] But this trial would take time, and the 1949 season was about to begin. Thus, Gardella and other players sought preliminary injunctions to allow them to play in 1949. These injunctions were never granted, and it was this fact that led Commissioner Chandler to settle these matters out of court and reinstate all of the blacklisted players. If he had not done so, a trial on the legality of the reserve rule would have been held, and perhaps the course of history would have been changed. But the out-of-court settlement seemed to satisfy everybody involved, as all pending antitrust litigation was dropped and nothing further was to be heard of these matters. Thus, baseball had been able to once again survive a war with a rival league and come out of it with its reserve clause unscathed. For the time being, it seemed that peace was finally at hand and that the players were destined to accept their fate as being bound to one club into perpetuity.

Perpetual Reservation and Further Court Action

While the Gardella trial was never held, and baseball remained under the 1922 antitrust exemption granted to it by the Supreme Court, nevertheless several congressmen acted as if the ruling of the Court of Appeals in the Danny Gardella case was a signal for things to come. Several bills were introduced in Congress which would have legislatively removed baseball from coverage under the antitrust laws of the United States. Of course, this exemption was already in place due to the Supreme Court decision, but several congressmen must have felt that a reversal was inevitable and that swift legislative action was needed to save the day.

These bills generated much publicity and featured extensive hearings, the outcome of which was a long report on *Organized Baseball* (see endnote 1 at the conclusion of this chapter). At these hearings, much testimony was taken on the reserve clause and whether it was a necessary element for the survival of the game of baseball. Club owners and league officials argued in favor of the clause, claiming that it was responsible for the equalization of competition among the various clubs, preventing the wealthiest clubs from buying up all of the best talent. Competitive balance was said to lead to closer pennant races, which in turn generated higher fan interest and a healthier economic climate for the game. The reserve clause was also seen as being very important in protecting the integrity of the game of baseball. Of course, the owners did not mention this but another aspect of player reservation to their liking was the fact that salaries could be kept down due to the club's superior bargaining power and the player's inability to negotiate with any other clubs in professional baseball. For their part, most players also testified as to the necessity for some form of a reservation system for the survival of baseball as a business, much as John Montgomery Ward had done several years earlier.

Arguments against the reserve clause focused on the lower salaries players received as compared to what they could have had were the baseball players' labor market completely free. Also, many argued that the perpetual nature of the reserve clause caused each player to surrender so much freedom as to place him in a state of slavery. Such a state of affairs was regarded as morally unjust. Even Ty Cobb, a star ballplayer in his own right and a staunch supporter of organized baseball, testified as to the limited bargaining power players had during salary negotiations due to the reserve clause. Cobb suggested that perhaps the clubs could agree to use some form of salary arbitration for players with over five years of major league service in order partially to balance the scales of power. (This idea was finally adopted in 1973; see Chapter 4.)

After hearing all of this testimony regarding the pros and cons of the reserve system, the committee essentially had five choices for action:[31]

1. Recommending legislation to outlaw the reserve clause.
2. Recommending passage of one of the bills granting baseball unlimited exemption from the antitrust laws.
3. Recommending the enactment of a baseball code that would

be comprehensive and enforced by a new government agency.

4. Recommending a limited antitrust exemption for the reserve clause.
5. Recommending that no legislation of any type dealing with baseball's reserve clause be enacted at this time.

The committee was of the opinion that baseball did need some sort of a reservation system and thus option one was discarded. The preponderance of evidence gathered was fairly conclusive on this point. Option two was also ruled out; it was felt that a blanket antitrust immunity would completely isolate baseball from prosecution due to any and all types of arbitrary uses of league, club, and commissioner power over the players. While abuses of such power were deemed to be rare, they had occurred in the past, and if they were to occur again in the future, it was felt that they ought to be subject to judicial review.

The third option would have required Congress to write a whole new set of rules for the game of baseball and then set up a new administrative agency to make sure that these rules were followed. Congressional leaders wanted no part of such a task, which they felt they were not competent to undertake in any event. It was also decided that it was best to leave baseball alone to work out solutions to its own problems rather than saddle the game with a new regulatory agency created and funded by the government. A fourth possible option for the committee was to recommend a limited exemption that would apply only to the reserve clause and not necessarily to the hundreds of other rules in existence in baseball. The committee seemed to favor this option more than any other discussed up to this point, but decided against such a recommendation based on the assurance from organized baseball that the reasonableness of the reserve clause and thus its legality under the antitrust laws would be tested through pending litigation. Not desiring to have an unwarranted influence on this pending litigation, the committee closed its report by indicating that it had chosen to recommend the last of the five options listed above—no legislative action at that time.

Thus it was that while baseball still enjoyed its antitrust exemption due to the 1922 Federal Baseball Club case, it did at least appear that the players were finally to have their day in court as to the legality of the reserve clause under the rule of reason. Or at least that is what most people closely associated with the hearings and with baseball thought as the hearings drew to a close. For at that very time, eight treble damage lawsuits against organized baseball were working their way up through the court system. As Sobel aptly points out, while organized baseball was assuring the committee members of its intention to have the legality of the reserve rule tested in court based on the rule of reason, at the very same time in pending litigation the club owners were using the argument that the rule of reason was irrelevant in the case of the reserve clause as baseball was intrastate commerce in nature and thus deserved to be totally exempt from antitrust prosecution.[32]

The Toolson Case

The most crucial of the pending cases at this time dealt with the situation of a New York Yankee player by the name of George Toolson. His case against organized baseball was eventually to be decided by the Supreme Court of the United States, which reaffirmed baseball's antitrust exemption in its 1953 decision.[33] Toolson was angered at the fact that he was assigned by the Yankees to their Binghamton, New York, minor league club and refused to report as ordered. He was then placed on Binghamton's ineligible list, which essentially barred him from playing organized baseball anywhere due to the reserve clause in his contract. As the reader will recall, this clause would enable Toolson to play for Binghamton and no other team; all other teams were precluded from negotiating with him. Toolson filed a treble damage suit against baseball alleging that the reserve clause in his uniform contract was in violation of the antitrust statutes. But as had been the case in the past, the Supreme Court sided with organized baseball and declared:[34]

> *In* Federal Baseball Club of Baltimore v. National League of Professional Baseball Clubs . . . *this Court held that the business of providing public baseball games for profit between clubs of professional baseball players was not within the scope of federal antitrust laws. Congress has had the ruling under consideration but has not seen fit to bring such business under these laws by legislation having prospective effect. The business has thus been left for thirty years to develop, on the understanding that it was not subject to existing antitrust legislation. The present cases ask us to overrule the prior decision and, with retrospective effect, hold the legislation applicable. We think that if there are evils in this field which now warrant application to it of the antitrust laws it should be by legislation. Without re-examination of the underlying issues, the judgments below are affirmed on the au-*

thority of Federal Baseball Club of Baltimore v. National League of Professional Baseball Clubs . . . *so far as that decision determines that Congress had no intention of including the business of baseball within the scope of federal antitrust laws. Affirmed.*

Thus, Toolson lost his case and baseball's reserve clause had once again passed inspection. But several other players were to test the applicability of the Sherman Act to baseball in later years; none of their attempts proved successful. As noted before, the ultimate demise of the reserve clause was to be brought about through collective bargaining and not through any legal mandate.

It should be noted that ever since the end of World War II, the reserve clause in the uniform player's contract in organized baseball has been deemed by the club owners to be *perpetual* in nature. While this reserve clause has been amended slightly from time to time in recent years, a fairly standard version of the pre-free-agency reserve clause is reprinted below from the 1973 collective bargaining agreement.[35]

On or before December 20 (or if a Sunday, then the next preceding business day) in the year of the last playing season covered by this contract, the Club may tender to the Player a contract for the term of that year by mailing the same to the Player at his address following his signature hereto, or if none be given, then at his last address of record with the Club. If prior to the March 1 next succeeding said December 20, the Player and the Club have not agreed upon the terms of such contract, then on or before 10 days after said March 1, the Club shall have the right by written notice to the Player at said address to renew this contract for the period of one year on the same terms, except that the amount payable to the Player shall be such as the Club shall fix in said notice; provided, however, that said amount, if fixed by a Major League Club, shall be an amount payable at a rate not less than 80 percent of the rate stipulated for the next preceding year and at a rate not less than 70 percent of the rate stipulated for the year immediately prior to the next preceding year.

The reader will note that the club is given the right to renew the contract on the same terms for the following year, provided only that the player's salary cannot be reduced by more than 20 percent. This 20-percent figure has been changed from time to time, but recall the fact that in contracts signed right after the Federal League War, the principle of establishing part of a player's pay for honoring his reserve clause and signing a contract was put into effect. Thus, as a remnant from this older system, we still see today the fact that reserved players who refuse to sign a uniform contract can be docked up to 20 percent of last season's pay as a penalty for not signing. The most important fact about this rule is that the club's right to renew the contract on these terms is itself one of the terms of the contract. Thus, once a player is reserved, the renewal clause in his new contract gives his club the option to renew his contract again and again, into perpetuity if they so desire.[36] This interpretation of the perpetual nature of the reservation clause would allow players Andy Messersmith and Dave McNally effectively to challenge and change baseball's reserve system for all time in the year 1975. But before the Messersmith/McNally grievances, we will cover one more legal attempt at abolishing baseball's reserve rule, the now famous case of St. Louis Cardinal outfielder Curt Flood.

The Flood Case

In the Flood decision, the Supreme Court noted that this case represented the third time in fifty years that the Court had been asked to rule on the applicability of the antitrust laws to baseball's reserve system.[37] Curt Flood was originally a member of the Cincinnati Reds for two years, but was traded to St. Louis prior to the 1958 season. He was a star outfielder at St. Louis for some twelve years when he was traded to the Philadelphia Phillies in October of 1969. Note that this trade occurred prior to the adoption of the so-called Santo clause in baseball's collective bargaining contract, where a player with ten years of professional experience, the last five of which were with the same team, could veto a trade not to his liking. (The term "Santo clause" is used as Ron Santo was the first player ever to invoke this veto right.) In 1969, when Flood was traded to Philadelphia, he had no such option available to him.

Flood complained about the trade and asked the Commissioner of Baseball, Bowie Kuhn, to declare him a free agent. This request was denied, and in January 1970 Flood filed suit against organized baseball, charging that the reserve clause was in violation of federal antitrust laws. Flood sat out the 1970 season even though offered $100,000 by the Philadelphia club. In 1970 he was again traded, this time to the Washington club. He did come to terms with Washington for $110,000 for the 1971 season but left the club in late April, never again to play professional baseball.[38]

Flood's case proceeded all the way to the Supreme Court after the rendering of both a District Court and a Court of Appeals ruling favoring the defendants, in this case the commissioner of baseball, the two league presidents, and all of the professional clubs in the National and American Leagues.[39] In both of these rulings, the earlier decisions in *Federal Baseball Club* and *Toolson* v. *New York Yankees* were cited as controlling. The Supreme Court agreed to hear the case to look once again at "this troublesome and unusual situation."[40]

Again in the case of Curt Flood, a majority of members on the Supreme Court ruled in favor of organized baseball based on the earlier *Federal Baseball Club* and *Toolson* decisions. It is interesting to note that the majority opinion clearly stated that they believed baseball to be a business engaged in interstate commerce and that the antitrust exemption provided to baseball through earlier Supreme Court decisions should be viewed as an anomaly, an aberration confined to baseball. Even though the ruling that baseball's reserve system is protected from antitrust prosecution might seem illogical, the court felt that it was a ruling that had been around for over fifty years and thus was entitled to the benefit of *stare decisis*. (The literal translation of this Latin phrase is "to stand by that which has been decided," or in the case of baseball, to let baseball's antitrust exemption stand based on the earlier decisions.) For this and other reasons, the court affirmed the earlier judgment of the Court of Appeals and Flood's case was dismissed. Thus, if the reserve clause was ever to be overturned as illegal, and if baseball was to lose its antitrust exemption, Congressional action would have to be forthcoming. The Supreme Court seemed clearly to indicate that as far as it was concerned, the next move was either up to the Congress or to the players and clubs through collective bargaining.

The Supreme Court ruling in the Flood case was not unanimous. Two justices (Douglas and Brennan) were of the opinion that earlier Supreme Court decisions regarding baseball's exemption from antitrust prosecution were clearly wrong and that the Flood case presented the court with a perfect opportunity to reverse a previous error. In a strongly worded statement, they declared that[41]

> There can be no doubt "that were we considering the question of baseball for the first time upon a clean slate" we would hold it to be subject to federal antitrust regulation . . . . The unbroken silence of Congress should not prevent us from correcting our own mistakes.

As was pointed out in a separate dissenting opinion by Justices Marshall and Brennan, just because the Supreme Court might decide to overrule *Federal Baseball Club* and *Toolson*, and thus subject baseball to the federal antitrust laws, this would not necessarily imply that Flood would automatically have won his case. A major hurdle that would still have to be overcome would be the fact that the reserve system was arguably a part of the collective bargaining contract agreed to by the club owners and the MLBPA and thus was a mandatory subject of bargaining. As such, would the federal labor statutes be the applicable laws instead of the antitrust statutes? This is a complicated legal issue that has not yet been addressed with regard to baseball because of its continuing exemption. However, the dissenting opinion in the Flood case would have remanded the case back to Judge Cooper's District Court for a consideration of this complex nexus of labor and antitrust legislation issues.[42] At this time, it does not look as if such a trial will ever be necessary as the parties have chosen to resolve their differences bilaterally through collective bargaining rather than do further battle in court. And in fact, it was in this same District Court where the Flood case was first heard that Judge Cooper interjected a personal opinion into his ruling that[43]

> *. . . negotiations could produce an accommodation on the reserve system which would be eminently fair and equitable to all concerned . . . the reserve clause can be fashioned so as to find acceptance by player and club.*

Reserve Options

The whole series of decisions reviewed above quite naturally gave rise to an extensive literature expounding on the pros and cons of baseball's antitrust exemption.[44] A good deal of this literature was quite favorably disposed toward the Supreme Court actions, while other authors were mildly critical. For example, one article summed up the problem of baseball's antitrust exemption by noting that the ". . . ultimate solution, therefore, to the predicament now facing the courts and organized baseball is legislation which would both exempt the reserve rule and guard it against abuse."[45] Almost all of these articles contained the suggestion that any solution to the problems caused by baseball's antitrust exemption would have to be forthcoming from Congress. Indeed, over time many bills were introduced, as we have seen above, but none have been passed. Additionally, further Congressional hearings have served to provide us with a list of options to the reserve system for Congress to consider:[46]

a.   Independent and competitive leagues.
b.   Limitation of player control to some fixed term.
c.   Free agency after an option year.
d.   Trade vetos for veteran players.
e.   Minimum salary progression.
f.   Fewer reserved players.
g.   Salary arbitration.
h.   Revenue division between clubs.

It is interesting to note the current status of each of the above suggestions for modification of baseball's reserve system. The reader should recall throughout this discussion that the players and clubs alike have been in general agreement on the point that *some sort* of a reserve system is a necessity for the game of baseball.

As we have already noted, option (a) above has not been seriously attempted in baseball since the Mexican League War of 1946. However, in other sports, such as basketball, football, and hockey, the existence of competitive leagues in recent years has been partly responsible for improved player salaries and benefits.

Option (b), a fixed-term reservation period to replace the former perpetual system, turns out to be the system finally agreed upon by the owners and the players in baseball through collective negotiations. As such, this system will be fully described later in this chapter and is reprinted in full in Appendix I at the end of this chapter.

The third possibility, free agency after one option year, has been experimented with in other sports, as we shall see in Chapter 6. The biggest problem with this type of a procedure as it existed in football and basketball was that the excessive and uncertain amount of compensation required from teams signing the free agents really put a damper on the free agent market altogether. This same issue of compensation for teams losing free agents now confronts baseball's bargainers, as we shall soon see. It might also be noted that the Seitz decision, which will be discussed shortly, would have changed baseball's perpetual reservation system into a one-year option rule. However, after this decision was rendered, the two sides were able to agree on a compromise six-year reserve system through collective bargaining.

Options (d), (e), and (g) are all currently included in the collective bargaining agreement signed by the owners and the MLBPA. In Chapters 4 and 5, we will have much more to say about salary arbitration, minimum salary progression, and the right to veto a trade as curbs on the owners' former unilateral and complete control over their player assets.

Option (f), a limited number of reserved players per team, has not been tried in recent years. The reader, however, is reminded that the original reserve clause in baseball agreed to in a secret meeting of club owners in 1879 was limited in nature in that only five players per club could be so reserved. As we have seen, this number has gradually been increased to include every player on every club.

Finally, as a replacement for the supposed equality of team playing strengths produced by the reserve system, some have argued for revenue division between clubs. A more equal split of the gate proceeds might enable all teams to bid for the services of free agent ballplayers. This proposal has never been seriously considered in baseball, given both sides' apparent interest in maintaining some form of a reserve clause. However, in other sports, gate receipts are split on a much more equal basis between the home and visiting clubs.

Thus, through the early 1970s, it became quite clear that the Supreme Court was not about to correct the anomaly that it had created in *Federal Baseball Club* and maintained in *Toolson* and *Flood*. Baseball was to continue to enjoy exemption from antitrust prosecution as it does to this date. Thus, many persons turned to the Congress to correct the deficiencies inherent in baseball's reservation system. However, Congress had failed to take action for over fifty years to overturn the *Federal Baseball Club* ruling and no immediate prospects for such legislation cropped up after the Flood decision. The players had two strikes against them at the time, but they still had one swing left. That remaining option was to try to mold some type of a compromise reservation system through the process of face-to-face collective negotiations with the club owners. Understandably, the owners were reluctant to make any changes in favor of the players unless they were forced to do so. Thus, the road toward free agency was to prove to be a rough one indeed. In fact, to this date, the parties have not been able to devise a system satisfactory to each of their interests. Yet some progress has been made and it is to a description and analysis of these recent events that we now focus our attention.

Bargaining Over the Reserve Clause

Realizing that court and/or legislative action to abolish the reserve clause was not likely to be forthcoming, the players decided to try to revamp the system through the process of collective bargaining. As if motivated to reach some compromise solution based on Judge Cooper's words (quoted above), the players and the owners did discuss the issue of the reserve clause and system at the bargaining table several times.

The first such discussions occurred during the negotiations over the initial collective bargaining contract in 1968. At this time, all the parties could agree to was provision for a joint study of their differences with regard to the reserve system. The 1970 collective bargaining contract dealt with the issue of the reserve clause using the following language:[47]

> *Regardless of any provision herein to the contrary, this Agreement does not deal with the reserve system. The parties have differing views as to the legality and as to the merits of such a system as presently constituted. This Agreement shall in no way prejudice the position or legal rights of the Parties or of any Player regarding the reserve system.*
>
> *It is agreed that until final and unappealable adjudication . . . of* Flood v. Kuhn, et al., *now pending in the Federal District Court of the Southern District of New York, neither of the Parties will resort to any form of concerted action with respect to the issue of the reserve system, and there shall be no obligation to negotiate with respect to the reserve system. Upon the final and unappealable adjudication . . . of* Flood v. Kuhn, et al., *either party shall have the right to reopen the negotiations on the issue of the reserve system. . . .*

Thus, at the time of the 1970 negotiations, the players were willing reluctantly to accept the reserve system as it stood so that they could challenge it through the court system in the case of *Flood* v. *Kuhn*. Further negotiations over the system were put on hold until after the final resolution of the Flood case. When Flood lost his case the players were once again anxious to use collective bargaining to try to get some compromise resolution over their difficulties associated with the reserve clause.

The 1973 collective bargaining contract featured the following language with regard to the reserve system:[48]

> *Except as adjusted or modified hereby, this Agreement does not deal with the reserve system. The Parties have differing views as to the legality and as to the merits of such system as presently constituted.*

This Agreement shall in no way prejudice the position or legal rights of the Parties or of any Player regarding the reserve system.

During the term of this Agreement neither of the Parties will resort to any form of concerted action with respect to the issue of the reserve system, and there shall be no obligation to negotiate with respect to the reserve system.

While the above language would seem to *remove* the "reserve system" from coverage under the collective bargaining contract and thus, leave disputes over such system *outside* of the jurisdiction of the grievance/arbitration procedure, consider the following language, also from the 1973 collective bargaining agreement:[49]

The form of the Uniform Player's Contract between a Club and a Player is attached hereto as Schedule A which is incorporated herein by reference and made a part hereof.

During the term of this Agreement, no other form of Uniform Player's Contract will be utilized. Should the provisions of any Contract between any individual Player and any of the Clubs be inconsistent with the terms of this Agreement, the provisions of this Agreement shall govern. Nothing herein contained shall limit the right of any Club and Player to enter into special covenants in the space provided in a manner not inconsistent with the provisions of this Agreement. The termination of this Agreement shall not impair, limit or terminate the rights and duties of any Club or Player under any Contract between any individual Player and any of the Clubs.

This Uniform Player's Contract, which was made part and parcel of the collective bargaining contract by the above clause in 1973, contained the reservation clause section that we quoted earlier. Thus, it would seem pretty clear that the reserve clause in the Uniform Player's Contract was now a part of the collective bargaining agreement and as such, was subject to the grievance/arbitration procedure. Or was it? Recall that Article XV quoted above specifically said that the collective bargaining agreement did *not* cover the reserve system. So we are left with a situation where the language in one clause (Article XV) seems to remove the reserve system from coverage under the negotiated contract while in the very same pact another section (Article III) clearly incorporates the Uniform Player's Contract (and thereby, the reserve clause) into the body of the collective bargaining agreement. This apparent contradiction in the contract was somehow going to have to be worked out, and as we shall see shortly, the final decision was to be in favor of the players.

The Jim "Catfish" Hunter Grievance

The first attempt to challenge the reserve clause through collective bargaining came in the case of Oakland pitcher Jim "Catfish" Hunter in 1974. An important thing for the reader to keep in mind is that the baseball clubs and the MLBPA had already agreed to the use of a grievance/arbitration procedure with impartial arbitration as the final and binding step in their 1973 collective bargaining contract. The history and importance of this negotiated grievance procedure will be covered in some detail in Chapter 4. At this juncture, however, the reader should be aware of the fact that baseball players were able to challenge the reserve system and have their complaints heard before a neutral arbitrator only because of the inclusion of this grievance/arbitration clause in their collective bargaining contract. Thus, the importance of this grievance procedure should not be minimized. It can be said that were it not for the grievance/arbitration procedure, baseball's former reserve system would probably have remained intact to date. Thus, the reader should be aware of the fact that of all the gains achieved through bargaining, the inclusion of a grievance/arbitration procedure in their negotiated collective bargaining contracts has to rate very near the top in terms of *importance* to the players. For as we shall soon see, while a grievance procedure is important in its own right, this grievance/arbitration procedure in baseball was essentially responsible for opening up the door through which players could challenge the perpetual reservation system. This they were able to do quite effectively.

The first such challenge came from Catfish Hunter in 1974. Hunter's 1974 contract specified that he was to be paid $100,000, half of which was to be for salary and the other half of which was to be applied in *any* manner which he chose. Trying to minimize his own tax burden, Hunter asked Oakland owner Charles Finley to use his other $50,000 to purchase a nontaxable annuity from a life insurance company in North Carolina. Finley was reluctant to do anything but pay his player in cash as he desired to use all of Hunter's salary as a deductible item on the team's tax return.

Based on Finley's refusal to purchase the annuity, Hunter took action under the terms of paragraph 7(a) of the Uniform Player's Contract that he had signed. (The Uniform Player's Contract is reprinted in full in Appendix I at the end of Chapter 5.) In essence, this contractual provision gave Hunter the right to terminate his contract if his club defaulted in payment or otherwise failed to satisfy any of the terms of the signed agreement. Hunter's contention was that Finley had failed to live up to all of the terms of their agreement by refusing to purchase the annuity. Hunter demanded that Finley pay him the amount due and that he be declared a free agent eligible to negotiate with any club in either league.

The dispute between Hunter and Finley could not be resolved in the early stages of the grievance procedure, and so Hunter's case was heard before arbitrator Peter Seitz. In December of 1974, Seitz ruled that Oakland owed Hunter $50,000 plus interest and that Hunter was a free agent. While the baseball club owners were surprised at the second part of this ruling, Finley decided to fight the decision with an appeal to the California Superior Court. However, these efforts proved unsuccessful, and as the faithful baseball fan will remember, Hunter eventually signed a five-year pact with the New York Yankees for $3.75 million, making him the highest paid baseball player at that time. Owners were quick to use this opportunity to point out again the necessity of a reserve clause to hold salaries in line and to preserve the financial integrity of the game of baseball. The players, on the other hand, felt that the Hunter case clearly demonstrated how the owners had used the cloak of the reservation system for a number of years to depress their wages artificially. Thus it was that the players looked forward with great anticipation to a future period of time when they would all be eligible to become free agents and test their value on baseball's open labor market. And they would not have to wait much longer before achieving this goal. For already, the seeds of discord leading to the filing of grievances by pitchers Andy Messersmith and Dave McNally were in evidence.

The Messersmith/McNally Grievances and the Seitz Decision

Andy Messersmith signed a one-year contract for $90,000 with the Los Angeles Dodgers in 1974. A dispute arose between Messersmith and the Dodgers prior to the 1975 season because the pitcher wanted a no-trade guarantee, or at least the right to approve any trade involving him, written specifically into his contract. The Dodgers balked at this, and Messersmith played the entire 1975 season without a signed contract. In essence, he was reserved to the Dodgers by the terms of paragraph 10(a) of his Uniform Player's Contract. Under this paragraph, the Dodgers could have cut Messersmith's salary by 20 percent to $72,000 in 1975. However, the record shows that he played the entire 1975 season and was paid the sum of $115,000. A similar situation existed for pitcher Dave McNally of the Montreal Expos. He had played the 1974 season under a signed contract and was then reserved by the Montreal club for the 1975 season under the terms of paragraph 10(a) in his Uniform Player's Contract. McNally then played a portion of the 1975 season for Montreal prior to his retirement from baseball.

At the conclusion of the 1975 championship season, each player declared that he was a free agent eligible to negotiate with any club in either league. The owners rejected this conclusion and instead argued that Messersmith and McNally were still bound to their respective teams by the provisions of the reserve clause in their Uniform Player's Contract. What the dispute boiled down to was the players' claim that this reserve clause was of the one-year variety while the owners insisted that it was perpetual in nature, a position they had taken for some time. The issue came to a head in October 1975, when the MLBPA filed grievances on the behalf of pitchers Messersmith and McNally seeking to have an arbitrator declare them both to be free agents, given that both players had already completed their one renewal year.

The clubs were quite anxious to prevent the players from winning these grievances; an affirmative decision for the players would most probably signal an end to the reserve system that the owners had come to relish so dearly. Thus, the clubs staged a several-pronged attack against these player grievances. Stage one was geared toward preventing these cases from reaching arbitration in the first place. One thing the parties could have done here was to reach an amicable out-of-court settlement. But this did not seem possible as neither side was willing to back down from its steadfast position. Thus, the owners collectively went to court to prevent these grievances from coming to arbitration. However, at the court hearing before Judge John W. Oliver, all sides involved agreed to go ahead with the scheduled arbitration hearing and let the arbitrator decide on the issue of jurisdiction and the merits of the case if necessary. Both sides also agreed that the determination of the jurisdictional question made by the arbitrator could then be appealed to Judge Oliver's U.S. District Court by either party.

Thus, at the arbitration hearings held on November 21 and 24 and December 1, 1975, the club owners argued that

1. The grievances were *not arbitrable* and therefore were not properly before the arbitration panel; that is, the panel had no jurisdiction to hear these grievances.
2. Even if the grievances were found to be properly before the panel, they should be denied based on the merits of the cases.

For their part, the players argued that the cases were arbitrable and that on their merits, each case should be decided in favor of the players. Each of these issues will be addressed in turn.

Arbitrability

The owners argued against the authority of the arbitration panel to hear the cases, while the players' case rested on the fact that the two cases were quite properly before the arbitration panel. It should be noted at this time that the panel of arbitrators referred to above included Marvin Miller, the Executive Director of the MLBPA, John Gaherin, the Director of the Player Relations Committee, and Peter Seitz, the same neutral who had made the earlier ruling in the Catfish Hunter case. This tripartite panel consisted of one union arbitrator, one management arbitrator, and the one true neutral, Peter Seitz. Thus, the decision of Peter Seitz would be controlling, as the positions of Miller and Gaherin on the issue had already been clearly stated.

The notion of arbitrability or the jurisdiction of the arbitration panel refers to whether or not the issue at dispute is properly before the arbitration panel. In this case the issue in dispute was whether the reserve clause in the Uniform Player's Contract was perpetual in nature as argued by the owners or of a one year nature as contended by the players. The first thing that had to be settled was whether this issue could be decided by an arbitrator.

The argument of the clubs in favor of nonarbitrability was based upon the language of Article XV of the 1973 collective bargaining contract quoted above. The reader will recall that in this section the statement that "this Agreement does not deal with the reserve system" was made. Given this clear statement, the authority of the arbitration panel to hear any grievances regarding the reserve system or any part thereof is singularly lacking. The reader should be aware of the fact that Article X of the 1973 collective bargaining agreement dealing with the grievance/arbitration procedure defined a grievance as any dispute which involved "the interpretation of, or compliance with, the provision of any agreement between the Association and the Clubs."[50] Since grievances could only be filed over matters dealing with the interpretation of issues in the current contract, and since the reserve system was clearly *not* a part of the current contract based on the language of Article XV, the clubs contended that these two grievances should be dismissed summarily as not being properly under the jurisdiction of the arbitration panel.

The counterargument of the players focused on the fact that the reserve system was not a clearly defined element but rather a conglomeration of several rules including paragraph 10(a) of the Uniform Player's Contract, Major League Rules 4-A (Reserve Lists) and Major League Rule 3(g) dealing with tampering with other teams' player personnel. As such, all of the various aspects of this reserve system could reasonably be argued to be subsumed under the collective bargaining contract language in Article III, reprinted above, in which the reserve clause was formally made a part of the collective bargaining contract, thus presumably subjecting it to the grievance/arbitration procedure. But then how could the players explain their acceptance of the Article XV language, which seemed to remove the reserve system from coverage under the collective agreement?

The explanation proffered by the MLBPA was that they had clearly expressed their dissatisfaction with the reserve system in bargaining sessions held in 1968 and 1970. Language included in these first two collective agreements and reprinted above clearly demonstrated that the players wished to change the reserve system. They reluctantly accepted the reserve system in the 1970 collective bargaining contract so that they could attack the legality of it in the then-pending Curt Flood litigation. The players argued that even though they viewed the reserve system as illegal under the antitrust laws of the land, they accepted compliance with it so that the Curt Flood case could be litigated. Having thus accepted a system which they believed to be illegal, the MLBPA needed to have some protection for itself against any possible claim by a player that his union was a co-conspirator with the baseball clubs in violation of the antitrust laws by accepting the reserve system. Thus, the MLBPA asked for and received the language of Article XIV quoted above that the Basic Agreement "does not deal with the reserve system." Thereby it was hoped that the Association would have some legal barrier against any player who might later decide to file suit against his union in such a fashion as described above.

While it can't be determined for certain how useful such a move might have proved in a court of law had a player chosen to file such a suit, the important thing was that Arbitrator Seitz viewed the above as an[51]

> . . . *understandable and reasonable explanation of the genesis and rationale of the provision in light of the apparent paradox and contradiction mentioned above. In exchange for such legal protection as might be afforded to the Association by Article XIV against a charge of linkage and federation with the leagues' historic reserve system (which it had been unable to modify or eliminate to its satisfaction in bargaining) it agreed, in 1970, pending the conclusion of the* Flood Case *not to engage in a) "any form of concerted action with respect to the reserve system," and b) not to negotiate with respect to the reserve system in that period.*

Thus, Arbitrator Seitz sided with the players on this first issue of arbitrability. He found that the two grievances were properly before him as nothing in Article XIV prevented the filing of such grievances. Additionally, the grievance procedure itself did exclude certain kinds of disputes from its scope but made no mention whatsoever of excluding issues dealing with the reserve system. Finally, it was noted that previous grievances had been filed over the reserve system (for example, the Catfish Hunter case) and that the owners had never before raised the claim that reserve system grievances were not arbitrable. Thus, for all of these reasons, and by the authority vested in arbitrators by the Supreme Court's "Steelworkers Trilogy" decisions of 1960,[52] Seitz ruled that the Messersmith and McNally grievances were properly before the panel. Thus, the cases could be decided upon their merits.

Merit

To decide these cases upon their merits would require Seitz to settle once and for all the basic issue at dispute, that is, whether the reserve clause paragraph 10(a) in the Uniform Player's Contract was perpetual in nature or was to be interpreted as providing the clubs with only a one-year option on a player's services after the expiration of an existing and signed individual player contract.

On this point, the argument of the clubs was that the reserve clause was perpetual in nature. Once Messersmith and McNally signed their original contracts with their respective clubs, they were bound to play for these teams until such time as they were traded, sold, or otherwise given an outright release. Being reserved for the 1975 season simply meant that these players were now playing under a new contract which also contained a similar reservation clause. Thus, the clubs believed that they did have the contractual right to the services of Messersmith and McNally for the 1976 season, and into perpetuity for that matter, if they so desired.

Further, based on Major League Rule 4-A(a), the clubs contended that by having duly placed these players' names on their reserve lists in November of 1975, they had reserved the exclusive rights to these players' services for the 1976 season under the published rules of baseball:[53]

> *(a) FILING. On or before November 20 in each year, each Major League Club shall transmit to the Commissioner and to its League President a list of not exceeding forty (40) active and eligible players, whom the club desires to reserve for the ensuing season. . . . On or before November 30 the League President shall transmit all of such lists to the Secretary-Treasurer of the Executive Council, who shall thereupon promulgate same, and thereafter no player on any list shall be eligible to play for or negotiate with any other club until his contract has been assigned or he has been released. . . .*

The clubs also argued that rule 4-A(a) was further supported by Major League Rule 3(g) dealing with tampering:[54]

> *(g) TAMPERING. To preserve discipline and competition and to prevent the enticement of players . . . there shall be no negotiations or dealings respecting employment, either present or prospective between any player . . . and any club other than the club with which he is under contract or acceptance of terms, or by which he is reserved . . . unless the club or league with which he is connected shall have in writing, expressly authorized such negotiations or dealings prior to their commencement.*

In summary, the clubs and leagues argued that Messersmith and McNally were still both the property of their respective clubs due to Major League Rules 4-A(a) and 3(g) and paragraph 10(a) of the Uniform Player's Contract. Given that the Los Angeles and Montreal clubs retained this exclusive right to these players' services, the clubs argued that the arbitrator should dismiss the grievances as being without merit.

The MLBPA simply argued that having once been reserved for the 1975 season, both of these players should be regarded as *no longer* being under contract to their former teams. Given that these players are no longer under contract, they should be declared to be free agents and be allowed to make the best possible deal for themselves with any club in either league. Thus, the arbitrator was faced with deciding whether the players were still under contract to their respective clubs and if not, whether the Major League Rules 4-A(a) and 3(g) cited above prevented these players and other clubs from dealing with each other for the purposes of negotiating an employment contract.

The Decision

As previously noted, Arbitrator Seitz sided with the players on all of the counts above. First, he ruled that the reserve clause explicitly guaranteed the clubs the right to renew a player's services for the period of *one year*. It is perfectly legal to write contracts with successive renewals in them. However, when this is done, such subsequent renewal rights have to be clearly stated in the terms of the contract. In the opinion of Arbitrator Seitz, there was nothing in paragraph 10(a) of the Uniform Player's Contract to indicate that the contract could be renewed for more than one year. The argument of the clubs that the renewed contract, being on the same terms as the previous contract, would also contain a reservation clause under which the player would remain the property of the same team, was dismissed by Seitz as being inappropriate. Thus, he ruled that players Messersmith and McNally were no longer under contract to their respective clubs.

Given this ruling, Seitz then had to decide whether Major League Rules 4-A(a) and 3(g) nevertheless would still prohibit these players from negotiating with any other clubs and similarly would prevent any other clubs from negotiating with them. His final ruling was that in the absence of an existing contractual relationship between the parties, a player could not be reserved. Reservation by simply placing a player's name on a Rule 4-A(a) list was not possible unless the player was under a signed Uniform Player's Contract. The signed contract allowed the teams to exercise one option of the reserve clause per player for a period of one year. After this one-year reserve period has run out, the player is no longer under contract and Rule 4-A(a) therefore does not serve to bind the player to his original team. Similarly, Seitz ruled that Major League Rule 3(g) led to the same conclusion—*no contract, no reservation.*[55]

Back to Court

Peter Seitz had shocked the world of baseball with this arbitration decision, declaring both Messersmith and McNally to be free agents and, more importantly, changing the nature of baseball's historic perpetual reservation system into a reserve system limited to but a single one-year option on a player's services. All clubs immediately realized that as soon as player contracts expired and these players had been reserved for a single season, they would all become free agents. Determined to prevent the certain bidding war that would ensue, the owners decided to take their case back to Judge Oliver's District Court, as was provided for in the agreement to arbitrate discussed earlier. The reader will recall that before arbitration had occurred, the clubs had filed a motion with Judge Oliver to prevent arbitration of these grievances based on the lack of jurisdiction of the panel to decide reserve system issues. However, both sides agreed to allow the arbitration proceedings to take place first, while reserving the right to appeal the arbitrator's decision to Judge Oliver at a later date. It was this right of appeal that the clubs were now exercising.

Judge Oliver refused to review the merits of the Seitz decision based upon the Supreme Court's precedent set in the "Steelworkers Trilogy" cases (cited in endnote 52 at the end of this chapter). He clearly stated in his opinion that:[56]

> The question of interpretation of the collective bargaining agreement is a question for the arbitrator. It is the arbitrator's construction which was bargained for; and so far as the arbitrator's decision concerns construction of the contract, the courts have no business overruling him because their interpretation of the contract is different from his.

However, Judge Oliver was willing to reconsider the jurisdictional issue raised by the clubs. His ruling was again based upon the precedent set in the Steelworkers Trilogy cases, that there was a presumption in favor of arbitrability unless an item was specifically mentioned as being outside of the realm of the grievance/arbitration procedure. Finding no such specific exclusion of the reserve system from the grievance/arbitration provision in baseball's collective bargaining contract, Judge Oliver ruled that the arbitration panel did have the jurisdiction to hear and decide the grievances. Thus, the rulings in the Messersmith and McNally grievances were upheld in court.

Seitz's Recommendations

Peter Seitz made it abundantly clear in his arbitration award that he was merely ruling on an issue of contract interpretation, as he was ordered to do by the parties, and was not by his decision rendering any personal opinion about the desirability of a reserve clause in baseball. In fact, he clearly pointed out that in previous years, clubs and players alike had testified as to the necessity for some type of a reservation system. Thus, he noted that:[57]

> It would be a mistake to read this Opinion as a statement of the views of the writer either for or against a reserve system or, for that matter, the Reserve System presently in force. It is not my function to do so! . . .
>
> It deserves emphasis that this decision strikes no blow emancipating players from claimed serfdom or involuntary servitude such as was alleged in the Flood case. It does not condemn the Reserve System presently in force on constitutional or moral grounds. It does not counsel or require that the system be changed to suit the predilections or preferences of an arbitrator acting as a Philosopher-King intent upon imposing his own personal brand of industrial justice on the parties. It does no more than seek to interpret and apply provisions that are in the agreements of the parties. To go beyond this would be an act of quasi-judicial arrogance!
>
> Indeed, the record in this case demonstrates abundantly that courts which have had the Reserve System under scrutiny, and the Congressional Committee of which Congressman Celler was chairman, reached the conclusion that a reserve system was indispensable to this sport; but that questions arise as to whether this reserve system, in some of its aspects or as interpreted and applied by the clubs, requires modifications.
>
> . . . the posture of the Players Association in these cases, as I understand it, is not to oppose a reserve system which accommodates the needs of the clubs with what it regards as the requirements of players in a society in which freedom to contract personal services is an important attribute.

Finally, it should be mentioned that Seitz seemed to be reluctant to hand down this decision and, indeed, even a bit apologetic when he did. This was not because of any concern on his part that the decision was improper or a poorly reasoned one, but rather based on his strong belief that the parties would be able to negotiate their own brand of a compromise reserve system through the process of collective bargaining. Seitz hoped that the concurrent bargaining sessions being held between the owners and the MLBPA would have produced a negotiated resolution to the reserve clause dispute, which would have rendered his decision unnecessary. But he couldn't delay his decision for too long as he was bound by the terms of the collective bargaining agreement to "render a written decision as soon as practicable" after the conclusion of the arbitration hearings. Thus, somewhat reluctantly, Seitz finally did issue his history-making ruling on December 23, 1975.

But even in this ruling, Seitz on several occasions pointed to the options of both sides to reach their own compromise agreement on player reservation through collective bargaining.[58]

> *If any of the expressed apprehensions and fears are soundly based, I am confident that the dislocations and damage to the reserve system can be avoided or minimized through good faith collective bargaining between the parties.*
>
> *. . . that a composition and resolution by them of their larger differences as to the extent and impact of the reserve system was a matter of paramount importance; that it was more desirable that those differences (and the issues in the current litigation before the panel) be resolved by the parties themselves in collective bargaining, than by a quasi-judicial arbitration tribunal . . . .*
>
> *The parties are still in negotiation however, and continue to have an opportunity to reach agreement on measures that will give assurance of a reserve system that will meet the needs of the clubs and protect them from the damage they fear this decision will cause, and, at the same time, meet the needs of the players. The clubs and the players have a mutual interest in the health and integrity of the sport and in its financial returns. With a will to do so, they are competent to fashion a reserve system to suit their requirements.*

Thus, as of December 23, 1975, baseball's older perpetual reservation system had been struck down by an arbitration decision which permitted the clubs but a single one-year option on a player's contract after which time the player was to be a free agent. Predictions of doom for the game of baseball abounded as many club owners and others connected with the sport reacted strongly to this near-abolition of the reserve system. Peter Seitz, while not agreeing or disagreeing with these dire predictions, nonetheless was himself seemingly convinced that baseball did need some sort of a reservation system. But his job was only to interpret the contractual dispute that the parties had brought before him. This he did, but in carrying out his prescribed duties as an arbitrator, Seitz was also able to interject his own personal view that the best resolution of the whole situation could be found through good faith collective negotiations. Seitz implored both sides to continue in their efforts at the bargaining table to reach some compromise solution that would be amenable to both the players and the owners. Just as others had done before him, Peter Seitz advised the parties to use the process of collective bargaining to strike a compromise solution. And the parties seemed to be receptive to Seitz's idea. For their part, the owners had nothing much more to lose, and perhaps a great deal to gain, from preserving some semblance of the reserve system through collective bargaining. The players also were of the opinion that some sort of player reservation system was important for the game of baseball. And so the stage was now set for the clubs and the players to strike a compromise somewhere between the perpetual reservation system of the past and the one-year option system provided for in the Seitz ruling. The outcome of these negotiations produced a new free agency/reservation system, which was first incorporated into the collective bargaining contract signed between the players and clubs to be effective as of January 1, 1976.

Subsequent Negotiated Changes to the Reserve System

As noted above, spurred on by the Seitz decision and suggestion for continued negotiations, the parties finally got down to the hard business of negotiating a reserve system that would meet the needs of both sides. Article XVII of the 1976 collective bargaining contract spelled out this compromise agreement between the parties in some detail.[59] Because of its historic interest, this article is reprinted in full in Appendix I at the conclusion of this chapter. The major elements of this compromise reserve system negotiated by the parties dealt with:

- Free agency.
- The reentry procedure and compensation.
- The right to require assignment of contracts.
- Repeater rights.

Each of these elements of the new reserve system will be discussed in turn.

Free Agency

As noted above, the parties were of the belief that some sort of reserve system was a necessity in the game of baseball. The players were certainly not willing to accept perpetual reservation after their victory in the Messersmith/McNally grievances, yet neither did they think that the one-year option system was ideal in meeting the needs of both sides. And so of all the possible options discussed earlier, both sides agreed upon a system whereby players could become free agents after having played for six seasons in the major leagues. Thus, the reservation system was not completely abolished but rather, team control over player services was now to be guaranteed only up to a maximum of six years.

The collective bargaining contract provided that any players who had signed Uniform Player's Contracts prior to August 9, 1976, were subject to be reserved by their clubs for a period of *one* year after said contracts expired. After the one-year reservation period, such players were to become free agents eligible to participate in the reentry draft to be described shortly. Thus, for example, if a certain player had signed a one-year contract for the 1976 season on July 1, 1976, he would be bound to his club for that season plus one additional year, 1977. At the conclusion of the 1977 season, if the player and the club had not agreed to new contractual terms, free agency status would be accrued for the player.

Any players with contracts signed on or after August 9, 1976, were eligible to become free agents after the completion of six years of major league service as noted above. For instance, let's say that a player signed his 1976 contract in early September of 1976, and that this was a one-year pact. Also assume that the 1976 season was this player's fourth year of major league baseball. According to the rules negotiated by the clubs and the MLBPA, whether this player eventually signed future contracts or not, he would be bound to this same club for at least two more seasons, 1977 and 1978. After the end of the 1978 season, he could become a free agent if he and his club were still unable to reach an agreement on salary.

Thus, what the newly bargained reserve system did, in essence, was to give each major league team a six-year guarantee on a player's services, after which time the player and club could agree to further contractual terms or the player could become a free agent. The clubs could no longer control players into perpetuity, but they could control them for six years, about the average career length of a professional baseball player. The players knew that they were bound to stick with the team they first signed with for at least six years unless traded, sold, or otherwise released. However, after six years, a player could look forward to testing his market value in a much more competitive environment than was previously the case in baseball.

The only requirement for becoming a free agent other than having six years or more of major league service was that each player desiring to become a free agent had to provide formal notification of such intent within a specified 15-day period beginning around October 15 of each year. Such notification by each player to the MLBPA was then to be passed along to a representative of the Player Relations Committee.

The Reentry Draft

Having thus addressed the problem of how a player was to become a free agent, the negotiators next set about the task of determining the procedure to be employed for negotiations involving free agent players. What they came up with is what has come to be known as the reentry draft. In early November of each year all major league clubs can participate in a "Selection Meeting." This meeting is convened by the Commissioner, and at this time clubs have the right to acquire negotiating rights to free agent players whose names are contained on the so called "Eligible List" for that year. Teams select players in inverse order of their finish in the previous season, such order to be determined by their respective won and lost percentages. Ties are broken by a coin flip, and the leagues alternate choices during this reentry draft.

The selection proceeds by rounds, with each club having the right to make one pick per round. Each player on the eligible list can be chosen by a maximum of thirteen teams. Additionally, the former club also can retain the right to negotiate with a player by so indicating this desire at the conclusion of the formal selection proceedings. Selections continue until such time as each eligible player has been chosen the maximum number of times or until every club indicates that it no longer desires to make any further choices.

It is important to keep in mind that these choices referred to above only entitle the club to negotiating rights with a particular player and do not guarantee that the club will actually be able to sign any player so chosen. Recall that a maximum of 14 clubs (13 from the reentry draft plus the original club) out of the 26 in professional baseball may opt to negotiate with any individual player. Players selected by fewer than 2 clubs immediately become free to negotiate with any of the 26 major league teams. In practice, this limit of 14 clubs has not been any great burden to the players. Many clubs do not participate in the reentry procedure and in recent years, only a few players have been chosen by the maximum allotted number of clubs. However, one should recall the recent dilemma of former San Diego outfielder Dave Winfield, who recently became baseball's richest player by going the free agency route and signing a 10-year, $13.75 million contract with the New York Yankees Club. Inasmuch as the Yankees had a very successful season in 1980 and therefore would pick near the end in the reentry draft, the thought occurred to Winfield that he might already be chosen the maximum number of times prior to the Yankees having a chance to make their first selection. Winfield was very interested in negotiating with the Yankees for two important reasons, the chance for the first time in his career to play on a pennant contender and the fact that New York was one of the richer clubs and had a tradition of signing free agents to lucrative contracts. Thus, in order to avoid being shut out, Winfield sent letters to several clubs in each league which indicated, for example, that he did not wish to live or play baseball in Chicago and, thus, it would be a waste of a selection for the Chicago team to choose him as he would not sign a contract to play baseball with Chicago in any event. There was some criticism of Winfield for employing this tactic and it is really rather hard to say whether it was successful or not. But, as noted above, Winfield was chosen by the Yankees as well as several other teams, and finally was able to come to terms with the Yankees.

Each club is limited in the number of free agent players who can be signed in any particular year by the terms of the collective bargaining agreement. These terms specify that if less than 14 players are on the eligible list, no club may sign more than one free agent player. If the number of eligible players is between 15 and 38, a maximum of two signings per club is permissible. Finally, if there are between 39 and 62 players on the eligible list, each club may sign a maximum of 3 players. However, regardless of the above rules, each club may sign as many free agent players as it loses in any particular season. Thus, if Cincinnati loses 5 free agents in a particular year when the eligible list contains 31 names, the Cincinnati club would be allowed to sign a maximum of 5 free agents that year.

Negotiations proceed between each player on the eligible list and those clubs selecting rights to bargain with him until a final agreement is reached with some club. Note that the player does not have to accept the highest salary offer presented to him if he doesn't want to. Dave Winfield, even though very well paid by the Yankees, reportedly turned down higher offers so that he could play with New

York. During the period reserved for bargaining, a player is able to test his free market worth. If he receives an offer of $150,000 from Detroit, he can then go to Cleveland and see if he can do better in his negotiations with that club. The player can collect all of his offers and choose one or decide to negotiate further with several of the clubs for which he is most interested in playing. Once a free agent player and a club come to terms, the League Office and the MLBPA are notified. Then, all other clubs holding negotiation rights to that player's services are informed that the chase is over.

Compensation. An important aspect of the free agency procedure in baseball as well as in many other sports to be considered in some detail in Chapter 6 is *compensation*. In short, compensation refers to what, if any, payment will be made to clubs that lose free agent players through the negotiated procedure described above. As we will see in Chapter 6, several other sports allow for free agency but require such heavy compensation as to essentially nullify the process. This is because teams are reluctant to sign free agent players where they face a heavy and often uncertain penalty in exchange for the acquisition of a certain player. The players were mindful of this situation and did not want to neutralize their free agency status because of excessive compensation rules. However, the owners were of the opinion then, as they are today, that some type of compensation was a necessity for teams losing free agents. Thus, a compensation formula was agreed to which covered all players who signed contracts on or after August 9, 1976. Players who became free agents through the initial route described above, signing contracts prior to August 9, 1976, were not covered by similar compensation rules. Thus, a team signing one of these latter types of free agents faced no compensation penalty whatsoever.

The compensation formula agreed to by the clubs and the MLBPA requires that the team signing a free agent player assign to that player's former team a single draft choice in the regular phase of baseball's June Amateur Player Draft. Thus, money and current professional players are not to be used as compensation payments, as is the case in several other sports. Instead, for example, when the Yankees signed Dave Winfield, they were forced to assign their first round draft choice in the next Amateur Player Draft to the San Diego Padres in exchange for the loss of Winfield. If the acquiring team is in the second half of the selecting clubs (as was the case with the Yankees), the compensation for the acquired player is the team's first-round draft pick. However, if the acquiring team is in the top half of the selecting clubs, the compensation for signing their first free agent is their second choice from the June Amateur Player Draft. Where clubs sign more than one free agent, they are required to give up their draft choices in successive rounds of the Amateur Draft until each team losing one of these free agent players has acquired one draft choice.

It should be fairly clear from the above description of baseball's compensation rules that while a compensation formula does in fact exist, it is a fairly weak one in comparison to those employed in other sports and to be discussed in Chapter 6. Consider that for the loss of Dave Winfield, the Padres received only the Yankees' first-round Amateur Draft choice. This is not like a first-round draft pick in basketball or football where teams are choosing players with four years of college experience, who are immediately ready to enter the professional ranks. In these sports, first-round draft picks often become regular players almost instantly. The baseball draft, however, is quite different. Most of the players chosen in the Amateur Draft are kids right out of high school who will be sent to the minor leagues for several years of training. And even then, with all of this extra training and expense to the clubs, these players may never achieve the playing potential to be promoted to the major leagues. Thus, a single choice in the June Amateur Draft is a very big gamble, and the likelihood of any one player becoming a major league star is quite small indeed. Knowing this, teams are quite willing to sign as many free agents as possible because they realize that they will probably accrue no major loss in so doing. The New York Yankees were quite pleased to be able to sign a player like Dave Winfield away from San Diego with only having to assign a single draft choice to the Padres in exchange. Player mobility in baseball has been quite high since the inception of the new free agency system. Hopefully, the reader will realize by now that a major contributing factor to this success has been the fact that the system has not been burdened by excessive compensation rules like those existing in other sports. Recently, the baseball owners have realized that one way to slow down the free agency machine they have jointly created with the players is to revise the compensation formula alluded to above, making it stricter to discourage wild bidding for free agent players. Teams might be a bit more cautious in their approach to and dealings with free agent players if they knew that in return for signing a free agent they might lose one or more of their present players plus cash. As we shall soon see, this is exactly the type of proposal the owners made during the 1980 negotiations, and it was this insistence on harsher compensation rules that almost precipitated a regular-season strike in May of 1980. To date, the issue of compensation for teams losing free agent players to other teams remains the single outstanding issue between the players and the clubs. But before we discuss these more recent bargaining events, several other aspects of the 1976 free agency procedure need to be covered.

Assignment of Contracts

Players who have signed contracts on or after August 9, 1976, and who have had five or more years of professional baseball experience, achieved another sort of freedom with the signing of the 1976 collective bargaining pact. For the first time, these players have acquired the right to *demand to be traded*. We have already seen how players earlier acquired the right to veto any trade not to their liking (the so-called "Santo clause"), and now players have also attained the right to demand to be traded. Any player with five years of baseball service can, at the conclusion of a season, require the assignment of his contract to another club by giving notification of his intention within a 15-day period beginning on October 15, or the day after the conclusion of the World Series, whichever occurs later. At the same time the player is allowed to name six teams which he will not accept as assignee of his contract. Thus, if a player demands a trade in the manner described above, he can do so and rest assured that he will not be traded to say, for example, Detroit, Montreal, Toronto, Atlanta, Philadelphia, and Seattle. His former club must try to make a deal for this player's services with one of the other 20 teams not on the above "veto list" submitted by the player.

The club then has approximately five months to work on a trade for this player. If no trade can be accomplished by the next March 15, the player immediately becomes a free agent eligible to negotiate with any club without restrictions. Finally, players are free to retract this demand to be traded at any time prior to the actual execution of a trade by their former club.

Repeater Rights

The final important aspect of the negotiated reservation system contained in the 1976 collective bargaining agreement deals with free agency repeater rights. In this regard, the contract specifies that a player who becomes a free agent and is signed by a new club pursuant to the rules we have described above will be bound to this new team for a maximum of five years. That is, such a player would become eligible to exercise his right of free agency again only after having completed an additional five years of major league service, presumably but not necessarily with the team that has signed him as a free agent. In a similar fashion, players who exercise their right to demand to be traded must accumulate another three years of professional baseball service before they may exercise this option for a second time.

Professional baseball has now accumulated five years of experience with its new free agency system. Much has been written about the pros and cons of such a system, and certainly it will continue to attract a lot of attention in the years to come. Before turning to a description of how the free agency system has operated to date, it is important to cover one last item, the recent bargaining between the players and the clubs regarding the revamping of this system.

Recent Events at the Bargaining Table

One of the reasons for the success of baseball's free agency system, at least from the standpoint of the players, is the fact that there is no burdensome compensation formula that causes teams to avoid dealing with free agents for fear of greater losses to their own team in the form of player personnel and/or cash. As we will see in Chapter 6, the amount of free agent movement from team to team in basketball and football has never approached anything like what we have seen in baseball. The plain and simple fact of the matter is that in these sports, harsh and at times uncertain compensation rules have prevented teams from contracting with free agent players in the same manner as has been done in baseball.

The language of the 1976 collective bargaining agreement clearly spelled out the fact that both sides viewed the newly bargained Article XVII Reserve System as being experimental in nature and as such, possibly subject to modifications in future rounds of negotiations. While this is essentially true for all items in every collective bargaining contract, the parties in baseball went so far as to include an attachment to the collective bargaining contract on this matter which read:[60]

The Parties recognize that the provisions of the Agreement con-
cerning player control establish a new dimension in their collectively
bargained relationship and, therefore, to a degree must be regarded as
experimental. Each of the Parties understands and accepts that there
is limited experience to guide them in what is now being agreed to and
that based on the operation of the new system either of them may find
it necessary to pursue in the course of future collective bargaining
contract provisions different from what they are accepting in this
Agreement.

1980 Negotiations

Both sides took the above attachment to heart during the 1980 negotiations. The players were fairly well satisfied with the new free agency system but, nevertheless, still desired to make the rules dealing with the acquisition of free agency rights a bit more lenient. Thus, they proposed shortening the current 6-year reserve system. The players were satisfied with the compensation formula they had agreed to back in 1976.

For their part, the owners were quite unhappy with the operation of the 1976 free agency system. Recall that the Seitz decision and these subsequent negotiated changes had severely limited the owners' former perpetual control over their player assets. In the past several years, many players each season had been able to become free agents and sign more lucrative contracts with new clubs. It is pretty clear that the owners expected this to happen, but perhaps not with quite the magnitude that was witnessed between the years of 1976 through 1980. In an effort to slow down this fast-paced system somewhat, the owners turned to a proposal for the revamping of the compensation principle as the hallmark of their 1980 negotiations with the players over the reservation system. In essence, the owners believed that more compensation was due to teams losing free agent players. One draft choice from the June Amateur Player Draft was neither enough to make the losing team "whole" for the loss of an established player nor to discourage teams from engaging in a free-for-all bidding war for these players' services. Thus, the owners proposed stricter compensation rules in the hopes of limiting the mobility of free agent ballplayers. And even if these ballplayers were still able to change teams, the owners hoped that the stricter compensation rules would suffice to make the player's former club whole for the loss of his services.

The proposal of the owners would work in the following fashion. The compensation formula negotiated in 1976 would be scrapped in favor of a new formula which would mandate increased compensation to be paid to teams losing "premier" free agents. The word premier was to be defined by such factors as the number of teams choosing a player in the reentry draft and/or by a player having achieved certain quantity statistics, such as games played or times at bat in the past. It is interesting to note that while the term premier seems to refer to a top-notch player, indeed, a bona fide star, the owners' proposal sounds more like the term "regular" player would have been more appropriate. For a generally accepted estimate is that under the owners' proposal, half of all present major league players would have premier status just by having accumulated a certain number of times at bat or the like. Recall that the definition of premier did not take into account things like batting average, slugging average, home runs, and the like. Thus, a run-of-the-mill starting second baseman, who perhaps batted .226 in the previous season but who accumulated a large number of games played or times at bat would be classified as a premier player. If such a player became a free agent and was signed by a new team, his previous club would be entitled to compensation for his services under baseball's newly proposed compensation formula.

This formula provided for the team signing the free agent player to be able to "freeze" or protect 15 to 18 players on its 40-man roster. After a certain number of players have been designated as protected, the player's former club would then be allowed to choose one of the remaining unprotected ballplayers as compensation for the loss of their former player. As one would expect, the MLBPA was not overly excited about the prospect of the adoption of this stricter form of compensation. Buoyed by their knowledge of the experiences in other sports, the players strongly rejected this proposal by the owners as one which would severely limit their opportunities for movement from club to club. The players correctly reasoned that if this plan was accepted, future free agents would face troubled times as clubs would not be as willing to sign them to huge contracts or at all with the knowledge that they would stand to lose one of their own major league players or some outstanding minor league prospect. For instance, where only 15 players can be protected, the team losing a free agent might be able to select a good relief pitcher or a first-rate backup player. Or, if this team knew of a particularly bright minor league prospect under contract with the other team, such a player might be chosen. If the team acquiring the free agent player wished to protect this minor league "phenom," it would have to unfreeze another one of its major league players and this player might be lost to the free agent's former team as compensation.

For all of these reasons and more, the professional baseball players desired to have no part of this revamped compensation formula. The heated bargaining over this issue and others led to a player strike during the final week of the 1980 exhibition season. With these issues still unresolved, both sides agreed to go back to the bargaining table so that the regular season could begin. The players' previous contract had expired on December 31, 1979; the players had been without a contract for a period of some three months. However, the two sides did set a new strike deadline of May 22, 1980. The parties agreed to return to the negotiating table for a period of about six weeks of intense bargaining sessions in an attempt to resolve the compensation issue and others that still remained at impasse. But the players made their intention clear that unless this new contract was finalized by the end of this period, a regular-season strike would ensue.

Bargaining continued during this period and to the credit of both sides, agreement was reached on all issues save for compensation for teams losing free agents. It certainly appeared that a regular-season strike was all but a certainty as the deadline of May 22, 1980, approached.

But then, just as fans and players alike seemed to be getting ready for a prolonged regular season strike, the parties were able to reach a negotiated solution that preserved the rest of the 1980 playing season. However, the issue of compensation was far from settled. Rather than have a strike over this single issue, the parties agreed to a new contract containing the terms of their bilateral negotiations on all issues except one, compensation. The former free agency/compensation system was extended for a period of one year under the same terms and conditions as those previously agreed to in 1976. Late into the night negotiations had saved the remainder of the regular season as both sides agreed to the following manner of resolving the compensation issue.

First, a joint player-management study committee was set up to focus their efforts on the free agent compensation issue. The report of this committee was due to be filed by the last day of 1980. The findings of the report of the committee were to serve as the basis for further negotiations between the players and the clubs on the compensation issue. The deadline for agreement on some new compensation formula (or the old formula, for that matter if the parties so choose) was February 19, 1981. If no agreement can be achieved by that date, the clubs are free to *implement their proposed compensation plan.*

The clubs announced their intention to implement their compensation proposal on February 19, 1981. This move by the clubs left the players with two choices: accept the owners' compensation proposal as is and thus allow it to continue in effect until the expiration of the current collective bargaining agreement on December 31, 1983, or reopen the agreement on the compensation issue and set a strike date for no later than June 1, 1981. The executive board of the MLBPA voted unanimously to follow the latter route and a walkout was set for May 29, 1981.

As of this writing, it seems that little progress has been made toward an amicable resolution of the compensation issue. Both sides remain steadfast in their original positions, the owners desiring to implement their new compensation formula while the players prefer to stick with the previous arrangement agreed to in 1976. As if resigned to the fact that a regular playing season strike is inevitable for 1981, club owners reportedly have been purchasing "strike insurance" to help them soften the financial blow that a regular season strike would bring to it. At this point, it would be pure speculation to make any predictions about the eventual outcome of negotiations over the compensation issue. However, the reader should be aware that this is clearly the single most important and volatile issue in the sphere of labor-management relations in the game of baseball at the present time. Hopefully, as they have done in the past, the two sides again will be able to work out their differences over the compensation issue through the process of good faith collective bargaining. But only time will tell and it does seem reasonable to assert that the issue of compensation and the broader issue of the reservation system in its entirety will continue to be the subjects of much heated discussion at the collective bargaining table as well as elsewhere quite a way into the foreseeable future. Given that this issue of player reservation has sparked so much interest and debate in recent years, it seems fitting that this chapter ends with a brief treatment of the impacts of free agency in baseball over the last several years.

The Impacts of Free Agency

We have now witnessed five years of experience under the collectively bargained six-year reservation system, and a preliminary analysis of its impacts on various aspects of the game of baseball certainly seems to be in order. Recall that as was apparent from the 1980 and current negotiations, neither the players nor the club owners were perfectly happy with the fruits of their 1976 agreement on the reserve system. The players have attempted to shorten the time period necessary in order to achieve free agency status, while the owners have attempted to interject their own formula for compensation for teams losing free agent players into the system. Neither of these proposals have been accepted to date and only time and further bargaining sessions will tell what the future may bring for baseball's reserve system.

Given the situation of future uncertainty, it is nevertheless quite possible to review what has happened in the five years since the reservation system has been changed from perpetual ownership to the 6-year collectively bargained system. The reader should note at this point that research in this area to date has been quite lacking. We simply do not have any definitive studies on the impacts of this new reservation system on various aspects of the game of baseball, as we do have for the case of salary arbitration covered in the following chapter. The problem does not seem to stem from a lack of interest in this subject, as many persons inside and out of the game of baseball seem to be willing to voice their opinions of free agency. For instance, Commissioner Kuhn might be quoted as saying that free agency and huge player salaries are bad for baseball and represent the game's number one problem to date. Or various club owners might be quoted on the pros and cons of free agency. The players and their executive director, Marvin Miller, are also often in the free agency limelight. And last but not least, hundreds and hundreds of sports fans and writers across the country and the world have voiced their opinions about free agency. No, the lack of research does not seem to stem from a lack of interest!

There do seem to be several possible explanations for the lack of scholarly research. Primary among these reasons is the sheer difficulty of such a project. For instance, a research project aimed at measuring the impacts of free agency on player salaries in professional baseball immediately faces two staggering problems. The first problem is how to obtain the required salary data. Newspapers carry reports of player salaries, but these in many cases may be based on rumors that are way off the mark. League and club officials, as well as individual players and the MLBPA, are notoriously reluctant to release this type of information so vital to research efforts. Another major problem that researchers must face, even were accurate salary figures available, is in the isolation of the effects of the reserve system on these salaries. In other words, player salaries have gone up in recent years for a whole host of reasons, including the right to employ salary arbitration, the right to demand and veto trades, inflation, and others. The researcher must be able to control for these other sources of increased salaries so as to isolate the statistically independent effect of free agency. While techniques are available that would enable researchers to resolve the above problems, they nonetheless represent major hurdles that are going to have to be jumped prior to the conducting of any major research studies in this area. To date, no one has been willing to exert the effort necessary to solve these problems. One hopes that this situation will be radically altered in the not-too-distant future.

Even if these problems are solved, some would argue that the newness of the reserve system adopted through collective bargaining would prevent the conducting of any meaningful research as to its effects on the game of baseball. Proponents of this argument would call for careful studies to be done, but only after we have had a longer time period under which to live with the system in its current form. Of course, if the parties change the system again in 1981, this point becomes moot as this newly bargained system would again have to be treated as another experiment, albeit one that is just beginning. And again the argument would be to be patient and wait to evaluate the system until after we have lived with it for a number of years.

This argument of the newness of the system would seem to be nullified given that we do have five full years of post-free-agency data available for our inspection. Thus, the biggest hangups for the interested researcher are in the areas of data unavailability and the extreme difficulties involved in doing the type of carefully controlled analyses that are befitting of the scientific method.

Having said all of this, and realizing that these latter two problems of data unavailability and *control* have yet to be resolved, it is nonetheless useful to make some exploratory comments on the types of research that might be done in this area and to reflect on what the findings of such research efforts might be. Thus, in turn we will briefly discuss the potential impacts of free agency on

- Player mobility.
- Player salaries.
- Competitive balance.
- Player performance.

While there are several other areas of interest that future researchers might consider, in the interest of brevity the comments to follow will be limited to a discussion of the aforementioned four items.

Player Mobility

It is clear that the situation in baseball has changed drastically from earlier times when players were never able to achieve free agency status. Today's ballplayer knows when he signs his initial major league contract that his first opportunity to test the free agency waters will come at the end of his sixth full season in professional baseball. Baseball has now had five full seasons of experience with the negotiated changes in the reserve system promulgated in the 1976 collective bargaining agreement. This experience clearly demonstrates that players have been making use of this free agency alternative, just as most people would have predicted. For a summary of the participants in baseball's free agency market since its inception in 1976, consult Appendix II at the conclusion of this chapter. In this appendix, data is reported on the players who have used the free agency mechanism in the five years that it has been in operation to date, 1976–1980. In each case we have listed the player's name, former club, new club, year of free agency, and the player's salary if available. As noted above, salary figures are not always readily available, and those figures that are published may not be accurate. Thus, the reader is warned to interpret the salary figures with some element of cautiousness and suspicion, as indeed the author has done.

The data in Appendix II reveal that just over 200 players (201 to be exact) have made use of baseball's new reservation/free agency system in the past five years. An even larger number of players have been eligible to employ this system but have come to terms with their teams on salary through individual bargaining. Thus, it would seem that the free agency mechanism has been good to the players in several ways. First, it may have caused clubs to bargain in good faith with those players the club intended on keeping. Knowing that a player is able to become a free agent in short order, clubs may do several things including offering much higher salaries in order to maintain their star players. Incidently, one would also predict that the advent of free agency would also bring with it longer-term player contracts as teams try to insure themselves of a player's services past his sixth season. For instance, if the Cincinnati club can sign a third-year superstar to a 10-year contract, this player cannot effectively become a free agent until the end of his thirteenth season. And by that time, the Cincinnati club may be glad to be rid of him. This tactic was recently employed by Baltimore in their signing of fourth-year star first baseman Eddie Murray to a multi-year multimillion dollar contract. Of course, players will realize that this tactic of longer-term contracts will tie them down and may not want to sign them, so as to be able to test the free agency waters after their sixth season. Another prediction that can be empirically tested deals with the trading of players nearing the 6-year mark. Since clubs at present receive practically nothing in exchange for the loss of a free agent, it seems likely that in those cases where signing is unlikely, teams might choose to trade or sell these young and budding stars so as to at least guarantee themselves of receiving something in exchange for the player's services. If the player or players they receive in exchange are themselves nearing the 6-year mark, the club will almost immediately face a similar situation to that described above.

In any event, it would also be quite interesting for some researcher to compare the set of players eligible to become free agents but who sign with their original clubs with those eligible players who actually use the free agency process to change teams. As the data in Appendix II report, the latter group's number approaches 200 while the number of players in the former group is small but not exactly known. Thus, it does seem that on average, 40 players per season have been able to employ baseball's free agency mechanism to change teams. When one considers that there are 26 professional teams each with 25 players, making for a total of 650 ballplayers, 40 players per season changing teams does not really seem like a lot. In any event, clearly less than 10 percent of all ballplayers have been eligible to use this free agency system each year. And far less than that, around 6 percent on average, have actually changed teams each season. However, when one considers that *no* players prior to 1976 could ever change teams and test baseball's open labor market just because they wanted to, this newly won freedom of mobility takes on a great deal of significance. Our tentative conclusion is that the free agency system has led to much more player mobility than was previously the case. Having said this, we remind the reader that there are a lot of unresearched and unanswered questions in this area that have yet to be addressed. The questions and issues posed above are just a representative sample of the larger universe of items that need to be considered.

Player Salaries

The second area for discussion mentioned above is the impact of free agency on player salaries in baseball. Again, this is a very hard subject to approach and discuss with the present unavailability of good, accurate salary data on players pre- and post-free agency. A cursory look at the Appendix II data reveals that those post-free agency salaries reported do seem to be quite high. The reader again should note that the author makes no claim for the accuracy of such figures. They have been culled from newspaper accounts and may or may not be correct. Also, note the large number of cases where no salary figures are available, illustrating the earlier point about how hard it is to find data in this area.

In theory, one would predict that salary payments to free agents should go up due to free agency. The interested reader is referred to the same argument made in Chapter 4 with regard to the impact of the availability of salary arbitration on player salaries. In essence, what has occurred in both cases is that the clubs have surrendered some aspect of their former monopsony (one buyer of labor) powers. These powers allowed them to pay players less than what these players would have made in a free market baseball environment. With the acceptance of free agency, the baseball owners have lost some of the monopsony power they formerly possessed and it can be predicted that salaries of player personnel will in fact go up. Teams will be forced to share more of their pie of resources with the players due to free agency. If the pie of resources stays the same, the level of team profits should fall due to the payment of these higher salaries. However, if the teams are able to increase their resources through means such as better attendance, more T.V. money, and the like, there is no reason why they shouldn't be able to maintain or even increase their profits even in the face of rising player payroll costs due to free agency. Having said all this, we again remind the reader of the extreme difficulty associated with the testing of the above hypothesis due to the lack of data and the problems associated with attempting to control for other factors that may also have been partially responsible for the increasing player salaries we have seen in baseball as of late.

Competitive Balance

A third area where one could perform research is on competitive league balance. The reader will recall that one of the owners' major arguments in favor of a reserve system since its inception has centered on the supposed league balance that it creates and maintains. This type of competitive balance is favored since it leads to tight pennant races which naturally induce more fan interest, that is, attendance. Where one or a few teams are quite rich and able to buy up all of the best talent in an open labor market, the owners argue that competitive balance will suffer and that general interest in the game will be lacking because outcomes become too certain. Thus, the owners are really arguing for maintaining an appropriate level of uncertainty in the minds of the fans of the game. The players and their union argue that there has never been such a thing as perfect competitive balance and that there have always been dynasties, even with the perpetual reservation system in place.

For example, the owners might point to the case of the New York Yankees and their recent signing of no fewer than ten free agent ballplayers. Table 3.1 presents a brief summary of the Yankees' fortunes in baseball's free agent market since 1976. Note that Catfish Hunter was signed in 1974, prior to the new system's inception, based on an arbitration ruling that he was a free agent (described earlier in this chapter). Now it is clear that the Yankees have had good success with the signing of these free agents. Yet the baseball fan will realize that the Yankees have had a long history of playing success that started long before they were able to buy free agents on the open market. Baseball has always had its dynasties. On the other hand, several teams like Texas, which has spent large sums of money in the free agent market, have not been as successful as the Yankees. Thus, the impact, if any, of free agency on competitive balance is far from certain at this time. We have not seen any research on this topic to date. Here again, potential researchers are faced with the

Table 3.1   New York Yankee Free Agents, 1974–1980

Name	Signing Date	Length of Contract	Salary Total
Catfish Hunter	12/31/74	5	$ 3,350,000
Don Gullett	11/18/76	6	2,096,000
Reggie Jackson	11/29/76	5	2,660,000
Rich Gossage	11/22/77	6	2,748,000
Rawly Eastwick	12/09/77	5	1,100,000
Luis Tiant	11/13/78	2	740,000
Tommy John	11/22/78	3	2,517,000
Rudy May	11/08/79	3	1,000,000
Bob Watson	11/08/79	3	1,710,000
Dave Winfield	12/15/80	10	25,000,000*

* *Note:* Winfield's salary total includes a yearly cost-of-living increase with a maximum of 10 percent, compounded annually.

problems of unavailable data, defining exactly what is meant by competitive balance, and once having done that, controlling for all other factors which might impact upon competitive balance, so that the independent effect of the free agency system, if any, can be isolated. Future researchers will have to tackle all of these problems if we are ever to get any meaningful answers about the impact of free agency on competitive league balance.

Player Performance

The final issue to be briefly addressed concerns the impact of free agency on player performance. There are a whole host of relevant issues here; only a few of the more salient ones will be discussed at present. One of the most interesting of these concerns the impact of knowing that one will soon be a free agent on one's performance record in baseball. One recent study by a pair of psychologists suggests that performance in the year prior to becoming a free agent actually *declines* as the player feels relatively underpaid as compared to other similarly performing ballplayers. These feelings of under-payment, according to what is referred to as equity theory, will cause players to hold back, either consciously or unconsciously, and thus perform worse.[61] On the other hand, economic theory would predict just the opposite, that is, that knowing that he is about to become a free agent, a player would try even harder to have a good record to present to several new teams in order to increase his bargaining power and, hopefully, his salary as well. As far as this writer is concerned, the issue of whether equity theory or labor market theory dominates is unanswered at this time. We have simply had no research that has attempted to sort out this problem to date. While the findings of the Lord and Hohenfeld study do seem to support equity theory predictions, the study has several problems, such as a very small sample size and a limited measure of player performance, so as to call its results into question. And in any event, even if player performance is found to decline, how do we ever separate out whether this is due to the equity theory predictions of players exerting less effort, or to the other reasonable explanation that these players were pressing so hard to do well that their overall statistics actually were worse? Performance statistics for baseball are very easy to come by and thus, hopefully, such research as suggested above will be forthcoming now that we have witnessed five years of experience with the free agency system.

Another issue deals with player performance after free agency. What is the effect of the signing of a long-term, multimillion-dollar contract on player performance? Do players, secure for the rest of their lives, relax a bit and not put out as much effort in an attempt to avoid injuries? Or does the competitive spirit burn so intensely within them that performance does not decrease? In this type of a study, we have to be sure to factor in the variable of age, which, of course, has an impact on performance. In baseball, players usually improve in performance up to around age 29, level off for a few years, and then decline until retirement. Finally, it would be interesting to compare performance levels of players not eligible for free agency against those who are eligible and sign contracts with either their former teams or some new club. All of the above would seem to be fertile areas for future research. Hopefully, data will become available that will cause young researchers to enter into the chase.

Summary

In this chapter, we have covered baseball's historic reserve clause and system from its earliest days until the present. From a beginning featuring a completely free labor market and marked by much player revolving, we saw how the club owners secretly met to adopt the first reserve rule. This rule was soon amended to bind every player in professional baseball perpetually to that club with which he signed his initial contract. Various attempts by the frustrated players to revise this rule through court actions and collective bargaining all proved futile due to baseball's antitrust exemption granted in the *Federal Baseball Club* court case in 1922.

However, two grievances brought by pitchers Andy Messersmith and Dave McNally, and the subsequent arbitration decision by Peter Seitz, finally began the process of tumbling the former player reservation system to the ground. Sustained efforts at the bargaining table enabled the parties to reach a compromise agreement on a 6-year player reservation plan. This new system has been in operation for five years and has recently been the subject of much heated debate. A player strike looms for the 1981 season if the two sides can't agree on some new formula for compensation, the only remaining issue in the current negotiations. No matter how this issue is eventually worked out, it can safely be predicted that the solution will come through collective bargaining, which has been extremely important in bringing about the various changes to the reserve system discussed in this chapter and certainly will remain a major tool for joint discussion, change, and progress in the future. The final portion of this chapter was reserved for a discussion of the impacts of free agency on the game of baseball in several respects. While not much research has been conducted in this area to date, it was pointed out that a huge potential exists as there are numerous interesting research hypotheses that await testing.

While it certainly can be argued that the elimination of the former perpetual reservation system was the players' biggest triumph through the usage of the process of collective bargaining, it would be very shortsighted to end our story here. For many other gains of both the monetary and nonmonetary varieties have been achieved at the bargaining table in recent years. Chapter 4 contains a thorough discussion of two other major rights that the players have won through collective bargaining, the right to have a grievance/ arbitration procedure and the right to demand salary arbitration. Finally, Chapter 5 will contain a brief discussion of the various other monetary and nonmonetary benefits now enjoyed by the players as a direct result of the collective bargaining process.

Endnotes

1. *Organized Baseball: Report of the Subcommittee on the Study of Monopoly Power of the Committee on the Judiciary*, House of Representatives, H.R. 2002, 82d Cong., 2d sess. (1952), p. 16.

2. *Ibid.*

3. *Ibid.*, p. 17.

4. *Ibid.*, p. 18.

5. *Ibid.*, p. 19.

6. *Ibid.*, p. 22.

7. Paul M. Gregory, *The Baseball Player: An Economic Study* (Washington, D.C.: Public Affairs Press, 1956) p. 150.

8. *Organized Baseball, op. cit.*, p. 23.

9. Gregory, *op. cit.*, p. 151.

10. Lionel Sobel, *Professional Sports and the Law* (New York: Law-Arts Publishers, Inc., 1977) pp. 84–85.

11. *Organized Baseball, op. cit.*, p. 32.

12. Sobel, *op. cit.*, pp. 85–86.

13. *Organized Baseball, op. cit.*, p. 24.

14. *Ibid.*, p. 25.

15. *Ibid.*, pp. 26–27.

16. *Ibid.*

17. *Ibid.*, p. 28.

18. *Ibid.*, p. 32.

19. See *Metropolitan Exhibition Co.* v. *Ward*, 24 Abb. N.C. 393, 400 (1890); *Philadelphia Ball Club, Ltd.* v. *Hallman et al.*, 8 Pa. Co. Ct. 57 (1890); *Metropolitan Exhibition Co.* v. *Ewing*, 42 Fed. 198 (1890).

20. *Organized Baseball, op. cit.*, p. 35.

21. *Ibid.*, p. 38.

22. *Philadelphia Ball Club* v. *Lajoie*, 51 Atl. 973 (Pa. S. Ct. 1902).

23. *Organized Baseball, op. cit.*, p. 53.

24. *Cincinnati Exhibition Co.* v. *Johnson*, 190 Ill. App. 630 (1914); *American League Baseball Club of Chicago* v. *Chase*, 86 N.Y. Misc. 441 (1914).

25. *Cincinnati Exhibition Co.* v. *Marsans*, 216 Fed. 269 (1914); *Weeghman* v. *Killefer*, 215 Fed. 289 (1914).

26. *Organized Baseball, op. cit.*, pp. 56–57.

27. *Federal Baseball Club of Baltimore, Inc.* v. *National League, et al.*, 259 U.S. 200 (1922).

28. *Gardella* v. *Chandler*, 79 Fed. Supp. 260 (D.C.S.D.N.Y., July 13, 1948); *Martin* v. *National League Baseball Club*, 174 Fed. 2d 917 (C.C.A.2, June 2, 1949).

29. *Organized Baseball, op. cit.*, p. 84.

30. *Gardella* v. *Chandler*, 172 F. 2d 402 (2d Cir. 1949).

31. *Organized Baseball, op. cit.*, p. 25.

32. Sobel, *op. cit.*, p. 25.

33. *Toolson* v. *New York Yankees*, 346 U.S. 356 (1953).

34. *Ibid.*, pp. 356–357, as cited in Sobel, *op. cit.*, p. 27.

35. *Basic Agreement Between The American League of Professional Baseball Clubs and The National League of Professional Baseball Clubs and Major League Baseball Players Association*, effective January 1, 1973, p. 37, paragraph 10(a).

36. *Organized Baseball, op. cit.*, pp. 112–113.

37. *Flood* v. *Kuhn*, 407 U.S. 258 (1972).

38. For an excellent account of the whole Curt Flood affair, see Curt Flood, with Richard Carter, *The Way It Is* (New York: Pocket Books, 1972).

39. *Flood* v. *Kuhn*, 316 F. Supp. 271 (1970); 443 F.2d 264 (1971).

40. *Flood* v. *Kuhn*, 407 U.S. 258, p. 259 (1972).

41. *Ibid.*, p. 288.

42. For an interesting treatment of this issue see Michael S. Jacobs and Ralph K. Winter, Jr., "Antitrust Principles and Collective Bargaining by Athletes: Of Superstars in Peonage," *Yale Law Journal*, 81 (November 1971), pp. 1–29.

43. *Flood* v. *Kuhn*, 316 F. Supp. pp. 282, 284.

44. For an excellent bibliography, see *Flood* v. *Kuhn*, 407 U.S. 258, pp. 280–281n.

45. "Monopsony in Manpower: Organized Baseball Meets the Antitrust Laws," *Yale Law Journal*, 62 (March 1953), p. 639.

46. Sobel, *op. cit.*, pp. 235–243.

47. *Basic Agreement Between The American League of Professional Baseball Clubs and The National League of Professional Baseball Clubs and Major League Baseball Players Association*, effective January 1, 1970, Article XIV.

48. *Basic Agreement Between The American League of Professional Baseball Clubs and The National League of Professional Baseball Clubs and Major League Baseball Players Association*, effective January 1, 1973, Article XV.

49. *Ibid.*, Article III.

50. *Ibid.*, Article X.

51. See *Professional Baseball Clubs*, 66 LA 101, p. 108 (December 23, 1975).

52. *United Steelworkers of America* v. *American Manufacturing Company*, 363 U.S. 564 (1960); *United Steelworkers of America* v. *Warrior and Gulf Navigation Company*, 363 U.S. 574 (1960); *United Steelworkers of America* v. *Enterprise Wheel & Car Corporation*, 363 U.S. 593 (1960). Also see *Gateway Coal Company* v. *United Mine Workers*, 414 U.S. 368 (1974).

53. *Professional Baseball Clubs*, *op. cit.*, p. 111.

54. *Ibid.*

55. *Ibid.*, p. 116.

56. *Kansas City Royals Baseball Corporation* v. *Major League Baseball Players Association*, 409 F. Supp. 233 (W.D. Mo. 1976); as cited in Sobel, *op. cit.*, p. 216.

57. *Professional Baseball Clubs*, *op. cit.*, pp. 111–112.

58. *Ibid.*, pp. 117–118.

59. *Basic Agreement Between The American League of Professional Baseball Clubs and The National League of Professional Baseball Clubs and Major League Baseball Players Association*, effective January 1, 1976, Article XVII, pp. 34–42.

60. *Ibid.*, Attachment 1, p. 45.

61. Robert Lord and J. G. Hohenfeld, Longitudinal Field Assessment of Equity Effects on the Performance of Major League Baseball Players," *Journal of Applied Psychology*, 64, 1979, pp. 19–26.

APPENDIX I: Article XVII—Reserve System

A. Reservation Rights of Clubs

Subject to the rights of Players as set forth in this Agreement, each Club may have title to and reserve up to 40 Player contracts. A Club shall retain title to a contract and reservation rights until one of the following occurs:

(1) The Player becomes a free agent, as set forth in this Article;

(2) The Player becomes a free agent as a result of

(a) termination of the contract by the Club pursuant to paragraph 7(b) thereof,

(b) termination of the contract by the Player pursuant to paragraph 7(a) thereof,

(c) failure by the Club to tender to the Player a new contract within the time period specified in paragraph 10(a) of the contract, or

(d) failure by the Club to exercise its right to renew the contract within the time period specified in paragraph 10(a) thereof; or

(3) The contract is assigned outright by the Club.

A Club may also reserve, under separate headings on a Reserve List, Players who properly have been placed on the Voluntarily Retired List, the Military List, the Suspended List, the Restricted List, the Disqualified List or the Ineligible List. (See also Attachments 12, 13 and 14.)

B. Free Agency

(1) *Player Contracts Executed Prior to August 9, 1976.* Following completion of the term of the contract as set forth therein, the Club may renew the contract, as specified pursuant to paragraph 10(a) thereof, for one additional year. The Player, unless he has executed a contract for the next succeeding season, shall become a free agent on the day following the last game played by the Club (in the championship season, or in the League Championship Series or the World Series if the Club participates in such Series) in the renewal year, subject to the provisions of Section C below.

(2) *Player Contracts Executed On or After August 9, 1976.* Following completion of the term of the contract as set forth therein, any Player with 6 or more years of Major League service who has not executed a

Source: Basic Agreement between The American League of Professional Baseball Clubs and The National League of Professional Baseball Clubs and the Major League Baseball Players Association, effective January 1, 1976.

contract for the next succeeding season shall become a free agent, subject to the provisions of Section C below, by giving notice as hereinafter provided within the 15-day period beginning on October 15 (or the day following the last game of the World Series, whichever is later). Election of free agency shall be communicated by telephone or any other method of communication by the Player to the Players Association. Written notice of free agency shall then be given within the specified time limits by the Players Association, on behalf of the Player, to a designated representative of the Player Relations Committee, and shall become effective upon receipt.

C.   Reentry Procedure

The procedure set forth in this Section C shall apply to Players who become free agents pursuant to Section B above. Players who otherwise become free agents under this Agreement shall be eligible to negotiate and contract with any Club without any restrictions or qualifications, shall be deemed not to have exercised rights of free agency for purposes of Section E of this Article XVII, and the Clubs signing such free agents shall do so without regard to the quota and compensation provisions of this Article.

(1) *Negotiation Rights Selection Procedure*

(a) A Selection Meeting of the Major League Clubs shall be convened by the Commissioner during the period between November 1 and November 15 of each year for the Clubs to select rights to negotiate and contract with free agent Players. Such Players shall be listed on an "Eligible List" certified by the League Presidents and the Players Association. Selections shall be made from the Eligible List.

(b) At the Selection Meeting, Clubs shall select in inverse order of their standing in the championship season just concluded. Percentage of games won and lost shall determine the order within each League without respect to Divisions. If two or more Clubs within a League have the same percentage, the order of selection among such Clubs shall be determined by lot. In 1976, the League drafting first shall be determined by lot and Leagues shall alternate choices thereafter. In succeeding years, the League which selected second in the previous year shall select first.

(c) Each of the 24 (26 beginning in 1977) participating Major League Clubs may make one selection in each round. As the proceedings advance, round by round, each Player may be selected by a maximum of 12 Clubs (13 beginning in 1977), not counting the Player's former Club which need not select such a Player. The selections will continue until each eligible Player has been selected by 12 Clubs (13 beginning in 1977) or until each Club has indicated that it desires to make no further selections. At the conclusion of the selections, the former Club of each Player will be asked to indicate whether it wishes to have negotiation rights with respect to that Player, and, if it does desire to have such rights, it will then be added to the list of Clubs eligible to negotiate and contract with that Player.

(d) If less than 2 Clubs select negotiation rights to a particular Player, the Player immediately will be free to negotiate and contract with any Major League Club, without restrictions or qualifications applicable to either the Player or the Club, in the same manner as a Player who becomes a free agent other than by virtue of Section B above.

(e) Any Player who, under these procedures, is unsigned on February 15 may elect, within 7 days after that date, to resubmit himself to a new drawing of lots by the Clubs for the selection of negotiating rights with him. The new drawing shall be held within 3 days after communication of the Player's election. Negotiating rights shall be granted to 4 Clubs determined by lot from Clubs which indicate at the time of the drawing that they are interested in signing such Player. The Player's former Club shall not be eligible to acquire negotiating rights pursuant to this paragraph. Of the 4 Clubs so determined, 2 shall be from each League, except, in the event less than 2 Clubs from one League indicate interest, more than 2 Clubs may be determined from the other League in order that a total of 4 Clubs are determined. If a Player elects to invoke the optional procedure provided for in this paragraph, all prior negotiation rights shall be cancelled and only the 4 Clubs drawn by lot would then have negotiation rights with the Player. Any such Club may sign the Player without regard to the quota provisions of this Article. If less than 2 Clubs select negotiation rights to a particular Player under this optional procedure, paragraph (d) above shall apply.

(2) *Contracting With Free Agents*

(a) Regardless of the number of Players for whom they have drafted negotiation rights, Clubs shall be limited in the number they may subsequently sign to contracts. The number of signings permitted shall be related to the number of Players on the Eligible List. If there are 14 or less players on the Eligible List no Club may sign more than one Player. If there are from 15 to 38 Players on the Eligible List, no Club may sign more than 2 Players. If there are from 39 to 62 Players on the Eligible List, no Club may sign more than 3 Players. If there are more than 62 Players on the Eligible List, the Club quotas shall be increased accordingly.

(b) Irrespective of the provisions of paragraph (a) above, a Club shall be eligible to sign at least as many Players as it may have lost through

Players having become free agents at the close of the season just concluded, under the provisions of Section B of this Article.

(c) No Player shall be prevented from negotiating with (and potentially signing with) at least 6 Clubs, or if less than 6 Clubs have selected negotiation rights with him, then the number of Clubs that have selected negotiation rights with him. Should the signing of other Players to contracts reduce the number of Clubs (excluding the Player's former Club) eligible to sign a particular Player below 6 (or below the number of Clubs drafting him if less than 6), then the Commissioner shall make an additional Club(s) eligible to sign such Player. The additional Club(s) shall be determined by lot from Clubs (excluding the Player's former Club) which

(1) originally drafted negotiation rights with the Player but became ineligible to sign the Player because of exhausting the limit of Player signings permitted under paragraphs (a) and (b) above, and

(2) indicate at the time of drawing of lots that they continue to be interested in signing such Player.

If the above procedure fails to restore the number of Clubs eligible to sign the Player to 6 (or the number of Clubs drafting him if less than 6), then the additional Clubs shall be determined by lot from all the remaining Clubs (excluding the Player's former Club) which, at the time of drawing, indicate interest in signing the Player, in order to so restore the number of Clubs. This procedure shall be followed and implemented on a weekly basis (and on a more frequent basis after January 1 of each year) to restore to the Player the minimum number of Clubs required to be available to negotiate (and potentially sign a contract) with him.

(d) When a Player and one of the Clubs which has selected negotiation rights to him reach agreement on terms, the Club will immediately notify its League Office of that fact together with a summary of the terms to which the Player has agreed. The Players Association will then be advised by the League Office of these facts and will promptly seek confirmation of them by the Player. Upon obtaining such confirmation, the Players Association shall notify the League Office, and all other Clubs holding negotiation rights to that Player shall be advised that the Player has come to terms and is no longer a free agent.

(e) A Club which signs a contract with a Player who became a free agent pursuant to Section B(1) of this Article, shall not compensate the Player's former Club. A Club which signs a contract with a Player who became a free agent pursuant to Section B(2) of this Article, shall, except as provided in Section C(1)(d) above, and the last sentence of Section C(1)(e) above, compensate the Player's former Club by assigning to it a draft choice in the Regular Phase of the next June Major League Rule 4 Amateur Player Draft. If the signing Club is among the first half of selecting Clubs, then the choice to be assigned for the most preferred free agent Player signed by such Club shall be its second choice, with choices in the next following rounds to be assigned as compensation for the signing of other Players in descending order of preference. If the signing Club is among the second half of selecting Clubs, then such compensation shall begin with the Club's first choice. In determining the order of preference among Players for this purpose, the Player selected by more Clubs will rank higher and, if the number of selecting Clubs is the same, the Player first selected by that number of Clubs will rank higher.

(3) *Conduct of Free Agents and Clubs Prior to Selection Meeting*

(a) During the period beginning on the day the Player becomes a free agent and ending 3 days before the Negotiation Rights Selection Meeting, any Club representative and any free agent or his representative may talk with each other and discuss the merits of the free agent contracting, when eligible therefor, with the Club, *provided, however*, that the Club and the free agent shall not negotiate terms or contract with each other. Notwithstanding the foregoing, the free agent and his previous Club may engage in negotiations and enter into a contract during said period. Should they enter into a contract during said period, the free agent shall be deemed not to have exercised his rights of free agency for purposes of Section E of this Article XVII, and the Club shall be deemed not to have signed a free agent for purposes of the quota provisions of this Article.

(b) During the period beginning 3 days before the Negotiation Rights Selection Meeting and ending with the conclusion of the Selection Meeting, free agents and Clubs may continue discussion as set forth in paragraph (a) above, but no terms shall be negotiated and no contracts shall be entered into.

(4) *Miscellaneous*

(a) Any Club selecting negotiation rights to and signing a contract with a Player under this Section C may not assign his contract until after the next June 15. However, notwithstanding the foregoing, such contract may be assigned for other Player contracts and/or cash consideration of $50,000 or less prior to the next June 16 if the Player gives written consent to such transaction.

(b) If a maximum number of Clubs select negotiating rights for a player who has become a free agent pursuant to Section B and, subsequent to the Selection Meeting, the Player does not contract with a Major League Club but does contract with a National Association Club, such Player shall not be eligible for assignment to or to contract with a Major League Club until he has been subject to the draft of National Association players, as provided for in Major League Rule 5, following the next playing season.* If the Player is not selected in such draft, a special Selection Meeting will be held for him during the first week of the next January pursuant to the procedures set forth in Section C.

(c) There shall be no restriction or interference with the right of a free agent to negotiate or contract with any baseball club outside the structure of organized baseball, nor shall there be any compensation paid for the loss of a free agent except as provided for in this Agreement.

D. Right to Require Assignment of Contract

(1) *Eligibility.* Any Player who signed a contract on or after August 9, 1976, and has 5 or more years of Major League service, may elect, at the conclusion of a season, to require that his contract be assigned to another Club. A Player who requires the assignment of his contract pursuant to this Section D shall not be entitled to receive a Moving Allowance. A Player shall not be eligible to require the assignment of his contract if his contract covers the next succeeding season, provided, however, that if his contract has been assigned by the Club which originally executed it, the Player shall be eligible to require the assignment of his contract notwithstanding the fact that it covers the next succeeding season. (See also Attachment 15.)

(2) *Procedure.*

(a) *Notice.* A Player may exercise his right to require the assignment of his contract by giving notice as hereinafter provided within the 15-day period beginning on October 15 (or the day following the last game of the World Series, whichever is later). Election to require the assignment of his contract shall be communicated by telephone or any other method of communication by the Player to the Players Association. Written notice thereof shall then be given within the specified time limits by the Players Association, on behalf of the Player, to a designated representative of the Player Relations Committee, and shall become effective upon receipt.

---

* If less than a maximum number of Clubs have selected negotiating rights for such a Player, the foregoing restriction on eligibility shall not apply, provided, however, that such Player shall not be eligible for assignment to or to contract with any Major League Club which has filled its quota for the signing of free agents until he has been subject to the Major League Rule 5 draft.

(b) *Player Veto Rights.* At the time notice is given as provided in paragraph (a) above, the Player may also designate not more than 6 Clubs which he will not accept as assignee of his contract, and the Player's Club shall be bound to assign his contract thereafter to a Club not on such list.

(c) *Free Agency if Assignment Not Made.* If the Player's Club fails to assign his contract, as set forth in this Section D, on or before March 15, the Player shall become a free agent immediately eligible to negotiate and contract with any Club without any restrictions or qualifications. The Player shall be deemed not to have exercised his right of free agency or his right to demand a trade, for purposes of Section E of this Article XVII, and the Club signing him shall do so without regard to the quota and compensation provisions of this Article. A Player who becomes a free agent pursuant to this paragraph shall not be entitled to receive termination pay. Such a free agent shall receive transportation and travel expenses in the same manner as he would if he had been unconditionally released except he shall be limited to receiving travel expenses to his new club if he reports to it directly, provided such expenses are less than to his home city.

(3) *Retraction by Player.* A Player who has elected to exercise his right to require an assignment of his contract may retract such election on or before March 15, by sending a telegram to his Club, provided that such telegram must be sent prior to the time a telegram is sent to him by his Club notifying him that his contract has been assigned. If such a Player has 10 or more years of Major League service, the last 5 of which have been with one Club, he shall, upon such retraction, be deemed to relinquish his right to approve any assignment of his contract to another Major League Club which is completed within 60 days after such retraction or until March 15, whichever is later. A Player who retracts his election shall be deemed not to have exercised his right to require an assignment for purposes of Section E of this Article XVII.

E.   Repeater Rights

(1) *Free Agency.* Any Player who becomes a free agent pursuant to Section B of this Article or whose contract was assigned as a result of a trade required pursuant to Section D of this Article shall not subsequently be eligible to exercise his right to become a free agent until he has completed an additional 5 years of Major League service.

(2) *Trade Demand.* Any Player who became a free agent pursuant to Section B of this Article or whose contract was assigned as a result of a trade required pursuant to Section D of this Article shall not subsequently be eligible to exercise his right to require the assignment of his

contract until he has completed an additional 3 years of Major League service.

F. Outright Assignment to National Association Club

(1) *Election of Free Agency.* Any Player who has at least 3 years of Major League service and whose contract is assigned outright to a National Association Club may elect, in lieu of accepting such assignment, to become a free agent. A Player who becomes a free agent under this Section F shall immediately be eligible to negotiate and contract with any Club without any restrictions or qualifications. Such Player shall not be entitled to receive termination pay. Such a free agent shall receive transportation and travel expenses in the same manner as he would if he had been unconditionally released except he shall be limited to receiving travel expenses to his new club if he reports to it directly, provided such expenses are less than to his home city.

(2) *Procedure.* Not earlier than 4 days* prior to the contemplated date of an outright assignment, the Club shall give written notice to the Player, with a copy to the Players Association, which shall advise the Player that he may either (a) accept the assignment or (b) elect to become a free agent. The Player shall also be informed in the notice that, within 3 days* after the date of the notice, he must advise the Club in writing as to his decision. If the Club fails to give written notice, as set forth herein, to the Player prior to the date of such assignment, the Player may, at any time, elect to become a free agent pursuant to this Section F, provided, however, that if the Club subsequently gives such written notice to the Player, he shall, within 3 days* thereafter, advise the Club in writing as to his decision.

G. Individual Nature of Rights

The utilization or non-utilization of rights under this Article XVII is an individual matter to be determined solely by each Player and each Club for his or its own benefit. Players shall not act in concert with other Players and Clubs shall not act in concert with other Clubs.

---

* Ten days, if during the period from the close of the championship season to the opening of spring training.

APPENDIX II

Participants in Baseball's Free Agency System, 1976–1980

Baseball 1976 Free Agents

Name	Old Team	New Team	Salary
Alexander, Doyle	New York (A.L.)	Texas	$1,000,000/6 yr.
Allen, Richie	Philadelphia	Oakland	$ 100,000/1 yr.
Bando, Sal	Oakland	Milwaukee	$1,406,000/5 yr.
Baylor, Don	Oakland	California	$1,675,000/6 yr.
Campaneris, Bert	Oakland	Texas	$1,010,000/5 yr.
Campbell, Bill	Minnesota	Boston	$1,050,000/5 yr.
Cash, Dave	Philadelphia	Montreal	$1,540,000/6 yr.
Colbert, Nate*	Oakland		
Dade, Paul	California	Cleveland	$ 92,500/2 yr.
Fingers, Rollie	Oakland	San Diego	$1,060,000/5 yr.
Fuentes, Tito	San Diego	Detroit	$ 90,000/1 yr.
Garland, Wayne	Baltimore	Cleveland	$2,300,000/10 yr.
Grich, Bobby	Baltimore	California	$1,650,000/5 yr.
Gullett, Don	Cincinnati	New York (A.L.)	$2,096,000/6 yr.
Hebner, Richie	Pittsburgh	Philadelphia	$ 600,000/3 yr.
Jackson, Reggie	Baltimore	New York (A.L.)	$2,660,000/5 yr.
Matthews, Gary	San Francisco	Atlanta	$1,875,000/6 yr.
McCovey, Willie	San Diego	San Francisco	$ 50,000/1 yr.
Nordbrook, Tim	California	Chicago (A.L.)	$ 100,000/2 yr.
Rudi, Joe	Oakland	California	$2,200,000/5 yr.
Soderholm, Eric	Minnesota	Chicago (A.L.)	$ 55,000/1 yr.
Smith, Billy	California	Baltimore	$ 97,500/2 yr.
Stillman, Royle	Baltimore	Chicago (A.L.)	$ 25,000/1 yr.
Stone, Steve	Chicago (N.L.)	Chicago (A.L.)	$ 60,000/1 yr.
Tenace, Gene	Oakland	San Diego	$1,590,000/6 yr.

* He was not chosen in the draft, and he did not sign.

Baseball 1977 Free Agents

Name	Old Team	New Team	Salary
Blomberg, Ron	New York (A.L.)	Chicago (A.L.)	$ 600,000/4 yr.
Bochte, Bruce	Cleveland	Seattle	$ 504,000/4 yr.
Bostock, Lyman	Minnesota	California	$2,250,000/5 yr.
Boswell, Ken	Houston	—	
Briggs, Dan	California	Cleveland	
Brohamer, John	Chicago (A.L.)	Boston	
Brown, Ollie	Philadelphia	—	
Burgmeier, Tom	Minnesota	Boston	
Crawford, Willie	Oakland	Los Angeles	
Drago, Dick	Baltimore	Boston	
Duffy, Frank	Cleveland	Cleveland	
Eastwick, Rawley	St. Louis	New York (A.L.)	$1,100,000/5 yr.
Forster, Terry	Pittsburgh	Los Angeles	$ 850,000/5 yr.
Fosse, Ray	Seattle	Milwaukee	
Gamble, Oscar	Chicago (A.L.)	San Diego	$2,850,000/6 yr.
Gomez, Luis	Minnesota	Toronto	
Gossage, Rick	Pittsburgh	New York (A.L.)	$2,748,000/6 yr.
Griffin, Tom	San Diego	California	
Grimsley, Ross	Baltimore	Montreal	$1,375,000/6 yr.
Guerrero, Mario	California	San Francisco	
Hendricks, Elrod*	New York (A.L.)	Baltimore	
Hisle, Larry	Minnesota	Milwaukee	$3,155,000/6 yr.
Hughes, James	Minnesota	Chicago (A.L.)	
Jorgenson, Mike	Oakland	Texas	
Kingman, Dave	New York (A.L.)	Chicago (N.L.)	$1,375,000/5 yr.
Maddox, Elliot	Baltimore	New York (N.L.)	$ 950,000/5 yr.
Marshall, Mike	Atlanta	Minnesota	
May, Carlos	New York (A.L.)	—	
Medich, George	New York (N.L.)	Texas	$1,000,000/4 yr.
Miller, Rick	Boston	California	
Mitterwald, George	Chicago (N.L.)	Seattle	
Moore, Alvin	Atlanta	Chicago (A.L.)	
Perez, Marty	Oakland	Oakland	
Rettenmund, Merv	San Diego	California	
Schueler, Ron	Minnesota	Chicago (A.L.)	
Terrell, Jerry	Minnesota	Kansas City	
Tolan, Bobby	Pittsburgh	—	
Torrez, Mike	New York (A.L.)	Boston	$2,507,249/7 yr.
Zisk, Richie	Chicago (A.L.)	Texas	$2,955,000/10 yr.

* He was not selected, but then he became a coach for the Orioles.

Baseball 1978 Free Agents

Name	Old Team	New Team	Salary
Bailey, Bob	Boston	—	
Barr, Jim	San Francisco	California	$1,000,000/4 yr.
Bouton, Jim	Atlanta	—	
Broberg, Pete	Oakland	Los Angeles	
Brye, Steve	Pittsburgh	—	
Bumbry, Al	Baltimore	Baltimore	$ 365,000/3 yr.
Carbo, Bernie	Cleveland	St. Louis	$ 115,000/1 yr.
Carty, Rico	Toronto	Toronto	$1,100,000/5 yr.
Colborn, Jim	Seattle	—	
Coleman, Joe	Toronto	San Francisco	
Dyer, Duffy	Pittsburgh	Montreal	
Etchebarren, Andy	Milwaukee	—	
Evans, Darrell	San Francisco	San Francisco	$1,000,000/5 yr.
Fitzmorris, Al	California	—	
Garrett, Wayne	St. Louis	—	
Gaston, Cito	Pittsburgh	—	
Gura, Larry	Kansas City	Kansas City	$1,200,000/5 yr.
Grote, Jerry	Los Angeles	—	
Hamilton, Dave	Pittsburgh	—	
Harrelson, Bud	Philadelphia	Philadelphia	
Harris, Vic	San Francisco	Los Angeles	
Horton, Willie	Toronto	Seattle	
John, Tommy	Los Angeles	New York (A.L.)	$2,517,000/3 yr.
Kendall, Fred	Boston	San Diego	
Knowles, Darold	Montreal	St. Louis	$ 150,000/2 yr.
Lacy, Lee	Los Angeles	Pittsburgh	
Lum, Mike	Cincinnati	Atlanta	
Marshall, Mike	Minnesota	Minnesota	
North, Bill	Los Angeles	San Francisco	
Paciorek, Tom	Seattle	Seattle	
Plummer, Bill	Seattle	—	
Renko, Steve	Oakland	Boston	$ 100,000/1 yr.
Roberts, Dave	Chicago (N.L.)	San Francisco	
Rose, Pete	Cincinnati	Philadelphia	$3,200,000/4 yr.
Slaton, Jim	Detroit	Milwaukee	$1,200,000/5 yr.
Sosa, Elias	Oakland	Montreal	$1,500,000/5 yr.
Stone, Steve	Chicago (A.L.)	Baltimore	$ 700,000/4 yr.
Thomas, Darrell	San Diego	Los Angeles	
Tiant, Luis	Boston	New York (A.L.)	$ 740,000/2 yr.
Unser, Del	Montreal	Philadelphia	
Williams, Charlie	San Francisco	California	
Wood, Wilbur	Chicago (A.L.)	—	

Baseball 1979 Free Agents

Name	Old Team	New Team	Salary
Alou, Jesus	Houston	—	
Blair, Paul	New York (A.L.)	New York (A.L.)	
Borgmann, Glenn	Minnesota	Chicago (A.L.)	
Chalk, Dave	Oakland	Kansas City	
Curtis, John	San Francisco	San Diego	$1,800,000/5 yr.
Ellis, Dock	Pittsburgh	—	
Goltz, Dave	Minnesota	Los Angeles	$3,000,000/6 yr.
Gross, Greg	Philadelphia	Philadelphia	
Hamilton, Dave	Oakland	Oakland	
Hassler, Andy	New York (N.L.)	Pittsburgh	
Hood, Don	New York (A.L.)	St. Louis	
Horton, Willie	Seattle	Seattle	
Hrabosky, Al	Kansas City	Atlanta	$2,200,000/5 yr.
Johnson, Tim	Toronto	Chicago (N.L.)	
Johnstone, Jay	San Diego	Los Angeles	
Kaat, Jim	New York (A.L.)	St. Louis	
Kessinger, Don	Chicago (A.L.)	—	
Kison, Bruce	Pittsburgh	California	$2,500,000/5 yr.
Kranepool, Ed	New York (N.L.)	—	
LaGrow, Lerrin	Chicago (A.L.)	Philadelphia	
Lockwood, Skip	New York, (N.L.)	Boston	$ 775,000/2 yr.
May, Milt	Chicago (A.L.)	San Francisco	
May, Rudy	Montreal	New York (A.L.)	$1,000,000/3 yr.
Montgomery, Bob	Boston	—	
Morgan, Joe	Cincinnati	Houston	
Norman, Fred	Cincinnati	Montreal	
Office, Rowland	Atlanta	Montreal	
Orta, Jorge	Chicago (A.L.)	Cleveland	
Patek, Fred	Kansas City	California	
Perez, Tony	Montreal	Boston	
Randle, Lenny	New York (A.L.)	Chicago (N.L.)	
Rettenmund, Merv	California	California	
Ryan, Nolan	California	Houston	$3,500,000/3 yr.
Scott, George	Boston	—	
Solaita, Tony	Toronto	—	
Stanhouse, Don	Baltimore	Los Angeles	$2,100,000/5 yr.
Stennett, Rennie	Pittsburgh	San Francisco	$3,000,000/5 yr.
Torres, Rusty	Chicago (A.L.)	Kansas City	
Twitchell, Wayne	Seattle	—	
Valentine, Bobby	Seattle	Montreal	
Watson, Bob	Boston	New York (A.L.)	$1,710,000/3 yr.
White, Roy	New York (A.L.)	Montreal	
Wise, Rick	Cleveland	San Diego	$1,950,000/5 yr.
Wohlford, Jim	Milwaukee	San Francisco	

Baseball 1980 Free Agents

Name	Old Team	New Team	Salary
Bahnsen, Stan	Montreal	Montreal	
Baker, Dusty	Los Angeles	Los Angeles	
Beniquez, Juan	Seattle	California	
Blitner, Larry	Chicago (N.L.)	Cincinnati	
Bird, Doug	New York (A.L.)	New York (A.L.)	
Borgmann, Glenn	Chicago (A.L.)	Cleveland	
Braun, Steve	Toronto	—	
Burris, Ray	New York (N.L.)	Montreal	
Cardenal, Jose	Kansas City	—	
Castro, Bill	Milwaukee	New York (A.L.)	$ 320,000/2 yr.
Chalk, Dave	Kansas City	Kansas City	
Cubbage, Mike	Minnesota	New York (N.L.)	
D'Aquisito, John	Montreal	California	
Dwyer, John	Boston	Baltimore	
Essian, Jim	Oakland	Chicago (A.L.)	
Figueroa, Ed	Texas	—	
Harrelson, Bud	Texas	—	
Harris, Vic	Milwaukee	—	
Hill, Marc	Seattle	Chicago (A.L.)	
Howell, Roy	Toronto	Milwaukee	
Jefferson, Jesse	Pittsburgh	California	
Kelleher, Mick	Chicago (N.L.)	Texas	
Kelly, Pat	Baltimore	Cleveland	
LaCock, Peter	Kansas City	—	
Leflore, Ron	Montreal	Chicago (A.L.)	
May, Lee	Baltimore	Kansas City	
McGraw, Tug	Philadelphia	Philadelphia	
Milner, John	Pittsburgh	New York (N.L.)	
Montanez, Willie	Montreal	Montreal	
Morales, Jerry	New York (N.L.)	Chicago (N.L.)	
Morales, José	Minnesota	Baltimore	
Oates, Johnny	New York (A.L.)	—	
Pattin, Marty	Kansas City	—	
Perry, Gaylord	New York (A.L.)	Atlanta	
Porter, Darrell	Kansas City	St. Louis	$ 3,500,000/5 yr.
Rader, Dave	Boston	—	
Randle, Lenny	Chicago (N.L.)	Seattle	
Roberts, Dave	Seattle (Pitcher)	New York (N.L.)	
Roberts, Dave	Texas (Catcher) (Infielder)	Houston	
Sadek, Mike	San Francisco	San Francisco	
Spikes, Charlie	Atlanta	—	
Spillner, Dan	Cleveland	Cleveland	
Staub, Rusty	Texas	New York (N.L.)	
Stein, Bill	Seattle	Texas	
Sutton, Don	Los Angeles	Houston	$ 4,500,000/5 yr.
Tiant, Luis	New York (A.L.)	Pittsburgh	
Tidrow, Dick	Chicago (N.L.)	Chicago (N.L.)	
Travers, Bill	Milwaukee	California	
Unser, Del	Philadelphia	Philadelphia	
Washington, Claudell	New York (N.L.)	Atlanta	$ 3,500,000/5 yr.
Winfield, Dave	San Diego	New York (A.L.)	$13,750,000/10 yr.
Zahn, Geoff	Minnesota	California	

Chapter 4

THE IMPACTS OF COLLECTIVE BARGAINING: GRIEVANCE AND SALARY ARBITRATION

In the previous chapter, the most significant gain made by the players through the process of collective bargaining, the modification of the reserve rule into its present form, was discussed in some length. While this change to a system of more liberal player movement from team to team was indeed a major achievement for the players, it would certainly be shortsighted to brush aside other crucial breakthroughs that have occurred at the bargaining table. This chapter and Chapter 5 will discuss the other major changes in the employment relationship in professional baseball brought about through the process of collective bargaining. The specific subject matter of this chapter is dispute resolution processes, while the ensuing chapter will cover a variety of other changes that have profoundly affected the game of baseball.

Dispute Resolution

In any industrial relations environment, there are basically two types of contractual disputes that may arise. These are generally referred to as rights/grievance disputes and interest/future terms disputes. The former type of dispute occurs during the existence of a collective bargaining contract and is usually based on a disagreement between labor and management over the interpretation, application, or compliance with the terms of the written contract. The latter type of dispute occurs over the content of *future* collective or individual agreements between the parties. A few examples of these two types of disputes should help the reader clarify this basic distinction between rights vs. interest issues, which will be an important distinction to keep in mind while reading the material in the balance of this chapter.

Grievance/Rights Disputes

When labor and management sign a collective bargaining agreement, it is usually for some fixed time period. That is, both sides agree to abide by the terms of the contract for, say, a period of three years. This usually includes a promise by labor not to strike and by management not to lock out over differences in opinions about contractual language during this three year period. But differences of opinion certainly must arise; and they do. A modern collective agreement can run several hundred pages and contain hundreds of clauses. To expect perfect harmony between labor and management regarding the specific interpretation of each and every paragraph in the agreement is simply unreasonable. In fact, the parties often will agree to vague language during negotiations so as to avoid strikes. Both sides then realize that the issue of the exact interpretation of this vague language will come up later during the life of the contract.

For instance, labor and management may disagree over the exact nature of a disciplinary sentence meted out to a tardy employee. Instead of the ten-day suspension without pay that management ordered, labor might contend that the contract specifies a much less harsh penalty, a written warning. Or, labor may disagree with management's decision to promote a junior employee over a senior employee, both of whom had applied for a higher position. Management might argue that the contract allows them to consider both seniority and ability in making promotion decisions, while the union might contend that the exact meaning of the contract allows management no such discretion. Promotion decisions must be based on seniority alone. To give one last example, consider the case where management grants a worker three days of paid funeral leave on the death of an immediate family member. However, the union and the employee believe that according to the contract, he is entitled to an additional two days of paid leave.

All of the above examples are typical of rights or grievance disputes. They are all concerned with the interpretation of an existing collective bargaining contract. But how can these disputes be resolved? Striking is one answer, but we have already noted that the parties usually prefer to handle these minor disputes in less reactionary manners.[1] The development of this posture stems from our country's experience during World War II, when the National War Labor Board was established to handle all industrial disputes peacefully, in an effort to halt any interruptions to industrial production, which was so vital to the war effort. Out of this experiment grew an attachment and appreciation for the process of grievance/ arbitration by both labor and management.[2] After the war most parties voluntarily wrote grievance/arbitration procedures into their collective bargaining agreements. They had found a procedure that worked well and all parties decided to stick with it. In fact, grievance/ arbitration procedures are so popular that today they can be found in well over 95 percent of major collective bargaining contracts. In these cases, the parties have agreed to pursue peaceful means to settle their grievance disputes rather than resorting to strikes or lockouts. Of course, not all contracts have grievance procedures or have binding arbitration on *all* possible contractual disputes. Thus, there is still some usage of the strike weapon to resolve contractual differences arising between labor and management during the life of a contract. These kinds of strikes are referred to as wildcat strikes and are prevalent in bituminous coal mining, among other industries. However, the vast majority of contracts specify that disputes over contract interpretation will be handled through the grievance/ arbitration procedure. It should be noted that this trend holds equally well for the private and public sectors of our economy. More will be said about the purposes and functions of a grievance/ arbitration procedure in the next section of this chapter where we focus specifically on the grievance procedure negotiated in baseball.

Interest Disputes

The second kind of dispute listed above was an interest dispute, or a dispute over items to be included in a future collective bargaining contract. Examples of these disputes include disagreements between labor and management over how much the basic wage specified in the current contract should be increased in the next contract and whether or not the upcoming contract should have a managerial prerogatives clause in it. These types of disputes can be over the magnitude or simply whether to include an item in a future contract or not. These disputes typically arise near the expiration date of a current contract, as the parties bargain in the hopes of a peaceful resolution of a new contract. These are also referred to as major disputes,[3] as in the collective sense they affect everyone covered by the contract, as compared with a grievance dispute which typically might affect only one person. However, it must be noted that even for grievance disputes, decisions rendered that instantly affect only one person nevertheless set precedents that definitely do impact on the entire workforce.

Interest disputes have not historically been resolved in the same manner as grievance disputes are settled, that is, through a voluntarily negotiated procedure that includes arbitration by a neutral party as a final step. Instead, in the private sector, the parties have typically preferred to resolve these types of disputes through bilateral negotiations with the strike/lockout threat as the ultimate weapon of force. Only rarely in the private sector have labor and management agreed in advance to resolve interest disputes through arbitration, thus precluding the possibility of strikes. Prominent among the examples of such arrangements which come to mind are the Experimental Negotiating Agreement in basic steel, the Council on Industrial Relations for the Electrical Contracting Industry, and indeed, the final-offer salary arbitration system employed in professional baseball.

The public sector represents an entirely different story. With strikes usually precluded in the name of maintaining essential public services, state legislatures have wrestled with the problem of how to replace the right to strike and preserve the true essence of the collective bargaining process. Their answer in many cases has been to mandate some form of interest arbitration when the parties are unable to resolve their disputes bilaterally by some budget submission deadline generally established by law. Thus, in the public sector we have witnessed much more experimentation with interest arbitration procedures than has occurred in private industry. In the private sector, both sides are usually willing to adopt arbitration for the resolving of grievance disputes, but this attachment to arbitration does not carry over into the realm of interest disputes. Here, both sides steadfastly cling to the right to bargain out their differences bilaterally, and if these efforts fail, to take concerted job actions in order to force their opponent into further concessions. Indeed, this unwillingness to adopt interest arbitration procedures has been buttressed by a National Labor Relations Board decision classifying interest arbitration as a nonmandatory item for bargaining.[4] That is, it is presently illegal to bargain to an impasse (and go on strike) over the demand to include a clause calling for interest arbitration in a future collective bargaining contract.

Given this labor relations background information on the nature and resolution of these two different types of disputes, we will now turn our attention to the specific application of this information to the realm of professional baseball.

The History and Development of Grievance/Arbitration in Professional Baseball

The use of a grievance procedure to resolve disputes has not had a long history in the game of professional baseball. In fact, prior to 1968 no formal system was available, and the resolution of disputes generally occurred when the player submitted to the punishment dictated by his club, the league, or the commissioner of baseball. Of course, it was possible for a club to discuss a grievance with a player and agree to some compromise solution that was satisfactory to all parties involved in the dispute. However, and this is the key point, the clubs were not mandated to take such action and often were quite satisfied with their unilateral decision-making powers. A player who didn't agree with the fine, suspension, or punishment meted out to him really had very few options available. He could find another job, but more likely he would choose to return to the game after paying his fine or serving out the appropriate suspension period.

The closest thing the players had to a grievance procedure prior to 1968 was the representation plan described in some detail in Chapter 2. This plan was a step in the proper direction, in that it had the proper ideals, but player representatives to the Executive Council had no voting privileges, and there was no provision for the submission of unresolved issues to a neutral party. In other words, management *always* made the final decisions! The players were quickly able to see through the facade the owners had set up through the representation plan and to realize that a more traditional grievance procedure was a necessity.

The Necessity for a Grievance Procedure

There were three reasons for the players' desire to obtain such a procedure.[5] First, a standard grievance procedure provides employees with an avenue through which to challenge and appeal employment decisions made by management which seem to run counter to contractual language or past practice. Without such a procedure in a contract, management is free to interpret contract language as they see fit and the union really has no recourse except to strike, go to court, or accept the determination made by management. A player who feels that he has been unjustly treated can appeal such treatment and ultimately have his case decided by an arbitrator only if there is a grievance procedure.

Second, no contract can ever anticipate all of the potential problems that can arise during the life of the agreement. Contract language may be either vague or, in some cases, nonexistent. When a new contract is signed, management's view is that the pact contains all of the items they have negotiated over and compromised on, and thus management expects all other decisions to fall under "managerial prerogatives," that is, those decisions they can make unilaterally. The union, however, takes a much different view of this situation. To them, the signing of a new collective agreement only means that one phase of bargaining has terminated for the time being. Specific changes won at the bargaining table are incorporated into the formal contract. But the union views the grievance procedure as a mechanism to be used during the life of the contract further to extend the gains won at the bargaining table. A second reason the players wanted a grievance procedure was to be able to continue the bargaining process during the life of the contract in the hopes of winning extended benefits and rights.

A third potential benefit of a grievance procedure both to the players and the club owners is through the transmission of valuable information about trouble spots within the employment relationship to both sides. Without such a procedure, these trouble spots may have gone unnoticed. However, if the clubs and players can make proper usage of the information conveyed to them through the grievance procedure, they may be able significantly to improve the climate and nature of the labor relations function.

Given the above positive elements associated with the institution of a grievance procedure, it is not surprising that the players would place the demand for such a procedure high on their priority list at the bargaining table.

Development of a Formal Procedure

The establishment of a formal grievance procedure in baseball dates back to the first collective bargaining agreement signed in the year

1968. The players were able to convince the owners that such a mechanism was much preferable to a whole host of legal actions that could be taken under Section 301 of the Taft-Hartley Act in its absence. This section of the law provides that any party who feels that the terms of a collective agreement have been breached may go to court for enforcement of the contract. However, as previously noted, the much more usual situation is for the parties to negotiate their own informal procedure to replace this potential battery of court proceedings. And this is just what the owners and the players did when they included a grievance/arbitration clause in their initial collective bargaining contract in 1968.

The first grievance procedure was a fairly standard one except in one respect, that is, the use of the commissioner of baseball as the "impartial" arbitrator in the last step of the procedure. Obviously, in the vast majority of private and public sector provisions, the arbitrator chosen to resolve disputes proceeding all the way to the final step of the grievance procedure is a neutral party, with no particular allegiance due to either side involved in the dispute. However, the players' goal of a truly impartial umpire was rejected by the owners in the 1968 negotiations. They would agree to a grievance procedure and to arbitration, but only if they could use Commissioner William Eckert as the arbitrator. Of course, what this implies is that management retains the power to make the final and binding decision on any and all disputes; the supposedly impartial arbitrator is in fact an employee of the owners. The commissioner is hired by, paid by, and can be fired by the owners when they become displeased with his performance. It seems reasonable to assume that one aspect of the commissioner's performance appraisal would deal with how effectively he performed his role as the arbitrator of contract disputes. In this manner, even though agreeing to a grievance procedure in principle, the owners were able to maintain the final authority over all issues at dispute.

Why were the players willing to accept such a weakened grievance/arbitration system? Why weren't they willing to hold out for a neutral arbitrator and use their strike weapon? To answer these questions, one must keep in mind that these were the initial collective negotiations between the owners and the players, and that both sides had to be willing to compromise somewhere. The players had already won many important gains through these talks and in the words of Richard Moss, counsel to the MLBPA,[6]

I don't know what, if any, issues would have been strike issues in 1968, but impartial arbitration clearly was not one of them. Other matters,

as to which we did make significant progress in the negotiations, were
considered much more important, for there was, even so recently, still
a general lack of appreciation of how basic the issue was. We
rationalized our defeat by deciding we would process grievances to
arbitration, and we were confident that the record of that experience
would conclusively demonstrate the importance of impartiality.

The situation of having a nonneutral arbitrator was not to last long. After only two cases were heard before Commissioner Eckert (one won by the players!), he was fired by the club owners who chose Bowie Kuhn to be his successor. Of course, Commissioner Kuhn is still in office today. In at least one sense, the hiring of Kuhn proved to be quite beneficial to the players. Since he had actually participated in the 1968 negotiations as one of the attorneys for the National League, both sides realized the absurdity of having him serve as the "impartial" arbitrator in grievance cases. Thus it was that baseball hired its first truly impartial arbitrator, David Cole.

Impartial Arbitration

When the 1970 Basic Agreement was signed, the principle of impartial grievance/arbitration was firmly established as the parties agreed to a tripartite arbitration panel consisting of two partisan arbitrators and a permanent impartial chairman. The first impartial chairman was Lewis Gill, who served for two years; Gabe Alexander was appointed upon his resignation. Other impartial arbitrators who have served baseball include Peter Seitz; Alexander Portor; and the current arbitrator, Raymond Goetz, a Professor of Law at the University of Kansas. The partisan arbitrators are appointed by their respective sides (one by the clubs, one by the players) and serve to make sure that the position of their side in each issue at dispute is clearly presented. However, it should be noted that with each side choosing one partisan arbitrator, it is clearly the *impartial* person on the panel who has the all-important tie-breaking vote and the power to making final and binding determinations on various matters of contract interpretation.

Since the inception of the system of industrial jurisprudence in 1968, players have filed hundreds of grievances, with many of these proceeding all the way to the final step in the grievance procedure, binding arbitration. But not all cases reach this stage and, indeed, not all cases can legally be submitted to the grievance/arbitration procedure in baseball. We now turn our attention to a brief discussion of the specifics of baseball's grievance/arbitration system and examples of several recent arbitration cases.

The Current Grievance Procedure

Appendix I contains a reprint of Article X, "Grievance Procedure," from the *Basic Agreement of 1976*.[7] While this procedure has undergone minor changes over time, the provisions from the 1976 collective bargaining contract remain pretty much intact today and certainly represent the thrust of the current grievance procedure used in baseball.

The first thing to note is that the agreement specifies that a grievance is defined as any complaint over the interpretation of or compliance with the terms of the collective bargaining contract and other agreements between the players and the clubs. Specifically excluded from the grievance/arbitration arena are disputes over the players' pension plan and dues check-off agreements. It should be noted that a separate dispute resolution procedure exists for pension plan disagreements. However, the fact that only pension and dues check-off disputes are specifically excluded from coverage implies that all other disputes (except where specifically exempted in other parts of the contract, as in the case of "integrity of the game" issues) will be subject to final and binding arbitration when the two sides can't reach an amicable solution. Recall the importance of this inclusiveness issue to Peter Seitz's decision involving pitchers Andy Messersmith and Dave McNally, described in detail in Chapter 3. The owners argued that the case was nonarbitrable, that is, not properly before a grievance arbitrator because it involved a rule (reserve rule) contained in the uniform player contract and not in the collective agreement. But Seitz ruled that the definition of a grievance was broad enough to include this type of dispute within its boundaries. It is important to realize how crucial the definition of what is grievable can be in shaping the future of employment relations in any industry. As the Seitz decision clearly illustrated, the impact can be monumental in scope!

Aside from pension and dues check-off complaints, the *Basic Agreement* specifies several other areas in which grievances are handled in a manner different from that specified in Article X. First, any and all complaints dealing with "the preservation of the integrity of, or the maintenance of public confidence in, the game of

baseball"[8] are to be decided solely by a decision of the commissioner. In such cases, his decisions have the same effect as if they
were grievance decisions of the arbitration panel. That is, they are
final and binding with no appeal possible. Another area in which
complaints are precluded from the grievance procedure is in the
area of disputes over section 3(c) of the uniform player's contract,
dealing with pictures and public appearances. Where disputes arise
over these issues (for example, the club's refusal to allow a player to
write a weekly newspaper column during the playing season), the
parties have agreed to the use of a court of law rather than the
grievance procedure for final and binding resolutions.

The formal procedures employed by a player who has a grievance
involve four steps. The typical grievance procedure in industry has
these steps to reflect various stages of the labor-management hierar-
chy at which a grievant can present his or her arguments and potentially have them resolved satisfactorily. Each step of the process
usually involves higher and higher levels of union and management
officials, who seek to resolve the issue prior to the final step, arbitration.

The Four-Step Procedure

The first step involves the oral discussion of the grievance between
the affected player and the representative of his club designated to
handle such matters. Where such discussions prove futile, the
player must then present his grievance in writing to his club within
45 days from the date of occurrence. The club must respond to the
player in writing within 10 days of the receipt of the written notice of
the grievance. At that time, the club makes its decision on the
grievance known to the player, and the player has 15 days to appeal
said decision to step two of the process.

Step two begins with the written notice of an appeal of a step-one
decision by the player or the MLBPA to the Player Relations Committee. The parties then must discuss the grievance within ten days,
and after such discussions have been concluded, the Player Relations
Committee must notify the grievant in writing of their decision
within ten days. The player then has fifteen days to appeal this
decision to step three.

The third step is initiated when the player involved (or the
MLBPA) appeals a step-two decision directly to the league president. The president must convene an informal hearing within

twenty days and then must render a written decision to the player within ten days after the close of the hearing. This written decision may be appealed by the player within fifteen days to the fourth and final step, arbitration.

When the chairman of the arbitration panel receives a written notice of appeal of a step-three decision, he must then move to set up and commence an arbitration hearing within twenty days. The decision of the panel is to be rendered as soon as practically possible (within five days if the case involves a disciplinary suspension), and such decision is final and binding on both parties. The arbitration panel is empowered only to interpret the agreements between the clubs and the players and is not allowed to add to, subtract from, or change said agreements in any way. Costs of arbitration are shared equally by the parties, and as noted previously, the neutral member of the arbitration panel is jointly appointed by the clubs and MLBPA and is subject to being terminated by either side on thirty days' notice. Figure 4.1 is a schematic diagram of the grievance/arbitration procedure as presently used in professional baseball. It should be noted that while most steps have clearly delineated time limits, there is no such limit in step four except in the case of disciplinary suspension grievances. However, it should be noted that the majority of arbitration decisions are rendered within thirty days of the close of the formal hearing, if no post-hearing briefs are filed. It also should be made clear that to process a grievance all the way through the four steps may take around 200 days. This may seem like a long time, but most cases do not require this much time, and even if some do, this is still considerably quicker than the usual alternative, the court system.

Article X also provides for grievances to be initiated by clubs. This is a typical procedure in private sector industry where, say, a firm might file a grievance against the union for engaging in a wildcat strike in spite of a no-strike pledge in the collective bargaining agreement. While these employer-initiated grievances are quite rare, it is important to recognize that they nonetheless are appropriate in certain situations. The reason these types of grievances occur so infrequently stems from the basic nature of the labor-management relationship itself, where it is typically management that takes some action, which is then called into question by the union: management acts and then the union has the right to react. This is a major hallmark of unionization, and a benefit whose importance is often underestimated when compared to other more fre-

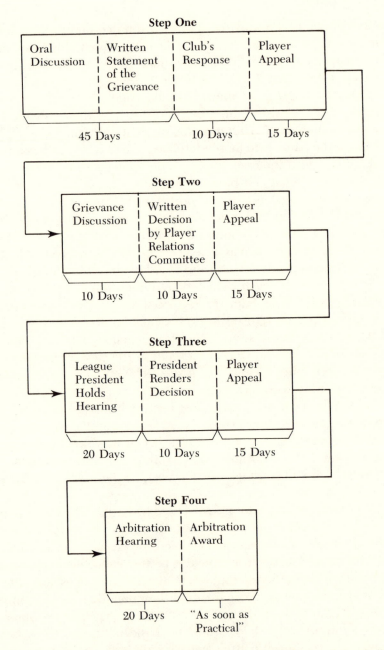

Figure 4.1   The Grievance/Arbitration System in Professional Baseball For Disputes Initiated by Players or the MLBPA

quently discussed items such as wage gains and fringe benefit improvements. In any event, in baseball as in other private and public sector domains, most grievances are filed by the union in protest against some management action deemed to violate the spirit of the collective agreement. However, management also has the right to file a grievance against a player or the MLBPA where such an action is deemed justifiable. The management-initiated grievance procedure has three steps instead of four, but the basic principle of successively higher levels of decision-making authority and a final decision made by a neutral arbitrator is preserved intact. Figure 4.2 is a schematic representation of the grievance procedure used for disputes initiated by management in professional baseball. Bypassing the third step used in the player-initiated grievance procedure should speed up the processing of club-initiated grievances without entailing any real compromises to the notion of due process.

The MLBPA may also file grievances on the behalf of a player or a group of players as they see fit. The only proviso here is that in the realm of disciplinary grievances, the MLBPA must receive player approval prior to appealing any decision. For all other types of grievance decisions, the MLBPA can initiate grievances or appeals on its own behalf.

During the twelve or so years in which baseball has had a formal grievance procedure with impartial arbitration as a final step in the dispute resolution process, many issues have been aired for the first time. It is important to note that most grievances are settled early on in the procedure and do not require impartial arbitration. For instance, one side or the other may decide to drop a grievance which is frivolous or without merit; the parties may be able to reach a genuine compromise pleasing to both sides in some early step along the way; or, feeling that the probability of a loss at arbitration is very high or that the cost of the proceedings will outweigh the benefits even if the case is won, one side or the other may simply let the issue die for lack of further appeal.

Cases That Reach Arbitration

Yet, there are a significant number of cases which do reach the arbitration step. Some of these are concerned with minor issues that would seem to be better resolved through bilateral negotiations. Others, however, have far-reaching consequences; decisions one way or the other can significantly alter the shape of the employment

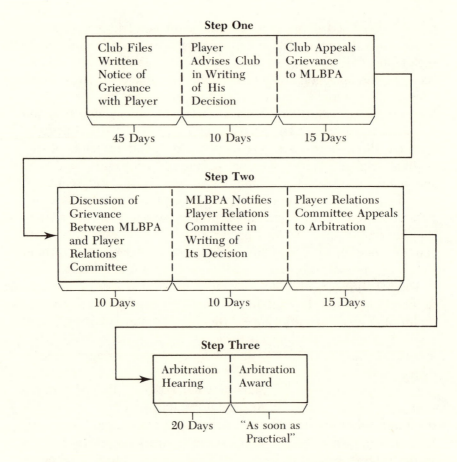

Figure 4.2   The Grievance/Arbitration System in Professional Baseball For Disputes Initiated by Clubs

relationship in the game of baseball for many years. For instance, there is no doubt that Peter Seitz's decision in the Messersmith/ McNally grievances over the reserve clause (described in detail in Chapter 3) has had a profound effect on the game. This decision clearly looms as the most important win for the players to date in the grievance/arbitration arena. As a result of this decision, baseball's perpetual reservation system tumbled and was replaced with the current six-year free agency system, leading to huge bidding wars and ever-escalating player salaries. As was noted in the previous chapter, baseball is exempt from antitrust legislation, so the reserve system could not be attacked from that legal angle. If it weren't for the grievance procedure made possible through collective bargaining, the former reserve system with its aspects of player slavery and salaries not commensurate with players' worths would quite possibly still be the order of the day. If only for this one case alone, the grievance/arbitration procedure in baseball would have to be considered a great success from the players' standpoint.

Other important cases have been decided through this procedure as well. One other case described in Chapter 3, that of pitcher Catfish Hunter vs. the Oakland Athletics owner Charles Finley, also dealt with the issue of free agency. Hunter was declared a free agent because Finley failed to live up to the terms of his player's contract. The bidding war that ensued for this prime player should have been a signal for owners and players alike as to just what was to come once the reentry draft procedure was instituted.

While it would be impossible to discuss all of the arbitration decisions in baseball since 1968 (indeed, this would be an interesting topic for a book or article), two more recent cases that have made national headlines will be discussed to give the reader a flavor for the types of issues that can be brought to arbitration. The first case involved Bob Horner, Atlanta Braves third baseman and National League Rookie of the Year in 1978.[9] The second case involved Texas Rangers pitcher Ferguson Jenkins.[10] In both cases, the arbitrator was Raymond Goetz, a professor of labor law at the University of Kansas.

The Horner Case.   The Horner case involved an attempt by the player and his agent (Bucky Woy) to achieve immediate free agency for Horner instead of having to wait for the mandatory six-year period as specified in the collective bargaining contract. Obviously, free agency for a player of Horner's talent would mean a big bidding war and a much higher salary for the player (and commission for his agent). In a way, this case was similar in nature to the Catfish Hunter case described earlier, in its attempt to achieve free agency for a player because of a supposed breach of the uniform player's contract. Horner's case was based on the fact that the Braves had offered him an invalid "conditional" contract for the 1979 season. The Braves originally offered Horner $100,000 for 1979 and then upped the offer to $146,000, conditional on the arbitrator's finding that Horner's 1978 bonus package was indeed a part of his salary. The arbitrator ruled in June of 1979 that the conditional contract was valid and that a good portion of the bonus payments that went to Horner were indeed to be considered as a part of his salary for 1978. The only exceptions were the payments for his college expenses, incentive bonus money earned, and scouting payments made to Horner's father. Thus, the ultimate outcome in this case was what would be known in boxing as a split-decision. Horner did not achieve the immediate free agency/millionaire status he desired and would have to remain with the Braves for the standard six-year period prior to entering the reentry draft. On the other hand, with the bonus payments considered to be part of his 1978 salary, Horner could receive no less than $146,000 for the 1979 season, even if the Atlanta club decided to impose the maximum salary cut upon him (20 percent) for his refusal to sign a contract for the 1979 season. The fact that arbitrator Goetz ruled that Bob Horner's 1978 salary equalled approximately $183,000 (through a combination of cash and bonus payments) proved to be a significant victory for Horner and his agent. And even if the arbitrator had ruled that the bonus money was not part of Horner's salary, all would not have been lost. As agent Woy put it, when discussing how he would feel if Horner lost his case on both counts, "I'll get sick. . . . We'll bite our lips, but at least we increased his salary to $100,000 through all this."[11]

The Jenkins Case.   The second recent arbitration case involved pitcher Ferguson Jenkins, who was suspended with pay for an indefinite period of time due to a drug arrest on August 25, 1980, while his team was playing in Toronto. His baggage was searched by customs officials who reportedly found approximately $500 worth of cocaine, marihuana, and hashish. Jenkins was arrested a few hours later during a practice session and was charged by Canadian authorities with the misdemeanor of "simple possession." A trial date of December 18, 1980, was set. However, the Commissioner of Baseball, Bowie Kuhn, decided that some action had to be taken in the interest of the integrity of the game. Kuhn appointed a committee to question Jenkins about the incident, but the pitcher refused to cooperate, on the advice of his attorney, Ed Greenspan. In essence, Jenkins had not yet had his day in court, and no plea had yet been filed in the case.

Perhaps Bowie Kuhn should have waited until Jenkins' innocence or guilt had been determined prior to taking some punitive action in the case, as would seem to be consistent with the U.S. Bill of Rights. However, Kuhn decided to suspend Jenkins with pay for his failure to cooperate with baseball's internal investigation. Kuhn noted that he felt it was "only fair" to remove the pitcher from uniform until after the case was settled, which presumably would have put Jenkins out of action for the remainder of the season. Incidently, the suspension became effective on September 8, 1980, after Jenkins had already started two games following his arrest and release in Toronto.

A grievance on Jenkins' behalf was almost immediately filed by the MLBPA, and in a ruling handed down some two weeks later, Raymond Goetz ordered that Jenkins be returned to active playing duty for the remainder of the 1980 season. Commissioner Kuhn declared that the decision of arbitrator Goetz was wrong and that baseball's investigation into the Jenkins affair would be continued.

On December 18, 1980, Judge Gerald Young decided that an indeterminate finding of guilt was to be registered in the Ferguson Jenkins case. In essence, this verdict means that Jenkins has no criminal record and is free to pursue his assault on 300 major league victories as far as the courts are concerned. After the verdict was announced in Canada, the Commissioner of Baseball announced that his own investigation into the matter was continuing. Early in February of 1981, it was announced that Jenkins would not be suspended from baseball by Commissioner Kuhn. Instead, Jenkins agreed to contribute $10,000 to a drug education and prevention program in Texas and to make public appearances in support of that program. He will also appear in a drug education film to be produced by major league baseball and has agreed to cooperate fully with the Rangers in their own drug education and prevention program.

One could go on and on with examples of grievance/arbitration decisions that have been rendered in professional baseball since 1968. However, by now, the essential point of all this discussion should be quite obvious. The development of a grievance procedure with impartial arbitration as a final step was a major victory for the players won through the process of collective bargaining. Prior to 1968, management made all decisions and management ruled on any and all appeals to these decisions. It is not surprising to hear that given such a structure, not many appeals were attempted. For to appeal a decision that one feels is grossly unfair to the exact same person who made that decision in the first place is not typical of the American ideals of justice and fair procedure. The inability to challenge club and/or league decisions led to mounting player resentment and stronger interest in unionization than would otherwise have been the case. The upshot of all of this discord was the establishment of a formal grievance procedure in 1968, followed by the inclusion of impartial arbitration as a final step in 1970. The current grievance/arbitration procedure is reprinted from the collective bargaining pact of 1976 in Appendix I. Perhaps the most compelling statement that can be made with regard to the significance of the adoption of a formal grievance/arbitration mechanism is attributed to Richard Moss, former counsel for the MLBPA, who noted,[12]

> In summary, I am convinced that of all the progress we have made as an organization through negotiations in the past six years, one of the most significant victories we have won has been agreement on impartial grievance arbitration. I mean that not only from the standpoint of effectively representing our membership, but also from the standpoint of healthy and stable relations between the parties.

Salary Arbitration

We shall now turn our attention to the second type of arbitration employed in professional baseball, final-offer salary arbitration. And just as we have seen was the case with grievance/arbitration, the implementation of salary arbitration made possible through collective bargaining has been responsible for major changes in the game of baseball.

Salary Bargaining Prior to 1974

Traditionally, the baseball industry has been in a very strong bargaining position when engaging in salary negotiations with baseball players. The salary bargaining that goes on is individual player bargaining and not collective bargaining as occurs in many other unionized private and public sector domains. That is, salaries are not negotiated "across the board" for all second basemen, relief pitchers, and the like. Rather, each player as an individual must, on the basis of his lifetime and previous season's performance record, bargain with his club over the appropriate salary figure for the upcoming season. It should be noted that length of contract is also a bargainable issue. That is, a player has the flexibility to sign a one-year contract for, say, $100,000, or a five-year pact for $150,000 per year. The amount of money per season, kind of payment to be received, and length of contract are all items up for negotiation, and the final settlement will depend on the initial bargaining postures and the willingness to concede of both parties.

A hallmark of private sector contract negotiations, as expressed in the philosophy underlying the National Labor Relations Act of 1935, is that equalization of bargaining power is a necessary ingredient for the promotion of "good faith" collective bargaining.[13] After all, where both sides are very powerful (or very weak), each will realize the nature of their joint dependency on one another and bargaining attitudes fostering concession and compromise will be forthcoming. And that is the way the process of bargaining is supposed to work.

However, in baseball, because of several institutional arrangements and court protection from antitrust prosecution, the balance of bargaining power prior to 1974 was clearly in the clubs' favor. For example, once a player was drafted by a particular club, he could negotiate with *only* that club. After signing his initial contract, he was the property of that club until such time as the club decided to trade, sell, or give the player an outright release. Even if a player wouldn't sign a contract, the powerful reserve clause (examined in detail in Chapter 3) bound players who wished to continue to play the game to their original team. Baseball teams acted as monopsonists in the labor market, as they were the only buyer of player services. Additionally, the clubs each had a product market monopoly, as they were the only seller of baseball entertainment in a particular geographic region. Note that some of the largest cities do have two teams, but always one from each league, thus precluding any direct intraleague competition for the sale of tickets. The monopoly (cartel) aspects of baseball described above were buttressed by a series of Supreme Court decisions which essentially removed baseball from any type of antitrust prosecution because of its nature as a "game." This series of decisions has been discussed in detail in the previous chapter and need not be repeated here. Suffice it to note that the impact of these decisions was to force baseball players to seek changes in the employment relations in the sport through the process of collective bargaining, while players in other major sports also had the added weapon of the courts on their side in many instances.

All of the aforementioned factors, added together, were responsible for an extremely unbalanced bargaining situation between clubs and players when it came time to discuss salary for the upcoming season. The owners, with the labor market and product market imperfections that they had created through the rules of baseball, were able to generate a set of economic rents, or monies that they would not have received had the industry been a perfectly competitive one. One of the factors which enabled the owners to generate such rents was their ability to pay players salaries that were far less than their fair market values. This they could do because the player in question could negotiate with this one club only, because of baseball's strict rules, obviously instituted by the owners to help keep salaries down, among other reasons, as noted in Chapter 3.

Consider now the plight of a ballplayer negotiating his salary for the upcoming season with his club. As one might expect, the player comes to the bargaining sessions armed with statistics that support his salary claims. Likewise, the club has facts and figures of their own to support some lower salary offer for the upcoming year. If the club is unwilling to compromise on their wage offer based on the information presented to them, what options does the player really have? Prior to 1974, these options were indeed limited. One thing the player could do was simply to acquiesce to the club's terms and try again next season. Or, if the player was convinced he was worth more, he could bargain harder and longer in an attempt to squeeze more money out of the club. If these attempts were unsuccessful, the player still possessed several alternatives. For one thing, he could hold out his services, thereby hoping to put pressure on the club to raise their salary offer to entice him back to the playing field. But, during such a holdout period, the player was not being paid and generally such strategies on the part of the player were doomed to failure. For all the club had to do was to hold steady to its position and insist that if the player wanted to play baseball in the United States again, he would have to do so on terms acceptable to the club owners. One could argue that superstar ballplayers could pressure management somewhat by staging a holdout and might possibly be able to secure higher salaries for their efforts. On the other had, the vast majority of ballplayers would not be able to exert this kind of pressure upon their respective clubs, and for this reason, the hold-out would not seem to be a very effective tactic.

Of course, players had a few other options they could pursue. They could always retire from baseball and pursue another career. However, this option presumes that these individuals in fact do have other skills which they could employ in alternative occupations. However, their opportunity wage, or the highest wage they might expect to earn in their most preferred alternative line of work, was often far below what they might earn in baseball, even with the unequal bargaining power that existed in the game. Retirement from baseball in the prime of one's career to pursue another job was a viable but not a very lucrative alternative strategy. Note that if a retired player later decided to reenter the game, his contract would still be owned by the last team on which he was an active player. Thus, a short period of retirement followed by reactivation as a player was not an effective means of gaining free agency status and greater bargaining power. Players could also request that they be traded to other teams, sold to other teams, or given an outright release by their home team. The impact of a trade or sale was such that the player involved no longer had to deal with a club owner who was particularly intransigent in salary negotiations. However, who was to say for sure that the player's new boss would react any differently to his demands? Once again, the player was faced with a situation of being forced to bargain with one and only one team until such time as this new team decided that the services of the player were no longer required. At that point, a player could be released outright, which essentially granted him the status of a free agent who could make the best bargain for himself with any club that was willing to negotiate with him. However, before a player could be released, he had to pass through waivers, a process whereby each club in both leagues could have one last chance to acquire the rights to that player's services for a very modest fee. If any club claimed a player on waivers, the original club had either to retain the player on their roster or to sell the player to the new club at the standard waiver fee. Once assigned to a new club in such a manner, the player was right back in the same powerless position as before, able to negotiate only with this new club. Any player who actually was passed over by all other teams during the waiver process would become a free agent. But consider the likely worth of such a player. If no team was willing to acquire monopoly bargaining rights to that player's services for the modest waiver fee, it stands to reason that the player was probably going to have a very hard time latching on with any team. Thus, this type of free agency is really quite meaningless in that by the time a player achieves this status, his value as a ballplayer is really quite minimal.

Another option that players who were dissatisfied with their salaries had was to retire from American baseball and go to play ball in Japan. In that country, the rules referred to above are not applicable and the player can become a truly free agent, able to negotiate with any Japanese team and sign a contract for the best possible terms. Several ballplayers have availed themselves of this option, but this move typically occurs late in a player's career, when his talents are on the wane. By moving to Japan at just the right time, a player can increase the length of his playing career and achieve a real modicum of financial security at the same time. Since Japanese baseball is not up to the high performance standards of the American game, an aging National or American League star can usually spend several quite successful seasons in the Orient. Supposedly, when Pete Rose winds up his playing days with the Philadelphia Phillies, he too is headed for Japan to extend his career for one or two more seasons.

While the picture painted to this juncture sounds pretty bleak from the players' standpoint, things actually get worse. The most powerful weapon at the clubs' disposal, the *reserve rule*, covered in great detail in Chapter 3, was yet another way that clubs could keep players' salaries lower than what they might have been under a system of perfect competition. The system has been described earlier, but it is important to review its significance in the salary bargaining process. Every player to engage in the game had to sign a uniform player's contract that contained the reserve rule section. In essence, any time a club and player failed to reach salary terms for the upcoming season, the club had the right to invoke the provisions of this reserve rule to force the player either to retire from baseball or to play with the club with which he had signed a contract in the previous year. Failure to sign a contract was punishable by a maximum cut in salary of 20 percent. Thus, the clubs could use this reserve rule as an added weapon to help them entice ballplayers to sign a contract on the club's terms. Consider, for example, the case of a moderately talented player demanding a salary of $100,000, when his club is willing to pay only $75,000, and his salary in the previous season was $60,000. The club won't pay any more than $75,000, and informs the player that a refusal on the part of the player to sign a contract for that amount will force them to invoke the conditions specified in the reserve clause. That is, the player must either sign now for a $15,000 raise in salary up to $75,000 or be forced to play the upcoming season at $48,000, a 20 percent cut from last season's salary. Put in those terms, the club's offer of $75,000 is some $27,000 higher than the player's alternative and looks pretty good. It is easy to see how the clubs pretty much had the individual ballplayers over a barrel. Bargaining power did lie almost solely in the hands of management. Sure, superstar players with lots of fan appeal could get more money than the run-of-the-mill player, but the important thing to remember is that even though they could command a higher salary, even they were exploited by the owners, as has been shown in several studies.[14] This system of paying ballplayers less than what they could have made in a competitive market was pervasive throughout baseball's salary structure and, as has been noted, was much to the liking of the owners.

On the other side of the table, players had been fuming for some time over the inequities inherent in the salary bargaining process. While many gains were sought through the process of collective bargaining, a demand high on the players' list was for some added salary bargaining power. This power was to come in the form of final-offer salary arbitration, which was instituted prior to the 1974 championship season.

Final-Offer Salary Arbitration: Background

As noted in the previous section, the imbalance in bargaining power between players and clubs engaged in salary disputes led to much player resentment and a growing concern that something had to be done to rectify this inequitable situation. The notion of using salary arbitration to aid in the resolution of the toughest of these salary disputes was not a new idea in baseball. Back in 1952, baseball Commissioner A. B. (Happy) Chandler testified before a House Subcommittee that it was his belief that players should possess the right to demand salary arbitration. The basic argument of Chandler and several others who testified in favor of arbitration was that it could serve to redress the balance of power problem that so favored management and forced individual players into the inferior bargaining posture of being able to only deal with one team. However, the mood of most owners was not receptive to this new idea, and little was heard of it for a period of almost twenty years.[15]

Then, during the hearings surrounding the Curt Flood case, described in Chapter 3, the stage was set for the negotiation of a formal salary arbitration procedure. Flood, a St. Louis Cardinal outfielder, had refused to be traded to the Philadelphia Phillies and decided once again to try to challenge baseball's seemingly invincible reserve system. While he was unsuccessful in this endeavor, the testimony presented at his trial did touch upon the issue of the possible usage of salary arbitration in baseball as one way of partially modifying the reserve system. Other suggested modifications included independent competitive leagues, fixed-term player control by clubs, trade vetoes for veterans, minimum salary progression, and a reduction in the number of players who could be reserved. It is interesting to note how many of these suggestions formed at the Flood trial are an integral part of the employment relations in the game today:

But getting back to the specific suggestion of salary arbitration, National League President Charles Feeney noted:[16]

> *This is a very difficult situation for any arbitrator because you can't judge a player strictly by his batting average or his home run total. There are lots of things players do to help win games that are not reflected in averages, and to see and know what he does you must be there and observe it. I think the players and the people who are negotiating with them at the present time are in a much better position to negotiate and know exactly what they are negotiating about than an arbitrator. Also I think you would end up having an arms length situation between the players and management with arbitration. I think that you would probably find yourself in a situation where the player rated his services very much higher than he really thought he was going to get and maybe management rated the services lower than they really felt because they knew arbitration was going to get into the picture. I don't think it would be a good thing as far as relations between clubs and players are concerned at all.*

But compare the pessimistic quotation above with the following lines attributed to owner Bill Veeck, who noted that:[17]

> *I think it would be a splendid idea . . . I think . . . it would help. I think that it would create a little better relationship. Just the right to have an arbitration, the right not to be feeling that you are singly, as an athlete, negotiating against the wealth of a ball club, I think it would improve relationships. I think on many occasions that the club itself might profit a little bit, that on occasion ballplayers have been somewhat unrealistic in their various demands. So I think it would be beneficial from both ways.*

The players viewed salary arbitration as a necessary first step to be taken in the direction of eventual freedom of movement from club to club. Club owners, however, viewed the inception of the procedure in a much narrower light. To them, salary arbitration by itself should have quieted any lingering doubts that the players might have had about the owners' sincerity in moving towards a more equitable bargaining relationship. That is, salary arbitration was viewed originally as a cure-all for the complaints that the players had over baseball's historic reservation system. But as we saw in Chapter 3, the owners' views in this area were quite shortsighted and in fact, final-offer salary arbitration was but the initial step in the players' quest for equality.

Final-Offer Salary Arbitration: The Procedure

On February 8, 1973, the owners proposed that salary disputes between club owners and players that could not be reconciled bilaterally be submitted to salary arbitration. Negotiations over the exact nature of the procedure dragged on for three weeks, culminating finally with an agreed-upon procedure that reflected compromises by both sides. The agreement was dated February 25, 1973, and the initial usage of final-offer salary arbitration was set for the months preceding the 1974 championship season.

While the procedure has been changed somewhat over the span of seven years through subsequent negotiations, the essential elements of the initial procedure agreed to in February of 1973 remain intact. Appendix II reprints Article V, Section E, entitled *Salary Arbitration*, from the 1976 Basic Agreement.[18] We will now discuss the major elements of this procedure, then look at the actual impacts of final-offer salary arbitration in baseball both on the process and outcomes of bargaining.

The salary arbitration rules in the collective bargaining contract specify that any player with between two and six years of major league experience may submit an unresolved dispute over salary to an arbitrator without obtaining the consent of the club involved. Any club may also request salary arbitration for any player at any time. Players who have six or more years of experience must receive consent from their club prior to an actual arbitration hearing. Failure to obtain consent precludes that player from using salary arbitration. Players and clubs choosing to employ arbitration must so signify their desires between the dates of February 1 and February 10, prior to the commencement of the playing season. The contract then calls for the actual arbitration hearings to be held as soon as possible, and in all cases prior to February 20th. The arbitrator must render his decision within 24 hours of the close of the hearing, and there is, in fact, no written award. The neutral must simply insert the salary figure he feels is the proper one in the appropriate place in paragraph 2 of the Uniform Player's Contract and then forward copies of the contract to the league office of the concerned player and club. Arbitrators are chosen by the mutual consent of the Player Relations Committee and MLBPA, and the hearings are held annually in Los Angeles, Chicago, New York, and any other major league cities upon which the two sides can agree. The hearings are private affairs and time limits for the presentation of each side's case are specified.

Costs of the proceedings are split equally between the player and club involved.

The most interesting aspect of the arbitration procedure is that it features what is known as the final-offer arbitration. That is, "the arbitrator shall be limited to awarding *only* one or the other of the two figures submitted."[19] In other words, if a player demands $125,000 and the club offers $93,000, the arbitrator may choose only one or the other of these salaries as the binding award. No compromise, such as one which would split the difference and award a salary of $109,250, would be permissible. *No compromise award of any kind is allowable.* The arbitrator must be satisfied to pick either the player's final demand or the club's final offer as the salary to be paid for the upcoming season. More will be said about the actual decision-making process of these arbitrators later in this chapter. For now, it is important to concentrate on why the owners and players chose to employ this type of arbitration procedure over the more conventional type where arbitrators have much more flexibility in rendering the award which they feel is fairest. In order to understand why final-offer arbitration was chosen, we need to explore the theory underlying this interesting arbitration technique.

Why Final-Offer Arbitration?

In essence, this technique is different because of the very limited flexibility that is accorded the arbitrator faced with coming up with the proper salary for the upcoming season. As noted above, that salary must be either the player's final demand or the club's final offer. This final-offer technique (alternatively referred to as "last best offer," "high-low," "either-or," or "one-or-the-other") stands in sharp contrast to the more conventional type of interest arbitration, where the neutral is allowed much flexibility in rendering the binding award. For example, if the players and owners had agreed to a conventional system and if a salary dispute arose where the player demanded $160,000 while the club offered $121,000, the arbitrator would have been free to choose *any* salary amount he thought proper. It could have been $121,000, $160,000, a split-of-the-difference at $140,500, or any other number between the two extremes. Additionally, if he so chose, the arbitrator chould award more than the player's final demand *or* less than the club's final offer, if he thought that one of these higher or lower salaries were more in line with the player's true worth. Compare this extreme amount of flexibility under conventional arbitration with the rigorous and inflexible decision making process forced upon the final-offer arbitrator. Why did both sides agree to employ final-offer arbitration instead of the conventional procedure? Certainly, arbitrators must prefer the flexibility inherent in the conventional procedure. And, they do![20] If this is the case, what benefits did the parties perceive from using final-offer arbitration to resolve their salary disputes?

First, it should be noted that the concept of final-offer arbitration is not a new one at all. The procedure has not been adopted all that often,[21] but the idea of final-offer arbitration has fairly long roots. The notion surfaced back in the early Taft-Hartley era (the late 1940s) when people were extremely concerned with finding ways to resolve national emergency disputes. Final-offer arbitration was discussed then as a possible alternative to the Taft-Hartley dispute resolution procedures.[22] The concept was revived by President Nixon as one potential mode of dispute resolution in his so-called "arsenal of weapons" to be available for use in handling emergency transportation disputes.[23] Neither of these proposals were enacted by Congress. However, several states have adopted final-offer arbitration for use in the resolution of interest disputes between the state and its public employees. But even in these cases, why might final-offer arbitration be preferred to conventional arbitration?

One simple answer in the baseball arena is that this is the technique that the two parties agreed upon. No one forced them to do it. It takes two to tango and two sides to make a bargain. Just the mere fact that the parties chose this technique might imply that both sides perceived that the benefits of final-offer arbitration would far outweigh its costs. The benefit/cost ratio for final-offer arbitration was greater than the benefit/cost ratio for the conventional procedure. But this really begs the question. So far, all we have said is that the reason the parties chose to employ final-offer arbitration is that they liked it better. It was the most preferred solution from the *joint* standpoint of labor and management. But one can always make this type of statement about any negotiated settlement. There must be more to it, and there is.

Drawbacks of Conventional Arbitration

The real reason for employing final-offer over conventional arbitration has to do with the impacts that these procedures have on the bargaining process itself. Consider the following example, which will help the reader grasp this vital distinction. Under a conventional arbitration system, it is theorized that the parties often suspect that the arbitrator will simply split the difference in arriving at the binding decision. And this type of a solution makes a good deal of sense in our compromise prone society—each side will get something. While neither party will feel that it has won the case completely, neither will either side feel demoralized due to a shattering loss. Arbitrators can keep both sides happy by a compromise solution and maximize their probability of reemployment by the parties. Conventional arbitration seems to contain something for everyone involved, the player, the club, and last, but certainly not least, the arbitrator.

But now consider the impact that this type of procedure might have on the process of bargaining. Ours is a society that values negotiated settlements, where those agreements are arrived at by the parties involved through good faith collective bargaining. All throughout our history, with some minor exceptions during war time, a high premium has been placed upon bilateral negotiations with a minimum of governmental or other third-party interference into the bargaining process. But what might happen to our record of bilaterally negotiated agreements under a system of conventional arbitration? Would bargaining break down completely? Well, maybe not, but the incentive to reach settlements without the aid of the neutral party would seem to be greatly reduced.

Where both sides (or one side) expect the arbitrator to split the difference or construct a compromise award, it can be hypothesized that the amount of good faith collective bargaining will diminish substantially. This is because instead of compromising and moving their positions closer together in an attempt to settle, the parties might actually set their sights higher (lower) in anticipation of the arbitrator's difference-splitting behavior. The player might demand $160,000 instead of $130,000 in the hopes that the arbitrator's award will then reflect some of this higher position. On the other side of the table, management might engage in a similar bargaining posture. Instead of the $100,000 they were prepared to offer, the club might only offer $70,000, again in the hope of saving some money through the arbitration process. Now obviously, if arbitrators *do* split the difference in the example above, the player's salary would turn out to be $115,000 whether the arbitrator was faced with the original or the deflated (inflated) positions of the parties. And that is a key point. For if each side believes that the arbitrator will split the difference, and if each side adjusts its position in a similar manner, the outcome of arbitration must necessarily be the same. But, how likely is this to happen? In my opinion, not very, and I think that this answer would probably reflect the sentiments of many persons knowledgeable in the labor relations area. The real truth is that each side, under a conventional arbitration system, might hope to do just a little better for itself by inflating (deflating) its position just a little more than their opponent. Then, when the arbitration decision is made, the compromise solution will favor the party that exhibited the more extreme position. Granted that this type of strategy will not always work, but the crucial thing to determine is if most parties behave as if arbitrators made their decisions in this fashion. If they do, we should find a large number of cases under a conventional arbitration system that actually require arbitration, as compared with the impasse rate under final-offer arbitration or a legal strike domain. Evidence that addresses this issue will be presented in the next section of this chapter. For now, it is enough to remember that many writers and practitioners feel that conventional arbitration suffers from several flaws which make it less than desirable as a dispute resolution technique.[24] First, if the parties think that the arbitrator will simply split the difference between their respective final positions, each side has an incentive to hold back in negotiations and maintain a position *from which* the arbitrator can effectuate the proper compromise. Second, this type of bargaining posture is said to have a chilling effect[25] on the parties' bargaining behavior. That is, good faith collective negotiations take a second or back seat to the process of arbitration, which the parties find to be much easier and to their liking. In other words, we would expect to find a high proportion of cases in a conventional arbitration domain that actually proceed all the way to arbitration, as compared with other dispute resolution techniques. Finally, this initial reliance on conventional arbitration is said to lead to a narcotic effect,[26] where the parties can actually become "hooked" on the arbitration procedure to such an extent that good faith negotiations will never again be feasible. That is, given that arbitration had been used in round one of the negotiations, the probability is very high that these same two parties will choose to employ arbitration again in round two. Arbitration, once used, is viewed as an easy alternative to the rigors of the bargaining table.[27]

Advantages of Final-Offer Arbitration

Given all these potential negative features of conventional arbitration, it is no wonder that the parties at the baseball bargaining table in February 1973 decided to choose an alternative procedure to settle their salary disputes, final-offer arbitration. As first discussed theoretically by Carl Stevens,[28] this procedure should be able to overcome all of the deficiencies noted above with respect to the conventional process.

First, by forcing the arbitrator to choose either the club's final offer or the player's final demand as the binding award, the procedure would seem to have a built-in protection against rote difference-splitting on the part of arbitrators. Since there is only one issue up for determination (player salary), no compromise among several issues can be made as may be the case in several states where issue-by-issue final-offer arbitration is mandated by law. Of course, some might argue that arbitrators still might be able to compromise in several ways. First, in any particular year, they might decide half of the cases for the clubs and the other half for the players. Or, alternatively, where individual players use the arbitration procedure for several years in a row, the arbitrator might strike an intertemporal compromise by favoring the player in one year, the club in the next year, and so on. In fact, there is some evidence that suggests that collectively, arbitrators have pursued the former strategy as the overall win-loss records of players and clubs using arbitration is close to a fifty-fifty split. This evidence will be reviewed in the next section of this chapter. However, at one point in time and for any particular player/club salary dispute, it is undeniably true that an arbitrator will not be able to render a compromise award. The award must be of the either-or variety and, it is the inflexibility of this award making process that can have a major impact on the nature of the parties' bargaining behavior.

Instead of chilling bargaining, as was hypothesized under conventional arbitration, many writers such as Carl Stevens argue that final-offer arbitration will actually promote good faith negotiations and predict that a very high proportion of cases handled under a final-offer arbitration umbrella will be settled bilaterally, without any need to resort to arbitration. The theory is that each party to the negotiations will be scared to death at the thought of final-offer arbitration, because each side will fear that the other party's final position will be considered the more reasonable one and will be chosen by the arbitrator as the binding award. Instead of increasing the spread between the final positions of the parties, as was shown to be the case under conventional arbitration, final-offer arbitration should have just the opposite effect. That is, each party will strive to become more and more reasonable in its bargaining positions and good faith negotiations will ensue. As the parties' positions become closer and closer, the likelihood of settlement prior to an arbitration hearing increases greatly. And even if arbitration is required, the arbitrator is forced to choose between two rather reasonable positions rather than the extremes exemplified in the conventional arbitration process. This will not always be the case (for example, Bruce Sutter), but in theory, this phenomenon should occur across all cases on average. Thus, final-offer arbitration is viewed as being a self-destructing mechanism that really works best when it promotes bilateral settlements and very little use of the arbitration procedure. The mere threat of final-offer arbitration as a potential weapon to be used by either side in the negotiations is predicted to spawn a great deal of good faith bargaining; there should be less of a chilling effect on the bargaining process associated with final-offer arbitration than with arbitration of the conventional variety. This hypothesis will be addressed shortly. Finally, proponents of final-offer arbitration argue that with fewer cases going to arbitration initially, the narcotic effect should also be less of a worrisome issue. It is true that some parties might become hooked on the technique, but as we shall see, the evidence thus far supports the notion that at least in baseball, the narcotic effect has not been very powerful.

The baseball players and the club owners were faced with a tough set of choices in their negotiations over salary arbitration in 1973. One possibility was to reject the notion of arbitration altogether. However, as noted earlier, mounting player resentment over the inequities inherent in the reserve system and in the salary bargaining process essentially precluded this option. The owners felt that the institution of the process of salary arbitration might be a cure-all for the growing player concerns. Once it was decided that arbitration over salaries would be used, the next question facing the negotiators was to choose the appropriate type of arbitration. For reasons mentioned earlier, conventional arbitration was rejected in favor of the final-offer procedure; one lasting hallmark of the baseball salary arbitration system is that the decision of the arbitrator is constrained to the extent that one of the two final positions submitted at the hearing must be chosen as the binding award.

A second interesting feature of baseball's final-offer salary arbitration procedure is that the collective bargaining contract clearly specifies the criteria which the neutral may and may not use in the decision-making process. As can be noted in Appendix II (Article V, section E, paragraph 12), the permissible criteria include such things as past season and career performance statistics, comparative baseball salaries, physical and/or mental defects on the part of the player, and the recent performance record of the team. Items specifically precluded from the arbitrators' decision-making information set include the financial positions of the respective parties, press testimonials, offers/demands made prior to the arbitration hearing, and salaries of players in other professional sports. The comparative salary information furnished to each arbitrator contains the salaries of all professional ballplayers in the previous season broken down by years of service and club. Names of all players are given, and the neutral is specifically instructed to consider the salaries of all comparable players in the decision-making process and not merely the salary of a single person or group of persons.

Thus, there are clear-cut criteria that the arbitrators involved in baseball's salary arbitration procedure are mandated to follow under the terms of the collective bargaining agreement. Of course, one would naturally ask, to what extent do arbitrators follow this mandate, and more specifically, how will we ever be able to tell whether they do or not? These questions address intricate aspects of the theory of how arbitrators make their decisions in baseball, which will be developed in the next section of this chapter.

Research on Salary Arbitration in Baseball

Given that we have now spent a good deal of time developing the historical and descriptive aspects of baseball's final-offer salary arbitration procedure, it is appropriate that we turn our attention at this point to research that has centered on the impacts of this arbitration system since its inception in 1974.

Impacts on the Process of Bargaining

The theory of final-offer arbitration, discussed above, stresses the self-destructing nature of the procedure. The parties should have such a disdain for this type of arbitration that they will bend over backwards to compromise and hopefully will be able to reach a settlement bilaterally. Thus, one measure of the success of any final-offer arbitration system is the extent to which the system is used and not used over time. In order to explore this notion more fully, Appendix III presents a summary of the extent of usage of the final-offer salary arbitration procedure in baseball since its inception in 1974. The most crucial aspects of the data presented in the appendix for each player and club involved in an arbitration case are the player's final salary demand, the club's final salary offer, and the arbitration award (that is, whether the neutral chose the club's or the player's position as the binding salary award).

Recall that one desirable aspect of final-offer arbitration is that it is supposed to promote bilateral settlements. To what extent is this theoretical expectation consistent with outcomes in practice? In other words, has the mere threat of the availability of the usage of salary arbitration of the final-offer variety served to replace the bargaining power embodied in the right to strike and given the players the additional clout necessary to force the club owners to bargain with them in good faith over salary.[29] If so, we should expect to see a high proportion of cases settled bilaterally; if the players still believe that their clubs are being unfair with them, they now have the added option of demanding salary arbitration. Let's take a look at the evidence to see how final-offer salary arbitration has affected the process of salary bargaining in baseball.

The first thing to note is that final-offer salary arbitration is indeed being used in baseball. Since 1974, a total of 115 players have had their salaries decided by an arbitrator, with the players winning 55 cases (48 percent) and the clubs winning 60 cases (52 percent). Data on 102 of these 115 individual salary arbitration cases has been culled from various sources and is presented in Appendix III. Table 4.1 presents a summary of the number of cases won by year by each side. As one can see from an examination of this table, the overall results of baseball's salary arbitration system have been very evenly split to date. That is, the clubs enjoy a very slight margin in the number of overall cases won. Note also that no cases were held in either 1976 or 1977 as the parties were operating without a signed collective bargaining contract and thus, under no mandate to continue to employ the procedure during those two years.

Merely to look at the data presented in Table 4.1 and Appendix III, and from these data to conclude that final-offer arbitration has been unsuccessful in baseball is misguided and from a scientific standpoint, quite inappropriate. It is true that final-offer arbitration has been used and thus has not been perfectly able to promote the resolution of *all* major league salary disputes at the bargaining table. But simply to view this fact and then pronounce the experiment a

Table 4.1   **Final-Offer Salary Arbitration in Baseball**

Year	Cases	Player Wins	Club Wins
1974	29	13	16
1975	16	6	10
1976	0	0	0
1977	0	0	0
1978	9	2	7
1979	14	8	6
1980	26	15	11
1981	21	11	10
Total	115	55 (48%)	60 (52%)

Sources: See the listing of sources in Appendix III. See also James R. Chelius and James B. Dworkin, "Arbitration and Salary Determination in Baseball," *Proceedings of the Thirty-Third Annual Meeting of the Industrial Relations Research Association*, Denver, September 1980, pp. 105–112.

failure is inappropriate. In fact, both sides in baseball seem to be quite pleased with the way the procedure has operated to date. Naturally, if given the opportunity, each side could suggest several improvements or changes that they would like to see made in the system. Nevertheless, on net, the participants who negotiated this system back in February 1973 seem to feel satisfied that final-offer salary arbitration has worked to the benefit of both sides.

It is obvious that some salary dispute cases have required the intervention of a neutral since the inception of the final-offer technique in 1974. But as we know by now, this is simply an artifact of the institutional salary bargaining arrangements that existed in baseball prior to the 1974 championship season. The club owners possessed a great deal more bargaining power than the players did and there was not much that an individual player could do to convince his club to adopt a more concessionary bargaining posture.

But all of this was changed by the inception of final-offer salary arbitration. The players for the first time had a stick in their closet, a weapon that they could use when management refused to offer them a fair salary. The mere threat of final-offer arbitration meant more bargaining power for the players: If the owners failed to realize this fundamental truth and attempted to negotiate exactly as in the past, one would expect to witness hundreds of arbitration cases, as players would surmise that they couldn't possibly do much worse at arbitration and perhaps, they could do much better.

Table 4.2   Final-Offer Arbitration and the Chilling Effect in Baseball

Year	Number of Players Eligible	Number of Cases Filed	Settled Prior to Hearing	Total Awards
1974	500	54	25	29
1975	500	55	39	16
1978	97	16	7	9
1979	110	40	24	14
1980	N.A.	64	38	26
1981	N.A.	98	75	21
Totals	1207	327	208	115

Source: Personal correspondence from Mr. C. Raymond Grebey, Director of the Major League Baseball Player Relations Committee, Inc., dated May 8, 1979. The 1980 and 1981 data are from *The Sporting News*, March 14, 1981 and March 15, 1980. The numbers in the fourth and fifth columns do not add up exactly to those in the third column because two players were released by their clubs in 1972 prior to an arbitration award. Additionally, in 1981 the status of two players who had filed for arbitration was yet to be determined. Carleton Fisk was declared a free agent through a grievance arbitration decision and signed a multi-year pact with the Chicago White Sox. The other player, Rick Burleson, filed for salary arbitration but his team (the Angels) and the Player Relations Committee argued that he was not eligible for salary arbitration. A grievance was filed by Burleson, with a hearing scheduled for sometime in April.

The evidence presented in Table 4.1 and Appendix III seems clearly to demonstrate that the threat of final-offer arbitration did serve to alter the bargaining strategy of the baseball owners. In sum, a very small number of cases actually proceeded all the way to the arbitration route. In fact, the vast majority of all salary negotiations in baseball during this period continued to be handled and settled between the owners and the players. Thus, final-offer arbitration, as predicted in theory, does not seem to have had a major chilling effect upon the salary bargaining process in professional baseball. Table 4.2 presents some time-series data relevant to this issue. As can be seen from this table, approximately 14 percent of the eligible players chose to file for salary arbitration from the years 1974 through 1979 (165 of 1207). Note that in the first two years *all* players in both leagues were eligible to file for arbitration. Of course, this was the period prior to the now famous changes to the reserve system which were described in detail in Chapter 3. In essence, in the years 1974 and 1975, salary arbitration was the only weapon that players had at their disposal and the fact is, it just wasn't used all that much. After the reserve rule changes of 1976, both sides agreed to modify the eligibility requirements for salary arbitration somewhat (see Appendix II). The feeling was that with free agency and the greater bargaining power that it brought with it, the more senior players no longer needed the salary arbitration threat as well. Additionally, many veteran players were now signing long-term contracts that would preclude the use of salary arbitration, in that future salary terms had already been agreed upon by both sides for, say, a period of five years. Thus, the number of players eligible for salary arbitration is drastically reduced for the years 1978 through 1981. The players who are eligible to invoke arbitration without their club's consent are those with less seniority, who have yet to accrue the right to test their fair market value through the free agency mechanism described in the previous chapter.

Incentive to Settle

But the 14 percent filing rate noted above does not tell the entire story. Under the contract, bargaining can and does continue right up to the time of the arbitration hearing in some cases. Any settlement reached prior to the actual hearing negates the need for the salary arbitration procedure. During the initial four years of experience with salary arbitration, 95 out of the 165 total cases filed have been settled bilaterally, prior to the actual holding of an arbitration hearing. That is, even after a player or club files for arbitration, there is still quite a strong incentive operating for both sides to get together and peacefully negotiate a salary that is acceptable to them, *prior* to using arbitration. And this incentive seems to be quite strong, to the extent that 64 percent (208 of 327) of all cases filed are eventually settled *without* the need for arbitration. It would seem that the threat of usage of final-offer arbitration becomes an even stronger one once either side has filed for use of the procedure. This action, assumedly taken by the side that feels it has the stronger case, should force the opponent to take a good, hard look at its own bargaining stance. If this stance seems unreasonable, and if one might reasonably expect an arbitrator to side with the other party, it would behoove the intransigent party to make concessions and try to improve the probability of getting a negotiated settlement. And this seems to be exactly the type of process that the filing for arbitration has brought on in a good percentage of the cases.

However, not all cases can be settled in this manner, and the fact remains that in the first six years under the operation of the final-offer salary arbitration system, some 115 cases were eventually decided by an arbitrator. This represents approximately 8 percent of the total eligible population. In other words, 8 out of every 100 players have used salary arbitration, while the other 92 have been able to come to salary terms with their teams using the more traditional forms of bilateral negotiations, perhaps buoyed by the threat of final-offer salary arbitration hanging over the heads of both sides. The obvious question becomes: Is this 8 percent figure good or bad, or is it impossible to tell? Has final-offer arbitration done a reasonable job in baseball? Has it had a benign effect on the bargaining process or not? Has it been able to preserve the true essence of collective bargaining by transferring bargaining power from the owners to the players or not?

These are obviously difficult questions to answer. We really have nothing with which to compare this baseball experience in the true sense of the scientific method of research. We are not able to impose the tight controls of a laboratory study which would enable us to say for certain that final-offer arbitration promotes bilaterally negotiated settlements better than does arbitration of the conventional variety. In the field research sense, we have no nice neat comparison that we can make, such as we would have had if baseball had used a system of conventional arbitration for a period of say, five years, and then switched over to their present final-offer salary arbitration system. The reader should realize the difficulty that one has in trying to make any definitive statements about the impacts of final-offer arbitration on the process of bargaining in baseball.

However, these caveats aside, we can look to some casual evidence from other field settings as compared to baseball in an attempt to make some generalizations about the usefulness of final-offer arbitration. These data are presented in Table 4.3, where the main issue being looked at is the incentive to negotiate under several different conflict resolution devices (that is, the strike, final-offer arbitration, and conventional arbitration). For our purposes, the final column of this table provides the most compelling evidence in favor of final-offer arbitration. There it can be seen that domains that have employed final-offer arbitration have had typically much lower usage rates of the procedure than has been the case under conventional arbitration schemes. It does appear that final-offer arbitration promotes bilateral settlements better than does conventional arbitration, where in some instances the impasse rate can be as high as 40 percent. Finally, it is interesting to note that the rate of impasse under final-offer arbitration schemes tends to be *less* than the average strike rate in United States manufacturing industry. While ap-

Table 4.3 Impasse Procedures and the Incentive to Negotiate

Domain	Years	Type of Impasse Procedure	Total Number of Negotiation Cases	Cases Employing Stated Impasse Procedure	Procedure Usage as a Percentage of Total Negotiation Cases
Baseball	1974–1975	final-offer	1,000	43	4.3%
Iowa	1975–1976	final-offer	372	25	6.7
Massachusetts	1975–1976	final-offer	548	36	6.6
Wisconsin	1973–1976	final-offer	549	64	11.6
Michigan	1973–1976	final-offer	540	88	16.3
Pennsylvania	1969–1974	conventional	276	83	30.1
New York	1974–1976	conventional	118	34	28.8
Canadian federal government	1967–1974	conventional	305	55	18.0
British Columbia schools	1969–1973	conventional	389	163	41.9
U.S. manufacturing	1969–1975	strike	3,144	641	20.4

Source: This table is reprinted from James R. Chelius and James B. Dworkin, "An Economic Analysis of Final-Offer Arbitration as a Conflict Resolution Device," *Journal of Conflict Resolution,* 24:2 (June 1980), pp. 293–310. See this article for a listing of data sources. Also see David B. Lipsky and Thomas A. Barocci, "Final-Offer Arbitration and Public Safety Employees: The Massachusetts Experience," *Proceedings of the Thirtieth Annual Winter Meeting of the Industrial Relations Research Association,* 1977, pp. 65–76.

proximately 20 percent of these negotiations in manufacturing lead to an impasse or strike, the highest corresponding impasse rate under final-offer arbitration is 16 percent, and most other domains exhibit impasse rates under final-offer arbitration significantly lower than this. When this data is coupled with the growing body of laboratory evidence demonstrating the superior bargaining incentives associated with final-offer arbitration when compared with other dispute resolution techniques, it seems clear that final-offer arbitration has lived up to the expectations held out for it in baseball.[30] However, it should be noted that this evidence notwithstanding, there remains today a considerable amount of controversy among academicians and practitioners in the field of industrial relations as to the extent to which final-offer arbitration really promotes bilateral agreements.[31] It will be interesting to watch how this controversy resolves itself as more and more theoretical and empirical studies both in the laboratory and in the field focus in on the process aspects of final-offer arbitration.

Aside from the data reported above, there are other interesting tests one could perform to assess the impacts of final-offer arbitration on the process of bargaining. For instance, even in those cases where arbitration is used, our theory would predict that the arbitrator would, on average, have to choose from two rather moderate final positions. Thus, we should expect that the spread between the final positions of the parties might be small if, indeed, the parties bargain in good faith, as the technique would predict, in a joint effort to present the most reasonable final offer to the arbitrator. If some particular parties do not understand the technique and continue to bargain in the old baseball style, we could predict that they would face many arbitrations. Witness the case of Oakland in 1979. In that year, out of 14 total arbitration cases, 5 players were from Oakland and all of these players won their cases. In a similar fashion, it is interesting to note the patterns of usage and nonusage by club presented in Appendix III. Why do some clubs get forced to use arbitration every year while others may never have had to use the procedure? It is also interesting to look at the pattern of player usage of the procedure over time. The reader can verify that several, but not many, players have used salary arbitration more than once. Does this reflect aspects of a narcotic effect associated with the usage of final-offer arbitration or merely that the side that lost at arbitration in the previous round expects to win the next time around and chooses to invoke arbitration? Recall that both sides in baseball have the right to invoke arbitration, and that since the inception of the system, the clubs have filed only a very small percentage of the cases (around 11 percent).

One could go on and on with such mental exercises, but the real problem lies in the relative newness of the system and the lack of a greater number of data points, that is, players using arbitration. These types of problems coupled with some of the earlier problems mentioned all lead to the same conclusion. That conclusion is that for the present, research aimed at identifying the impacts of final-offer arbitration on the process of salary bargaining in baseball is extremely difficult to perform and the results of such exercises need to be carefully scrutinized and cautiously interpreted. For now, about the most we can say is that final-offer salary arbitration in baseball has not destroyed the process of bilateral salary negotiations. A great percentage of the total salary negotiations cases on a year-by-year basis continue to be resolved at the negotiating table, without the need for arbitration. And that, after all, is the theory behind how final-offer arbitration is supposed to work.

Impacts on Bargained Outcomes

While the previous paragraphs have dealt with the impacts of final-offer salary arbitration on the process aspects of collective bargaining in baseball and found that the procedure worked as expected, another potential impact of the mere availability of final-offer arbitration is on bargained outcomes. In this section, we will review the evidence with regard to this second type of impact for the years 1974–1975. In this way, we are able to control for any contaminating influences of the new reserve system which baseball instituted in the year 1976. In other words, had we considered the years 1976–1980, we would also have to realize that any results obtained in our analyses might have been caused by the reserve system changes instead of the institution of final-offer arbitration. Thus, an important point to keep in mind is that the results presented herein control for this contaminating possibility by looking at salary determination *only* during the first two years of baseball's experience with this procedure. During this two-year period, the availability of salary arbitration was the only major change to occur in the game's employment relationships. Thus, there was what might be termed a naturally occurring field experiment during that two-year period, and after we control for a whole host of other factors to be discussed, it seems likely that remaining differences in salaries pre- and post-arbitration can be attributed to the availability of the arbitration procedure during the latter set of years. The same type of causal statement could not be made if, for instance, the effect of the new free agency system was also operating at the same time. If one found that salaries increased by 10 percent between 1975 and 1976, it is hard to separate out the effects due to the reserve system from the effects due to final-offer arbitration. In addition, the only salary data available to the author was for two years prior to the start of final-offer arbitration and for the 1974–1975 seasons. Even if one could separate out the impacts referred to above, the problem of data unavailability would need to be tackled first. Thus, the results presented herein control for reserve clause changes by considering only the first two years of the salary arbitration system, both of which were prior to any reserve clause and free agency breakthroughs that were initially instigated by Peter Seitz's arbitration decision involving pitchers Messersmith and McNally in December 1975. Hopefully, all of these careful controls will enable us to pinpoint the independent impacts of final-offer salary arbitration on the outcomes of salary bargaining.

To begin with, it must be reiterated that the monopolistic nature of the baseball industry over time had placed the club owners in a relatively enviable position, as compared to what would have been the case were they in an industry that featured perfect competition both in product and labor markets. In the first place, the product market monopoly that each club enjoyed historically (only one team per league in each major city) allowed the teams to charge higher ticket prices than would have been possible under a competitive product market situation. In addition, as we have already seen, the owners also possessed what amounted to a labor market monopsony as they were the only purchasers of players' services. No other team within baseball had the right to tamper with any of the players under contract to any other team. The reserve rule essentially allowed the owners to pay salaries that were far less than they would have been under a more competitive labor market situation. Thus, these product and labor market imperfections allowed the owners to generate a set of economic rents that they would not have otherwise had. When analyzing the outcome impacts of final-offer arbitration, it is convenient to think in terms of how this pie of economic rents (or excess profits) was divided up between the clubs and the players prior to and after the institution of salary arbitration. As we shall see, the threat of final-offer salary arbitration provided the players with the bargaining power they needed to force their respective club owners to begin sharing their wealth with the players in a more equitable fashion than was previously the case.

Theoretical Impact

Now, let's consider what the impact of the availability of final-offer arbitration in baseball should be in theory. After this brief theoretical treatment, in which three basic hypotheses will be stated, empirical evidence bearing on each of these hypotheses will be presented.

When players are restricted to one team in their salary bargaining, owners will be able to discriminate among players on the basis of their opportunity wages outside of baseball, that is, the highest alternative wage that players could earn in some alternate occupation. If a player currently earns $75,000 per season in baseball and if the highest wage he could earn outside of the game (given the skills he currently possesses) is $23,000 as an insurance salesman, then this $23,000 is said to be that player's opportunity wage. A set of players who are equally productive in baseball but who have varying nonbaseball opportunity wages will generate the upward sloping supply curve to the team depicted in the graph in Appendix IV. An owner who paid the same wage to all equally productive players would pay wage *OF* with the corresponding total wage bill being *OFBC*. But we have already noted that prior to the inception of final-offer arbitration, owners discriminated against players of equal productive talents based upon their varying opportunity wages; players with lower opportunity wages were typically paid less.

Now, it is pretty tough for the club owners to perfectly discern each and every one of their players' opportunity wages. If they could do so, they would pay each player according to where his position was on the supply curve and be able to *save AFB* dollars. However, the difficulty of trying to perfectly discern opportunity wages, coupled with the potential morale problem associated with not paying similarly performing players the same wage, would imply that the actual schedule of wages paid prior to final-offer arbitration was less steeply sloped than the schedule based on opportunity wages alone. The schedule of actual wages paid prior to final-offer arbitration is labelled *GB* in the diagram.

The advent of final-offer arbitration in 1974 meant that a dissatisfied player could now invoke the procedure and present evidence at an arbitration hearing with regard to his productivity and the comparative wages paid to other players. As noted above, the threat of using final-offer arbitration provided owners with a rather strong incentive to try to settle these salary disputes bilaterally. Thus, one would predict that because of the threat of final-offer arbitration, owners would offer salaries above the *GB* schedule in an attempt to avoid arbitration and the possibility of having the arbitrator choose the player's final offer as the binding award. The higher wage offered will be up to a limit of *OF*, which represents the marginal value or contribution to the team of that player. It is clear that the mere availability of final-offer arbitration should serve to increase the players' bargaining power and impact upon the outcomes that they can reasonably expect to achieve. In general, where one side is in some sense weaker than their opponent, prior to the adoption of final-offer arbitration, the theory predicts that bargaining power will be more equal after the technique becomes available for usage. The equalizing of bargaining power is in fact a public policy goal and so it is interesting to look at the extent to which final-offer arbitration might promote the achievement of this goal.

The above analysis implies three testable hypotheses about the impact of the availablility of final-offer arbitration on salary outcomes:

1. The availability of final-offer arbitration should lead to higher average wages for baseball players. On the graph in Appendix IV, the total wage bill prior to arbitration was *OGBC*. After arbitration, this wage bill increased to *OFBC*. Since *OFBC* is greater than *OGBC* and since the number of players per team *OC* is fixed at twenty-five, average wages should increase.

2. Before arbitration, profits to the team owners were defined by *GEB* = *OEBC* − *OGBC*. After arbitration, profits were *FEB* = *OEBC* − *OFBC*. Given that FEB is less than GEB, it is predicted that the return to owning a baseball team declined after the availability of final-offer arbitration.

3. In the prearbitration period, players similar in performance were paid a range of wages from *OG* to *OF* depending upon their opportunity wages outside of baseball. After arbitration, all equally productive players should receive wage *OF*. Thus,

the range of wages paid to equally performing baseball players should decline after the adoption of final-offer arbitration.[32]

Statistical Testing

As noted above, these three hypotheses were tested using data on baseball players' salaries for two years prior to the adoption of final-offer arbitration, as compared to the years 1974 and 1975, the first two years of experience under the then newly negotiated procedure. During the years of the analysis, the only major change in the employment relationship in the game of baseball was the adoption of the final-offer salary arbitration procedure. Thus, one can make some reasonably strong statements about its effects if changes are indeed found in the data after arbitration was implemented.

First, it should be noted that all three of the hypotheses stated above were confirmed through empirical analyses. The financial rewards for playing baseball did increase substantially and significantly during the period under study. Table 4.4 shows that both nominal (actual dollar salaries) and real (corrected for inflation) salaries did increase significantly after the availability of final-offer arbitration. Thus, just as the theory would predict, after arbitration became available, club owners did begin to pay players more in line with their real values to their teams. The owners were forced to share a larger part of their revenue pie with the players for the first time. Alternative explanations for this result of higher post-arbitration salaries were examined and found to be lacking in explanatory power. Thus, changes in opportunity wages and increased performance levels in baseball were both looked at as possible alternative explanations for this increase in player salaries. Neither of these explanations proved satisfactory, as baseball wages actually increased more than did opportunity wages during the relevant time frame and performance was seen to be unchanged based on several em-

Table 4.4 Pre- and Postarbitration Salaries in Baseball*

	Prearbitration	*Postarbitration*
Average Nominal Salaries	$30,204	$50,169
Average Real Salaries	$29,366	$33,475

* *Note:* Salaries reported above are averages for one league, excluding rookies and players who actually used arbitration to have their salaries determined. The differences between pre- and postarbitration average salaries are statistically significant at the .01 level.

pirical tests.[33] It does seem likely that the availability of final-offer salary arbitration was associated with an increase in the average wage of baseball players.

The second hypothesis, that club profits would decrease after the inception of final-offer arbitration, was also supported through empirical tests. While it is not easy to gather data on the exact nature of the revenues and costs associated with the operation of a professional baseball team, a procedure first described by Scully can be used as an approximation technique.[34] According to this technique, team revenues are assumed to come from four main sources: (1) home ticket sales, (2) visiting team road ticket shares, (3) local broadcast rights, and (4) network broadcast rights. The other side of the profit calculations (that is, total costs) is more troublesome. The only aspect of costs for which good data were available was in the area of player salaries. Having no real data on nonsalary expenses, Demmert's assumption that player payroll costs equalled one fifth of total team costs was employed.[35] Given these data and assumptions, the team profit calculations are straightforward. They require the summing of all aspects of revenues referred to above and then, from this total revenue figure, the subtraction of total costs. As noted, total costs are defined as player payroll expenses times five. If this profit estimating procedure is consistent both before and after the availability of final-offer arbitration, the estimates will help determine whether the salary increases noted above were at the owners' expense. By the method described above, average real team profit in the prearbitration years was $2.6 million per year, while the profit level per team fell to around $2.2 million per year during the arbitration years of 1974 and 1975.[36] Thus, these results support the hypothesis that final-offer arbitration may have been partially responsible for neutralizing some of the owners' previous excess of bargaining power by lessening their ability to discriminate in salary payments among players of equal productivity.

The final hypothesis has to do with the relationship between pay and performance in baseball before and after the availability of arbitration. Prior to arbitration, teams paid equally productive players a range of wages based upon their best alternatives outside of baseball. The prediction of the theory is that after final-offer arbitration became available, the pay of players with similar performance should be less variable. That is, teams should tend to pay all players of equal talent more or less the same wage.

This particular hypothesis can be tested by means of a regression equation relating pay to performance. But in order to perform such analysis, one must first have some model of the wage determination process in baseball. Several authors have attempted to build just such a model,[37] but their attempts are all subject to the same basic criticism. That is, there is really no way theoretically to know which performance variables should be employed in analyzing the wage-determination process. Some authors might suggest the use of home runs and runs batted in as the major determinants of salary for hitters, while other authors might prefer to use slugging average and seniority. The point is that there is no way, in theory, that we can ever say who is right or wrong, or even who is more right in the above example.

Given this severe problem, the method developed by Chelius and Dworkin seems to be a preferred solution.[38] Realizing that the problem of which performance variables to use could not be solved in theory, these authors, rather than choosing their explanatory variables based upon their own value judgments, instead chose to use a statistical technique known as principal components analysis to solve this problem. Basically, this technique takes a larger set of interrelated variables (in some cases, highly correlated variables such as home runs and runs batted in), and reduces this larger set to a much smaller set of totally independent (orthogonal) principal components. Appendix V presents the results of these principal components analyses for both the hitter and pitcher samples. It should be noted that in each case, the variables chosen to be employed in the larger set for the analyses were all permissible factors which an arbitrator could consider if called upon to make a salary award. (These factors were discussed earlier in this chapter and can be found in the collective bargaining contract in Appendix II.)

The principal components analyses led to the establishment of three major determinants for player salaries in the case of both hitters and pitchers. For hitters, these variables were labelled *production*, *power*, and *seniority*, while for pitchers, the three variables were called *work load*, *inefficiency*, and *seniority*. To see which of the variables in the larger set were important to each of these factors (what the statisticians refer to as "high loadings"), the reader need only glance down the column associated with each factor in Appendix V and pick out those variables with correlations of above, say, .70. For instance, the variables which load highly on the seniority factor for both hitters and pitchers are numbers one and two respectively, that is, years in the major leagues and age. None of the other variables employed had a similarly high loading on the seniority factor. A similar exercise can be performed by the reader for each of the other two factors found in the hitters' and pitchers' models. Given this factor structure found through the principal components analyses, the equations the authors used to relate performance to salary were:[39]

Equation 1. $\text{Salary}_{\text{hitters}} = \alpha_0 + \alpha_1 \text{ Production}$
$+ \alpha_2 \text{ Power} + \alpha_3 \text{ Seniority} + \mu$

Equation 2. $\text{Salary}_{\text{pitchers}} = \alpha_0 + \alpha_1 \text{ Work Load}$
$+ \alpha_2 \text{ Inefficiency} + \alpha_3 \text{ Seniority} + \mu$

Recall that the third hypothesis was that after final-offer arbitration became available, the range of wages paid in baseball to similarly performing ballplayers should decline. Using the two equations specified above, regression analyses were performed for hitters and pitchers for the years prior to and after the inception of arbitration. These results are presented in Appendix VI. While all of the factors derived through the principal components analyses do turn out to be significant and independent predictors of baseball players' salaries, the crucial aspect of the results in the table in Appendix VI are contained in the column labelled $\overline{R}^2$, where the results for the exact test of hypothesis three are reported, and as can be seen from the data, this hypothesis is also confirmed. In brief, the statistic $\overline{R}^2$ describes the amount of total variation in the dependent variable (in this case, players' real salaries, adjusted for inflation) that is accounted for by the combination of independent or explanatory variables included in the model. Or put in another way, if the total variation in player salaries equals 100, by what amount is that variation *reduced* due to the inclusion of the set of independent variables used in the particular model? This calculation is then adjusted for the number of degrees of freedom, or the number of observations (data points on player salaries) in the sample.

If hypothesis three is to be supported, we should find a closer fit between pay and performance after final-offer arbitration is available. And that is exactly what was found as in the hitters' model; the increase in $\overline{R}^2$ was from .65 to .69. In the pitchers' model, the corresponding increase was from .56 to .65. Both of these differences are statistically significant at conventional levels. What all this means is that in fact, as predicted by the theory, owners did tend to pay similarly performing players more similar salaries after the advent of final-offer arbitration. Thus, we do tend to observe a tighter fit between pay and performance in major league baseball after the inception of salary arbitration. This manifests itself in the better explanatory power of the models presented in the table in Appendix VI for the years after salary arbitration was implemented.

Thus, as we have seen, all three of the hypotheses with regard to the impact of the availability of final-offer arbitration on the outcomes of bargaining have been confirmed. It does seem that the mere presence of final-offer salary arbitration in baseball has greatly enhanced the bargaining power of the players at the expense of the owners, as the theory of final-offer arbitration would predict. We now turn our attention to an analysis of the decision-making process employed by the arbitrators in baseball's salary arbitration procedure.

How Final-Offer Arbitrators Make Their Decisions

The results reported in the previous section focused in on the availability of arbitration in baseball and the impacts such availability has had on bargained outcomes. As such, primary interest was not on those players who actually used salary arbitration but on those others whose salaries were increased by the mere presence or threat of going to arbitration. And as we saw in an earlier part of this chapter, over 90 percent of the eligible ballplayers were able to come to terms with their clubs over salaries without actually using arbitration. The mere threat of arbitration was usually enough to bring about good faith bargaining on both sides. But why were the owners so afraid of using arbitration? Perhaps it was because they knew they had been underpaying their players for some time and that an arbitrator was likely to realize this and award the player's demand as the binding salary. But arbitrators should not blindly favor the player in each and every case; if they did, all players would soon learn that a good way to increase their salaries was by invoking arbitration. We have already seen that this is clearly not the case in baseball. A very small percentage of players and clubs do choose to use arbitration, and in those cases where arbitration was actually used, the breakdown of management as opposed to player victories was just about an even split.

All this leads one to the conclusion that it would be quite useful to be able to model the decision-making process employed by arbitrators in baseball's salary arbitration cases. It seems reasonable that prior to invoking arbitration, both players and clubs would probably try to estimate their probabilities of success. These probabilities must necessarily reflect the parties' respective guesses of what factors the neutral is likely to employ in his decision making and how each of these factors might be weighed. A player who feels he can get more by using arbitration than through accepting his club's final offer at the bargaining table will most certainly choose to use arbitration. Similarly, a club will seek arbitration whenever the owners feel that an arbitrator will award a player a salary lower than the player's final demand at the bargaining table. Since both sides determine their own actions based on their presumptions about the most likely behavior on the part of the arbitrator, it seems crucial that we focus some attention on the process employed by these neutrals in choosing between the club's final offer and the player's final demand on a case-by-case basis.

Theory

Theoreticians and practitioners alike have assumed that final-offer arbitrators go through a two-stage decision-making process in the rendering of their awards. First, the arbitrator comes up with his own estimate of the player's worth for the upcoming season (call this estimate parity) using all of the past performance data and comparative salary figures available to him under the collectively bargained procedure (see Appendix II). After coming up with this notion of parity, the arbitrator is then presented with two final offers, one from the club and the other from the player. In the second step of his decision-making process, it is assumed that the arbitrator will compare his estimate of parity with these two positions submitted to him at the hearing and then choose that position which comes closest to parity as the salary award for the upcoming season. For example, if parity equals $83,550, the player has demanded $110,000, and the club has offered $78,500, it is predicted that the arbitrator will choose the club's offer, $78,500, as the binding award. Of course, one could easily come up with other types of decision rules that arbitrators might follow, but the essential point is that it is usually assumed that the parties feel that arbitrators behave in the manner described above. Thus, as a starting point, it might prove extremely useful to test the above description of arbitrator behavior to see if it indeed is an accurate one.

A more formal statement of the above theory of arbitrator behavior is presented in Equation 3 below:

Equation 3. $Y = \alpha + \beta\,[(Sp - S) - (S - Sc)]$, where

Y = the arbitrator's decision and equals 1 if the decision favors the club, 0 if the decision favors the player;

α = a constant term;

β = the parity coefficient, to be estimated through a regression analysis;

Sp = the player's final demand;

Sc = the club's final offer; and

S = the arbitrator's notion of parity for a particular player

In order to facilitate understanding of the above model, the reader may wish to refer to the diagram presented in Appendix VII. In the diagram, the vertical axis represents the arbitrator's decision, while the horizontal axis refers to the quantity $[(Sp - S) - (S - Sc)]$. The actual decision an arbitrator can render is of the either-or variety (1 or 0), but prior to that decision being made, the parties can make predictions regarding the probability of their side prevailing at arbitration. These probabilities, of course, might range anywhere from zero to one. For instance, a player might rate his chances of winning at arbitration as 80 percent while a club might think their chances of winning are 60 percent.

The quantity measured on the horizontal axis gets at the notion of our assumption that the arbitrator chooses the final offer presented to him that most closely approximates parity as the binding award. One way to write this assumption mathematically is as we have done, $[(Sp - S) - (S - Sc)]$. Of course, this also assumes that the player's final offer is greater than the club's final demand, an assumption that is by definition true in all cases where salary disputes arise. It is not necessary that the arbitrator's conception of parity lie within the bounds of Sp and Sc. The model works equally well when it does not; for example, if S is less than Sc. In such a case, the prediction would simply be that the arbitrator would choose the club's offer as the binding award. In actuality, both of these situations are reasonably likely to occur, and do occur in the baseball salary arbitration procedure.

The upward sloping line labeled the parity curve in the diagram in Appendix VII represents two basic notions. First, the fact that this line passes through .5 is not accidental. When both sides' final offers are equidistant from the arbitrator's notion of parity, the neutral will be indifferent between choosing between these positions. That is, the probability of a management win at arbitration will be .5, and likewise, the probability of a player win will be .5. This situation might occur where, for instance, the club offers $50,000, the player demands $80,000, and the arbitrator thinks the player's true value (parity) is $65,000. In this case, the theory can not predict a winner. The best we can do is say that each side has a fifty-fifty chance of having its position chosen.

But this type of an exact split between the final positions of the parties is not very likely to occur. More normally, in a case at arbitration, one of the final positions submitted to the arbitrator will be much closer to his concept of parity. And according to the theory, that is the position which will be chosen. The graph in Appendix VII indicates that as the spread between the player's final demand and parity increases in relation to the spread between parity and the club's final offer, the chances of the club prevailing at arbitration increase. That is, the arbitrator is more likely to choose the club's final offer when it is closer to parity than is the player's final demand. Alternatively, where the spread between the player's final demand and parity is less than the spread between the club's final offer and parity, the arbitrator is more likely to choose the player's demand as the binding award. This is so because where the player's final offer is closer to parity, the arbitrator views the player's position as the more reasonable of the two offers put before him. Thus, in the diagram, the parity curve is seen to have a positive slope, and in the ensuing analysis, a direct test of this parity hypothesis can be performed by looking at the sign of the coefficient β generated through the statistical analyses. A positive value of β indicates support for this so-called parity theory of how final-offer arbitrators make their decisions.

Practice

In order to test the model presented in Equation 3, four pieces of information are necessary. Three of these, Y, Sp, and Sc, are readily available and pose no problem. Recall that these symbols stand for the arbitrator's decision, the player's final demand, and the club's final offer, respectively. The fourth piece of data required is the arbitrator's notion of parity, or the fair wage, for each player involved in arbitration. This is the salary figure that the arbitrator has arrived at using his own decision-making calculus described in stage one of his thought process reviewed above. Obviously, this piece of information is not readily available and presents a real difficulty to the researcher attempting to make the model more tractable. One possibility is to ask the actual arbitrators what the parity salary was in each case; but they may not remember and, even if they did, may not wish to reveal such information. Another method had to be found in order to estimate parity.

Happily, such a procedure is readily available, based on the Chelius and Dworkin salary determination model discussed in the previous section and represented in Equations 1 and 2. In essence, the equations were originally run omitting those players who had actually used arbitration. A substantial explanatory and predictive power was shown to be present in the three variables used in both the hitters' and pitchers' models. Given the results presented in Appendix VI, one could easily estimate a predicted salary for players using arbitration and then employ these salary figures as estimates of parity in each player's case. The procedure first requires that the composite indices of player performance (seniority, workload, and the like) be computed for each player who used arbitration. This is done by multiplying the standardized values of each player's performance measures (gathered from the *Baseball Encyclopedia, 1979*) times the relevant factor score coefficients. Once these composite indices are computed, they in turn are multiplied by the regression coefficients reported in the table in Appendix VI for players and pitchers, respectively. The result is an S value for each player who used arbitration, that is, an estimate of what the arbitrator felt that player was worth. These parity estimates can then be used directly along with values of S, Sp, and Sc to evaluate Equation 3. The exact procedure for doing this evaluation is quite technical and will not be reported here.[40] However, it should be noted that the parity coefficient β did turn out to be positive and statistically significantly different from zero, as predicted in theory. The constant term α, instead of the expected .5, came out to be around .37. What this means is that when both sides' final positions are equally close to parity, management has only a 37 percent chance of winning the case. That is, there appears to be some form of a built-in bias in the arbitrator decision-making process that tends to favor the players over the clubs. To further explicate the interpretation of these results, the interested reader is referred to the table appearing in Appendix VIII. The column labeled $[(Sp - S) - (S - Sc)]$ presents various possible values of the above expression. For instance, in the fifth row, the value shown is $27,480. The reader can verify that one way this figure could be arrived at is if the arbitrator's estimate of parity was $100,000, the player demanded $154,960 and the club offered only $72,520. What the second column tells us is that in fact, even though the club's offer is $27,480 closer to parity than is the player's offer, this is the point where the club just has a fifty-fifty chance of having its position chosen by the arbitrator. In other words, for the eighty-one cases analyzed to date, arbitrators seem to be requiring the clubs to be quite a bit more reasonable than the players before adopting their positions as the final settlement. Thus, while the overall theory is confirmed in that the coefficient β is positive and significant, the results seem to indicate that the theory is not as precise as would have been predicted. It is true that lower values of $[(Sp - S) - (S - Sc)]$ tend to be associated with player wins and vice-versa. However, for management to have even a fifty-fifty chance of winning at arbitration, their final offer must be some $27,480 closer to parity than the union final demand has to be. The process appears to have built into it a bias in favor of awards for the players. It seems clear that if the owners realize this, they should be even more prompted to try to settle all of their salary disputes with the players bilaterally. And thus, the nature of the arbitrator decision-making process itself seems to have a large impact on the owners' behavior. Coupling this observed behavior on the part of the arbitrators with the other incentives to settle that final-offer arbitration provides (discussed earlier in this chapter), it is no wonder that only a very small proportion of all possible cases wind up at arbitration.

One final note about the analysis above is in order. Using the very simple model outlined above, one is able to correctly classify 84 percent of the arbitration cases. That is, based on the predictions of the model above, 80 percent of the hitters' and 90 percent of the pitchers' cases can be properly predicted as to whether it is most likely that the club or the player will prevail at arbitration. Thus, it would seem that the model might provide a useful tool for both player and management representatives who are trying to decide whether or not to proceed to arbitration. On average, the model could correctly tell 9 out of 10 pitchers (clubs) whether they are likely to win (lose) at arbitration. The corresponding prediction for hitters is a bit lower, at 8 out of 10.

Given the great gains that the players have been able to derive through the threat and actual usage of salary arbitration, it is not surprising to find out that in recent negotiations the club owners have attempted to invoke changes in the salary arbitration procedure that would tip the balance of power more in their favor. A short description of the most recent of these attempts will be the subject of the following section.

Recent Management Proposals to Alter the Final-Offer Salary Arbitration System

As noted above, the most recent round of labor-management negotiations in baseball featured an attempt by the owners to revamp substantially the final-offer salary arbitration system that had been in operation since the 1974 season. The change the owners proposed in the 1980 negotiations would have restricted the arbitrator to considering *only* the criteria of seniority and the pay of players with similar seniority levels in rendering their decisions. Compare these two criteria with the broad range of items originally available for usage, described earlier in this chapter and reprinted in Appendix II. In effect, the owners' proposal amounted to a concerted attempt to regain some of their lost monopsony powers. Instead of tending to pay all similarly performing players the same wage as would occur under competitive market conditions, the new proposal would have, if adopted, tended to impose a salary schedule for all players with five or fewer years of experience. Thus, all second basemen with three years of experience would earn, say, $82,000, regardless of their performance disparities. Such artificial equality would most certainly imply some degree of discrimination against the better players.

As described in Chapter 3, the heated bargaining that ensued over this issue and proposed changes to the reserve clause indeed almost led to a regular season strike. Finally, the owners dropped their demands for restructuring the final-offer salary arbitration system, and the procedure first negotiated in 1973 remains essentially intact today. As was noted in Chapter 3, the issue of compensation for teams losing free agents is still unsettled and the threat of a regular season strike on May 29, 1981, over this issue looms larger all the time.

Summary

In this chapter, we have reviewed the implementation and impacts of two forms of arbitration that have come to be used in various aspects of the employment relationship between professional baseball players and their club owners. First, grievance/arbitration was discussed, and the importance of this procedure in shaping several of the major changes in the game's employment relationship was emphasized. Next, final-offer salary arbitration was described in some detail, followed by a rather lengthy review of research that has focused on the impacts of this procedure on the process and outcomes of bargaining and on the decision-making process used by arbitrators involved with this system. Again, as was the case in Chapter 3 where we discussed the free agency system, heavy emphasis has been placed on the fact that these two forms of arbitration were made possible only because of collective bargaining between the owners and the players. The gains which the players have been able to attain through the process of bilateral negotiations seem extensive indeed! We have now concluded our discussion of the three primary gains achieved through collective bargaining, free agency, grievance/arbitration, and final-offer salary arbitration. But to stop here would be to only tell part of the story. For the players have won significant improvements in many other aspects of their employment relationship, in the areas of both pecuniary and non-pecuniary benefits. The next chapter will present a brief review of these other important gains achieved through collective bargaining.

Endnotes

1. A. C. Pigou, *The Economics of Welfare* (London: Macmillan and Company, 1950), pp. 451–461.
2. R. W. Fleming, *The Labor Arbitration Process* (Urbana, Illinois: University of Illinois Press, 1965), pp. 1–30.
3. Pigou, *op. cit.*, pp. 451–461.
4. *Columbus Printing Pressman*, 219NLRB268, 89LRRM1553 (July 18, 1975).
5. Neil Chamberlain, Donald Cullen, and David Lewin, *The Labor Sector* (New York: McGraw-Hill, 1980), pp. 235–238.
6. Barbara Dennis and Gerald Somers, *Arbitration of Interest Disputes*, Proceedings of the Twenty-Sixth Annual Meeting, National Academy of Arbitrators (Washington, D.C.: Bureau of National Affairs, 1974), p. 110.
7. *Basic Agreement between The American League of Professional Baseball Clubs and The National League of Professional Baseball Clubs and Major League Baseball Players Association*, effective January 1, 1976, Article X, pp. 18–27, 66–69.
8. *Ibid.*, p. 19.
9. *The Sporting News*, May 5, 1979, p. 22; *The Sporting News*, June 16, 1979, p. 40.

10. *The Sporting News*, September 13, 1980, p. 47; *The Sporting News*, September 27, 1980, p. 21; *The Sporting News*, October 11, 1980, p. 45.

11. *The Sporting News*, May 5, 1979, p. 22.

12. Dennis and Somers, *op. cit.*, p. 115.

13. *Labor Management Relations Act*, Section 1.

14. Gerald Scully, "Pay and Performance in Major League Baseball," *American Economic Review*, 64 (December 1974), pp. 915–930.

15. *Hearings on Organized Baseball Before the Subcommittee on the Study of Monopoly Power of the House Committee on the Judiciary*, 82nd Congress, 1st Session, Sec. 1, Pt. 6, pp. 298–299 (1951). As cited in Mark Goldstein, "Arbitration of Grievance and Salary Disputes in Professional Baseball: Evolution of a System of Private Law," *Cornell Law Review*, 60 (August, 1975), p. 1065.

16. Goldstein, *ibid.*, p. 1067.

17. Goldstein, *ibid.*

18. *Basic Agreement, op. cit.*, pp. 7–11.

19. *Ibid.*, p. 8.

20. Fred Witney, "Final-Offer Arbitration: The Indianapolis Experience," *Monthly Labor Review*, 96 (May, 1973), pp. 20–25.

21. States that have adopted final-offer arbitration for the resolution of public sector interest disputes include Connecticut, Iowa, Massachusetts, Michigan, New Jersey, and Wisconsin.

22. Goldstein, *op. cit.*, p. 1069.

23. *Ibid.*

24. Peter Feuille, *Final-Offer Arbitration*, (Chicago, Illinois: International Personnel Management Association, 1975), p. 56.

25. John C. Anderson and Thomas A. Kochan, "Impasse Procedures in the Canadian Federal Service: Effects on the Bargaining Process," *Industrial and Labor Relations Review*, 30 (April, 1977), pp. 283–301.

26. Anderson and Kochan, *ibid.*

27. Address by Willard Wirtz before the National Academy of Arbitrators, February 1, 1963. Reprinted in *Daily Labor Report* (Washington, D.C.: Bureau of National Affairs, February 1, 1963), pp. F1–F4.

28. Carl Stevens, "Is Compulsory Arbitration Compatible with Bargaining?" *Industrial Relations*, 5 (February, 1966) pp. 38–52.

29. See James B. Dworkin, "The Impact of Final-Offer Interest Arbitration on Bargaining: The Case of Major League Baseball," *Proceedings of the Twenty-Ninth Annual Meeting of the Industrial Relations Research Association* (1976), pp. 161–199, for a further treatment of this issue for the years 1974 and 1975.

30. W. W. Notz and F. A. Starke, "Final-Offer versus Conventional Arbitration as a Means of Conflict Management," *Administrative Science Quarterly*, 23 (June, 1978), pp. 189–203.

31. Henry Farber and Harry Katz, "Interest Arbitration, Outcomes, and the Incentive to Bargain," *Industrial and Labor Relations Review*, 33 (October, 1979), pp. 55–63.

32. James R. Chelius and James B. Dworkin, "An Economic Analysis of Final-Offer Arbitration as a Conflict Resolution Device," *Journal of Conflict Resolution*, 24 (June, 1980), pp. 293–310.

33. Chelius and Dworkin, *ibid.*, pp. 302–304.

34. Scully, *op. cit.*, pp. 915–930.
35. Henry G. Demmert, *The Economics of Professional Team Sports* (Lexington, Massachusetts: D.C. Heath, 1973), p. 106.
36. Chelius and Dworkin, *op. cit.*, p. 303.
37. Scully, *op. cit.*, pp. 915–930.
38. Chelius and Dworkin, *op. cit.*, pp. 307–310.
39. Chelius and Dworkin, *op. cit.*, p. 304.
40. James B. Dworkin and Mario F. Bognanno, "A Model of Final-Offer Arbitrator Behavior," working paper, 1980.

APPENDIX I: ARTICLE X—GRIEVANCE PROCEDURE

For the purpose of providing an orderly and expeditious procedure for the handling and resolving of certain grievances and complaints, as hereinafter provided, the following shall apply as the exclusive remedy of the Parties.

A. Definitions

As used herein the following terms shall have the meanings indicated:

1. (a) "Grievance" shall mean a complaint which involves the interpretation of, or compliance with, the provisions of any agreement between the Association and the Clubs or any of them, or any agreement between a Player and a Club, except that disputes relating to the following agreements between the Association and the Clubs shall not be subject to the Grievance Procedure set forth herein:

(i) The Major League Baseball Players Benefit Plan.

(ii) The Agreement Re Major League Baseball Players Benefit Plan.

(iii) The Agreement regarding dues check-off.

Any procedures or remedies available to the Parties for the resolution of disputes arising under said agreements which were available as of their respective execution dates, shall continue to be available and shall not be altered or abridged in any way as a result of this Basic Agreement between the Association and the Clubs.

1. (b) Notwithstanding the definition of "Grievance" set forth in subparagraph (a) above, "Grievance" shall not mean a complaint which involves action taken with respect to a Player or Players by the Commissioner involving the preservation of the integrity of, or the maintenance of public confidence in, the game of baseball. Within 30 days of the date of the action taken, such complaint shall be presented to the Commissioner who promptly shall conduct a hearing in accordance with the Rules of Procedure attached hereto as Appendix A. The Commissioner shall render a written decision as soon as practicable following the conclusion of such hearing. The Commissioner's decision shall constitute full, final and complete disposition of such complaint, and shall have the same effect as a Grievance decision of the Arbitration Panel. In the event a matter filed as a Grievance in accordance with the procedure hereinafter provided in Section B gives rise to issues involving the integrity of, or

Source: Basic Agreement between The American League of Professional Baseball Clubs and The National League of Professional Baseball Clubs and the Major League Baseball Players Association, effective January 1, 1976.

public confidence in, the game of baseball, the Commissioner may, at any stage of its processing, order that the matter be withdrawn from such procedure and thereafter be processed in accordance with the procedure provided above in this subparagraph (b). The order of the Commissioner withdrawing such matter shall constitute a final determination of the procedure to be followed for the exclusive and complete disposition of such matter, and such order shall have the same effect as a Grievance decision of the Arbitration Panel. (See also Attachment 6.)

The Players Association may reopen this Agreement, with reference solely to Section A 1(b) and Section C of this Article, upon the giving of 10 days' written notice at any time, based upon experience under the aforesaid Sections which, in its opinion, is unsatisfactory. Also, in the event either of the incumbent League Presidents leaves the Office, the Association may reopen this Agreement, with reference solely to Section C of this Article as it affects the role of the League Presidents, upon the giving of 10 days' written notice. (See also attachment 7.)

1. (c) Notwithstanding the definition of "Grievance" set forth in subparagraph (a) above, "Grievance" shall not mean a complaint or dispute which involves the interpretation or application of, or compliance with the provisions of the first sentence of paragraph 3(c) of the Uniform Player's Contract. However, nothing herein shall alter or abridge the rights of the Parties, or any of them, to resort to a court of law for the resolution of such complaint or dispute. (See also Attachment 8.)

2. "League" shall mean The American League of Professional Baseball Clubs or The National League of Professional Baseball Clubs.

3. "Commissioner" shall mean the person holding the office of Commissioner of Baseball as defined in the Major League Agreement.

4. "Player" or "Players" shall mean a Player or Players on the active roster of a Major League Club or on a disabled, restricted, disqualified, ineligible, suspended or military list of a Major League Club. The term "Player" shall also include a former Player or Players who have a grievance or complaint arising by reason of their former status as a Player as defined in the preceding sentence.

5. "Club" or "Clubs" shall mean a Club or Clubs with membership in a League.

6. "Association" shall mean the Major League Baseball Players Association.

7. "Player Relations Committee" shall mean the Player Relations Committee established by the Clubs.

8. "Grievant" shall mean a party who initiates or appeals a Grievance.

9. "Arbitration Panel" shall mean the tripartite panel of arbitrators empowered to decide Grievances appealed to arbitration. One arbitrator shall be appointed by the Association, one arbitrator shall be appointed by the Clubs and the impartial arbitrator, who shall serve as the Chairman of the Panel, shall be appointed by agreement of the two party arbitrators. In the event the party arbitrators are unable to agree upon the appointment of the impartial arbitrator, they jointly shall request that the American Arbitration Association furnish them a list of prominent, professional arbitrators. Upon receipt of said list, the party arbitrators shall alternate in striking names from the list until only one remains. The arbitrator whose name remains shall be deemed appointed as the impartial arbitrator.

At any time during the term of this Agreement either of the party arbitrators may terminate the appointment of the impartial arbitrator by serving written notice upon him and the other party arbitrator. Within 30 days thereafter, the party arbitrators shall either agree upon a successor impartial arbitrator or select a successor from an American Arbitration Association list, as set forth above.

Decisions of the Arbitration Panel shall be made by majority vote or, with the agreement of the party arbitrators, by the impartial arbitrator alone.

B. Procedure

Step 1. Any Player who believes that he has a justifiable Grievance shall first discuss the matter with a representative of his Club designated to handle such matters, in an attempt to settle it. If the matter is not resolved as a result of such discussions, a written notice of the Grievance shall be presented to the Club's designated representative, provided, however, that for a Grievance to be considered beyond Step 1, such written notice shall be presented within (a) 45 days from the date of the occurrence upon which the Grievance is based, or (b) 45 days from the date on which the facts of the matter became known or reasonably should have become known to the Player, whichever is later. Within 10 days (within 2 days if disciplinary suspension) following receipt of such written notice, the Club's designated representative shall advise the Player in writing of his decision and shall furnish a copy to the Association. If the decision of the Club is not appealed further within 15 days of its receipt, the Grievance shall be considered settled on the basis of that decision and shall not be eligible for further appeal.

Step 2. A Grievance, to be considered in Step 2, shall be appealed in writing by the Grievant or by the Association to a designated representative of the Player Relations Committee within 15 days following receipt of the Club's written decision. The Grievance shall be discussed within 10 days (within 2 days if disciplinary suspension) thereafter between representatives of the Player Relations Committee and representatives of the Association in an attempt to settle it. Within 10 days (within 2 days if disciplinary suspension) following such discussion, the designated representative of the Player Relations Committee shall advise the Grievant in writing of his decision and shall furnish a copy to the Association. If the decision of the Player Relations Committee representative is not appealed further within 15 days of its receipt, the Grievance shall be considered settled on the basis of that decision and shall not be eligible for further appeal.

Grievances which involve (a) more than one Club, or (b) a Player who is not under contract to a Club which is party to the Grievance, may be filed initially in Step 2, provided that written notice of the Grievance shall be presented to the designated representative of the Player Relations Committee within (a) 30 days from the date of the occurrence upon which the Grievance is based, or (b) 30 days from the date on which the facts of the matter became known or reasonably should have become known to the Player, whichever is later.

Step 3. In order for a Grievance to be considered further, it shall be appealed in writing by the Grievant or by the Association, within 15 days of receipt of the Step 2 decision, to the President of the Club's League, for his consideration. Upon receipt of the notice of appeal, the President of the League shall designate a time and place for an informal hearing, which hearing shall be commenced as soon as practicable but no later than 20 days from the date of receipt of the appeal. The League President shall render a written decision within 10 days following the conclusion of such hearing, and may affirm, modify or reverse the decision appealed from. If the decision of the League President is not appealed further within 15 days of its receipt, the Grievance shall be considered settled on the basis of that decision and shall not be eligible for further appeal.

The parties may, by mutual consent, waive the necessity of the Step 3 procedure and permit the appeal of a Grievance from Step 2 directly to arbitration.

Grievances which relate to League disciplinary action and which are not covered by the procedure set forth in Section C, below, may be filed initially in Step 3, provided that written notice of the Grievance shall be presented to the League President within 30 days following the date on which the Player receives written notification of the discipline.

Arbitration. Within 15 days following receipt of the decision of the League President (or, in the event the parties have agreed to waive the Step 3 procedure, within 15 days following receipt of the Step 2 decision), the Grievant or the Association may appeal the Grievance in writing to the Chairman of the Arbitration Panel for impartial arbitration. Upon receipt of the notice of appeal, the Chairman of the Arbitration Panel shall set a time, date and place for hearing the appeal, which hearing shall be commenced as soon as practicable but no later than 20 days (5 days if disciplinary suspension) following receipt of the notice of appeal. Such hearing shall be conducted in accordance with the Rules of Procedure attached hereto as Appendix A. The Arbitration Panel shall render a written decision as soon as practicable (within 5 days if disciplinary suspension) following the conclusion of such hearing, and may affirm, modify or reverse the decision appealed from. The decision of the Arbitration Panel shall constitute full, final and complete disposition of the Grievance appealed to it.

With regard to the arbitration of Grievances, the Arbitration Panel shall have jurisdiction and authority only to interpret, apply or determine compliance with the provisions of agreements between the Association and the Clubs or any of them, and agreements between individual Players and Clubs. The Arbitration Panel shall not have jurisdiction or authority to add to, detract from, or alter in any way the provisions of such agreements.

All costs of arbitration, including the fees and expenses of the impartial arbitrator, shall be borne equally by the parties, providing that each of the parties shall bear the cost of its own party arbitrator, witnesses, counsel and the like.

C.   Special Procedure with Regard to Certain Disciplinary Action

Complaints involving a fine or suspension imposed upon a Player by a League or by the Commissioner for conduct on the playing field or in the ball park shall be subject exclusively to this Section C, as follows:

(1) Any Player who believes that he has a justifiable complaint regarding such discipline may, within 30 days of his receipt of written notification of the discipline, appeal in writing to the League President if the discipline was imposed by him, or to the Commissioner, if the discipline was imposed by him, for a hearing. Upon receipt of the notice of appeal, the League President or Commissioner, as the case may be, shall designate a time and place for hearing the appeal, which hearing shall be commenced within 10 days from the date of receipt of the appeal. Such hearing shall be conducted in accordance with the Rules of Procedure attached hereto as Appendix A. The League President or Commissioner, as the case may be, shall render a written decision as soon as practicable following the conclusion of such hearing, and may affirm, modify, or revoke the disciplinary action originally imposed. The decision of the League President or Commissioner, as the case may be, shall constitute full, final and complete disposition of the complaint and shall have the same effect as a Grievance decision of the Arbitration Panel.

(2) Notwithstanding the provisions of paragraph (1) above, if any such discipline imposed upon a Player by a League involves a fine in an amount which exceeds $500 or a suspension exceeding 10 days, complaint relating thereto shall be appealable from the decision of the League President to the Commissioner for determination in the same manner and with the same effect as provided in subparagraph 1(b) of the Section A hereof.

(3) With respect to discipline imposed upon a Player by a League or the Commissioner, the League or the Commissioner shall immediately give to the Players Association notice by mail of fines, and telegraphic notice of suspensions and of an appeal for a hearing.

D. Grievances Initiated or Appealed by a Club

Step 1. Any Club which believes it has a justifiable Grievance shall present a written notice of the Grievance to the Player with a copy to the Players Association, provided, however, that for a Grievance to be considered beyond Step 1, such written notice shall be presented within (a) 45 days from the date of the occurrence upon which the Grievance is based, or (b) 45 days from the date on which the facts of the matter became known or reasonably should have become known to the Club, whichever is later. Within 10 days following receipt of such written notice, the Player shall advise the Club in writing of his decision and shall furnish a copy to the Player Relations Committee. If the decision of the Player is not appealed further within 15 days of its receipt, the Grievance shall be considered settled on the basis of that decision and shall not be eligible for further appeal.

Step 2. A Grievance, to be considered in Step 2, shall be appealed in writing by the Club or the Player Relations Committee to the Players Association within 15 days following receipt of the Player's written decision. The Grievance shall be discussed within 10 days thereafter between representatives of the Player Relations Committee and representatives of the Players Association in an attempt to settle it. Within 10 days following such discussion, the Players Association shall advise the Player Relations Committee in writing of its decision. If the decision of the Players Association is not appealed further within 15 days of its receipt, the Grievance shall be considered settled on the basis of that decision and shall not be eligible for further appeal.

Grievances which involve (a) more than one Club, (b) more than one Player, or (c) a Player who is not under contract to a Club which is party to the Grievance, may be filed initially in Step 2, provided that written notice of the Grievance shall be presented to the Association within (a) 30 days from the date of the occurrence upon which the Grievance is based, or (b)

30 days from the date on which the facts of the matter became known or reasonably should have become known to the Club, whichever is later.

Arbitration.   Within 15 days following receipt of the Step 2 decision of the Players Association, the Player Relations Committee may appeal the Grievance in writing to the Chairman of the Arbitration Panel for impartial arbitration. The procedures to be followed in arbitration and the jurisdiction of the Arbitration Panel shall be as set forth in Section B above.

Nothing contained in this Section D shall be deemed to limit or impair the right of any Club to impose discipline upon a Player or Players or to take any other action not inconsistent with the Uniform Player's Contract or any agreement with the Association to which the Club is a Party. Any complaint or dispute which may be a subject for discipline shall not constitute a proper basis for a Club Grievance under this Section D.

E.   Grievances Initiated or Appealed by the Association

(1) The Association may on its own motion appeal Grievances or complaints on behalf of a Player or Players as provided in this Grievance Procedure, except that the Association will not appeal a Grievance or complaint involving player discipline without the approval of the Player or Players concerned.

(2) The Association may on its own motion initiate Grievances or complaints on behalf of a Player or Players on all matters not involving player discipline. Nothing herein shall interfere with the right of a Player who initiates a disciplinary Grievance or complaint to be represented by the Association at any Step of the Grievance Procedure.

F.   Miscellaneous

(1) Each of the time limits set forth herein may be extended by mutual agreement of the Parties involved.

(2) If any Grievance is not processed in accordance with the prescribed time limits in any Step, unless an extension of time has been mutually agreed upon, either Party, after notifying the other Party of its intent in writing, may appeal to the next Step.

(3) Any decision which is appealable under this Grievance Procedure but which is not appealed within the time allowed or within any time mutually agreed upon by the Parties shall constitute a full, final and complete disposition of the Grievance involved.

(4) In any discussion or hearing provided for in the Grievance Procedure, a Player may be accompanied by a representative of the Association who may participate in such discussion or hearing and represent the

Player. In any such discussion or hearing, any other Party may be accompanied by a representative who may participate in such discussion or hearing and represent such Party.

(5) The Parties recognize that a Player may be subjected to disciplinary action for just cause by his Club, League or the Commissioner. Therefore, in Grievances regarding discipline, the issue to be resolved shall be whether there has been just cause for the penalty imposed.

(6) A Player who is disciplined shall have the right to discover, in timely fashion, all documents and evidence adduced during any investigation of the charges involved.

(7) Nothing contained in this Grievance Procedure shall excuse a Player from prompt compliance with any discipline imposed upon him. If discipline imposed upon a Player is determined to be improper by reason of a final decision under this Grievance Procedure, the Player shall promptly be made whole. (See also Attachment 9.)

(8) During the term of this Agreement, the right of a Player to terminate his Uniform Player's Contract pursuant to the provisions of the first sentence of paragraph 7(a) of such contract shall be limited to defaults or failures to perform which are material in nature. Should such a material breach on the part of a Club be alleged, the Club, the Player involved, the Player Relations Committee and the Players Association will cooperate in scheduling the handling of any Grievance brought with respect to such alleged breach so that such Grievance may be submitted to arbitration on an expedited basis.

RULES OF PROCEDURE

Grievance Arbitration Hearings Before
The Arbitration Panel

1. Granting of Hearings.

Hearings will be granted in all cases properly appealed to the Arbitration Panel unless the Parties by mutual agreement request a finding of facts and a decision based upon briefs submitted.

2. Attendance at Hearings.

Persons having a direct interest in the arbitration are entitled to attend hearings. The Arbitration Panel shall have the power to require the retirement of any witness or witnesses during the testimony of other witnesses. It shall be discretionary with the Arbitration Panel to determine the propriety of the attendance of any other persons.

3. Conduct of Hearings.

Hearings will be conducted in an informal manner. The arbitration hearing shall be regarded as a cooperative endeavor to review and secure the facts which will enable the Arbitration Panel to make just decisions. The procedure to be followed in the hearing will be in conformity with this intent.

4. Representation of Parties.

A Player or Players may be accompanied by a representative of the Players Association who may participate in the hearing and represent the Player or Players. Any other Party may be accompanied by a representative who may participate in the hearing and represent such Party.

5. Adjournments.

The Arbitration Panel for good cause shown may adjourn the hearing upon the request of a Party or upon its own initiative, and shall adjourn when all the Parties agree thereto, provided that no adjournment hereunder shall exceed 10 days unless all Parties so agree.

Source: Basic Agreement between The American League of Professional Baseball Clubs and The National League of Professional Baseball Clubs and the Major League Baseball Players Association, effective January 1, 1976.

6.   Order of Proceedings.

The Arbitration Panel may, in its discretion, vary the normal procedure under which the initiating Party first presents his claim, but in any case shall afford full and equal opportunity to all Parties for presentation of relevant proofs.

7.   Arbitration in the Absence of a Party.

The arbitration may proceed in the absence of any Party who, after due notice, fails to be present or fails to obtain an adjournment. An award shall not be made solely on the default of a Party. The Arbitration Panel shall require the other Party to submit such evidence as it may require for the making of an award.

8.   Evidence.

The Parties may offer such evidence as they desire and shall produce such additional evidence as the Chairman of the Arbitration Panel may deem necessary to an understanding and determination of the dispute. The Chairman of the Arbitration Panel shall be the judge of the relevancy and materiality of the evidence offered and conformity to legal rules of evidence shall not be necessary. All evidence shall be taken in the presence of all of the Parties except where any of the Parties is absent in default or has waived his right to be present.

9.   Testimony.

All testimony shall be taken under oath or by affirmation. All witnesses whose testimony shall be introduced as evidence at the hearing shall be made available for cross-examination by the other Party. The Arbitration Panel may receive and consider the evidence of witnesses by affidavit, but shall give it only such weight as it deems proper after consideration of any objections made to its admission.

10.   Stenographic Record.

The Arbitration Panel will make the necessary arrangements for the taking of an official stenographic record of the testimony whenever such a record is deemed necessary by it or it is requested by either Party. The cost of such record shall be borne equally by the Parties unless, at the opening of the hearing, both the Chairman of the Arbitration Panel and the other Party indicate their desire not to receive a copy of the transcribed record, in which case the entire cost shall be borne by the requesting Party.

11.   Closing of Hearings.

The Chairman of the Arbitration Panel shall inquire of all Parties whether they have any further proofs to offer or witnesses to be heard. Upon receiving negative replies, the Chairman of the Arbitration Panel shall declare the hearings closed and a minute thereof shall be recorded. If briefs or other documents are to be filed, the hearings shall be declared closed as of the final filing date set by the Chairman of the Arbitration Panel.

12.   Reopening of Hearings.

At any time before the award is made the hearings may be reopened by the Arbitration Panel on its own motion, or on the motion of either Party for good cause shown.

13.   Issuance of Decision.

Two signed copies of the Arbitration Panel's written decision will be provided to each Party.

14.   Settlement by the Parties.

When cases appealed to the Arbitration Panel are thereafter settled by agreement between the Parties, either prior to or after the arbitration hearing, the Arbitration Panel shall be so notified promptly by the Party which appealed the case. The Arbitration Panel shall thereupon treat the case as closed, and shall have no obligation to render a decision or further process the Grievance.

15.   Expenses.

The expenses of witnesses, counsel and the like for either side shall be paid by the Party producing such persons.

16.   Communication with the Chairman of the Arbitration Panel.

Copies of all written communications sent by a Party to the Chairman of the Arbitration Panel in connection with arbitration cases shall immediately be made available to the other Party. There shall be no oral communication by a Party with the Chairman of the Arbitration Panel in connection with arbitration cases unless the other Party or his representative is present.

17.   Commissioner and Section C Hearings.

These Rules of Procedure shall also apply to hearings conducted by the Commissioner pursuant to Section A, subparagraph 1 (b), or by the Commissioner or a League President pursuant to Section C of the Grievance Procedure.

APPENDIX II

E.   Salary Arbitration

Effective with the 1976 championship season, the following salary arbitration procedure shall be applicable:

(1) *Eligibility.*   The issue of a Player's salary may be submitted to final and binding arbitration by any Player or his Club, provided the other party to the arbitration consents thereto. For the 1978 and 1979 seasons, any Club, or any Player with both a total of two years of Major League service and Major League service in at least three different championship seasons, but with less than six years of Major League service, may submit the issue of the Player's salary to final and binding arbitration without the consent of the other party (subject to the provisions of subparagraph (6) below).

(2) *Six Year Player—Club Consent to Arbitration.*   Upon request of a Player with 6 or more years of Major League service, his Club shall, on or before October 15, in writing notify him as to the Club's position regarding salary arbitration should the Player's contract for the next season not be agreed upon by February 1. (See also Attachment 4.)

(3) *Notice of Submission*

(a) *Player Submission.*   Election of submission shall be communicated by telephone or any other method of communication by the Player to the Players Association. Written notice of submission shall then be given, within the specified time limits, by the Players Association on behalf of the Player to the designated representative of the Player Relations Committee. Within three days after the notice of submission has been given, the Players Association and the Player Relations Committee shall exchange salary figures. It shall be the responsibility of the Players Association during this three-day period to obtain the salary figure from the Player, and the Player Relations Committee shall have a similar responsibility to obtain the Club's figure.

(b) *Club Submission.*   Written notice of submission by the Club shall be communicated to the Player by registered letter mailed between January 29 and February 7 (both inclusive) to the last address the Player has supplied to the Club, with copies to the Players Association and the Player Relations Committee. The submission shall be deemed to be made on the third day following the date of mailing by

Source: Basic Agreement between The American League of Professional Baseball Clubs and The National League of Professional Baseball Clubs and the Major League Baseball Players Association, effective January 1, 1976.

the Club. Salary figures shall be exchanged by the Players Association and the Player Relations Committee as soon as practicable thereafter.

(4) *Form of Submission.*   The Player and the Club shall each submit to the arbitrator and exchange with each other in advance of the hearing single salary figures for the coming season (which need not be figures offered during the prior negotiations). At the hearing, the Player and Club shall deliver to the arbitrator a Uniform Player's Contract executed in duplicate, complete except for the salary figure to be inserted in Paragraph 2. Upon submission of a salary issue to arbitration by either Player or Club, the Player shall be regarded as a signed Player (unless the Player withdraws from arbitration as provided in subparagraph (6) below).

(5) *Timetable and Decision.*   Submission may be made at any time between February 1 and February 10. In the event the offer of the Club is reduced on or subsequent to February 10, the Player's right to submit to arbitration shall be reinstated for a period of 7 days. Arbitration hearings shall be held as soon as possible after submission and, to the extent practicable, shall be scheduled to be held before February 20. The arbitrator may render his decision on the day of the hearing, and shall make every effort to render it not later than 24 hours following the close of the hearing. The arbitrator shall be limited to awarding only one or the other of the two figures submitted. There shall be no opinion and no release of the arbitration award by the arbitrator except to the Club, the Player, the Players Association and the Player Relations Committee. The arbitrator shall insert the figure awarded in paragraph 2 of the duplicate Uniform Player's Contracts delivered to him at the hearing and shall forward both copies to the League office of the Player and Club concerned.

(6) *Withdrawal from Arbitration.*   In the event the Club submits the matter to arbitration, the Player may within 7 days after receipt of the Club's salary arbitration figure notify the Club that he does not wish to arbitrate and the matter shall be deemed withdrawn from arbitration. In such event, or in the event that neither the Club nor the Player submit to arbitration, the rights and obligations of the Club and Player shall be unchanged from those which existed prior to the adoption of this salary arbitration procedure. In the event the Club and Player reach agreement on salary before the arbitrator reaches his decision, the matter shall be deemed withdrawn from arbitration.

(7) *Selection of Arbitrator.*   The Players Association and the Player Relations Committee shall annually select the arbitrators. In the event they are unable to agree by January 1 in any year, they jointly shall request that the American Arbitration Association furnish them lists of

prominent, professional arbitrators convenient to the hearing sites. Upon receipt of such lists, the arbitrators shall be selected by alternately striking names from the lists.

(8) *Location of Hearings.* The hearing sites will be located in Los Angeles, Chicago, New York and such other Major League cities as the parties may agree upon. The hearings shall be held at the site closest to the home city of the Club involved.

(9) *Conduct of Hearings.* The hearings shall be conducted on a private and confidential basis. Each of the parties to a case shall be limited to one hour for initial presentation and one-half hour for rebuttal and summation. The aforesaid time limitations may be extended by the arbitrator in the event of lengthy cross-examination of witnesses, or for other good cause.

(10) *Continuances, Adjournments or Postponements.* There shall be no continuances or adjournments of a hearing, but the commencement of a hearing may be postponed by the arbitrator upon the application of either the Player or Club based upon a showing of substantial cause. Any request for the postponement of a scheduled hearing shall be made to the arbitrator in writing, with copies to the Players Association and the Player Relations Committee.

(11) *Hearing Costs.* The Player and Club shall divide equally the costs of the hearing, and each shall be responsible for his own expenses and those of his counsel or other representatives; provided, however, that the Club and Player shall divide equally the total of (a) the round trip air fare for one Club representative from the Club's home city to the arbitration site plus (b) the round trip air fare for the Player or one representative from the Player's residence to the arbitration site.

(12) *Criteria.* The criteria will be the quality of the Player's contribution to his Club during the past season (including but not limited to his overall performance, special qualities of leadership and public appeal), the length and consistency of his career contribution, the record of the Player's past compensation, comparative baseball salaries (see subparagraph (13) below for confidential salary data), the existence of any physical or mental defects on the part of the Player, and the recent performance record of the Club including but not limited to its League standing and attendance as an indication of public acceptance (subject to the exclusion stated in (a) below). Any evidence may be submitted which is relevant to the above criteria, and the arbitrator shall assign such weight to the evidence as shall to him appear appropriate under the circumstances. The following items, however, shall be excluded:

(a) The financial position of the Player and the Club.

(b) Press comments, testimonials or similar material bearing on the performance of either the Player or the Club, except that recognized annual Player awards for playing excellence shall not be excluded.

(c) Offers made by either Player or Club prior to arbitration.

(d) The cost to the parties of their representatives, attorneys, etc.

(e) Salaries in other sports or occupations.

(13) *Confidential Major League Salary Data.* For his own confidential use, as background information, the arbitrator will be given a tabulation showing the minimum salary in the Major Leagues and salaries for the preceding season of all Players on Major League rosters as of August 31, broken down by years of Major League service. The names and Clubs of the Players concerned will appear on the tabulation. In utilizing the salary tabulation, the arbitrator shall consider the salaries of all comparable Players and not merely the salary of a single Player or group of Players.

APPENDIX III

A Summary of the Participants in Major League Baseball's Final-Offer Salary Arbitration Procedure, 1974–1980

Player	Club	Year	Hitter/Pitcher	Demand	Offer	Award*
Bando	Oakland	1974	H	$100,000	$ 75,000	0
Blair	Baltimore	1974	H	70,000	60,000	1
Braun	Minnesota	1974	H	31,000	25,000	0
Evans	Atlanta	1974	H	52,500	47,500	0
Foli	Montreal	1974	H	55,000	40,000	1
Gaston	San Diego	1974	H	50,000	42,000	1
Grich	Baltimore	1974	H	49,000	46,000	1
Hisle	Minnesota	1974	H	29,000	23,000	0
R. Jackson	Oakland	1974	H	135,000	100,000	0
Kubiak	Oakland	1974	H	42,500	37,000	1
C. May	Chicago White Sox	1974	H	85,000	70,000	1
N. Miller	Atlanta	1974	H	35,000	30,000	0
Michael	New York Yankees	1974	H	65,500	55,000	1
M. Perez	Atlanta	1974	H	39,500	27,500	1
Rojas	Kansas City	1974	H	80,500	67,500	1
Rudi	Oakland	1974	H	67,500	50,000	1
Sims	New York Yankees	1974	H	56,000	50,000	1
Tenace	Oakland	1974	H	52,500	45,500	1
Tepedino	Atlanta	1974	H	23,000	20,000	1
Sudakis	New York Yankees	1974	H	30,000	25,000	0
Bahnsen	Chicago White Sox	1974	P	82,500	70,000	1
K. Brett	Pittsburgh	1974	P	40,000	35,000	1
Fingers	Oakland	1974	P	65,000	55,000	0

A Summary of the Participants in Major League Baseball's Final-Offer Salary Arbitration Procedure, 1974–1980 (continued)

Player	Club	Year	Hitter/Pitcher	Demand	Offer	Award*
Granger	New York Yankees	1974	P	$ 46,000	$ 42,000	0
Holtzman	Oakland	1974	P	93,000	80,000	0
Knowles	Oakland	1974	P	59,000	55,000	0
McNally	Baltimore	1974	P	115,000	105,000	0
Woodson	Minnesota	1974	P	30,000	23,000	0
Bando	Oakland	1975	H	125,000	100,000	1
Braun	Minnesota	1975	H	41,000	36,000	1
Carbo	Boston	1975	H	60,000	50,000	1
Carew	Minnesota	1975	H	140,000	120,000	1
Cey	Los Angeles	1975	H	56,000	47,000	0
Fosse	Oakland	1975	H	68,500	50,000	1
Garr	Atlanta	1975	H	114,000	85,000	0
R. Jackson	Oakland	1975	H	168,500	140,000	1
Kubiak	Oakland	1975	H	47,500	42,000	0
Blyleven	Minnesota	1975	P	85,000	65,000	1
Burgmeier	Minnesota	1975	P	35,000	29,000	1
Fingers	Oakland	1975	P	89,000	75,000	0
Holtzman	Oakland	1975	P	112,000	93,000	1
Sedecki	St. Louis	1975	P	52,000	47,000	0
Smalley	Minnesota	1978	H	110,000	85,000	1
Dilone	Oakland	1979	H	42,000	34,000	0
Essian	Oakland	1979	H	90,000	68,000	0

Name	Team	Year				
Hampton	California	1979	H	33,000	20,000	1
Newman	Oakland	1979	H	58,000	45,000	1
Scott	Montreal	1979	H	75,500	50,000	0
Youngblood	New York Mets	1979	H	91,000	78,000	0
Farmer	Texas	1979	P	35,000	23,000	0
Heaverlo	Oakland	1979	P	95,000	70,000	0
Langford	Oakland	1979	P	67,000	45,000	0
D. Miller	California	1979	P	110,000	72,000	1
Murray	New York Mets	1979	P	100,000	72,000	1
Spillner	Cleveland	1979	P	80,000	67,000	0
Collins	Cincinnati	1980	H	167,500	126,000	1
Cruz	Seattle	1980	H	130,000	95,000	0
Essian	Oakland	1980	H	125,000	100,000	1
Harlow	California	1980	H	75,000	50,000	0
Howell	Toronto	1980	H	133,000	110,000	1
Ron Jackson	Minnesota	1980	H	150,000	115,000	0
Kemp	Detroit	1980	H	210,000	150,000	1
Knight	Cincinnati	1980	H	175,000	112,500	0
Newman	Oakland	1980	H	150,000	85,000	0
Page	Oakland	1980	H	100,000	85,000	0
Scott	Montreal	1980	H	185,000	125,000	1
B. Smith	Baltimore	1980	H	95,000	65,000	1
Trammell	Detroit	1980	H	130,000	100,000	0
Whitaker	Detroit	1980	H	130,000	100,000	0
Aase	California	1980	P	100,000	77,500	1
Andujar	Houston	1980	P	130,000	90,000	0
Kravec	Chicago White Sox	1980	P	175,000	150,000	0

A Summary of the Participants in Major League Baseball's Final-Offer Salary Arbitration Procedure, 1974–1980 (continued)

Player	Club	Year	Hitter/Pitcher	Demand	Offer	Award*
Lacey	Oakland	1980	P	75,000	$ 50,000	0
Langford	Oakland	1980	P	115,000	82,500	0
Lemanczyk	Toronto	1980	P	175,000	130,000	1
McEnaney	St. Louis	1980	P	125,000	65,000	1
Montague	California	1980	P	95,000	70,000	1
Parrott	Seattle	1980	P	130,000	82,500	1
Sambito	Houston	1980	P	213,000	143,000	0
Sutter	Chicago Cubs	1980	P	700,000	350,000	0
Zahn	Minnesota	1980	P	200,000	130,000	0
Armas	Oakland	1981	H	500,000	210,000	1
Castino	Minnesota	1981	H	200,000	150,000	0
Cerone	New York Yankees	1981	H	440,000	350,000	0
Collins	Cincinnati	1981	H	360,000	267,500	1
Cruz	Seattle	1981	H	160,000	106,000	1
Jackson	Minnesota	1981	H	200,000	130,525	0
Kemp	Detroit	1981	H	600,000	360,000	0
LeMaster	San Francisco	1981	H	155,000	135,000	0

Nordhagen	Chicago White Sox	1981	H	255,379	160,000	1
Scott	St. Louis	1981	H	225,000	180,000	0
Skaggs	California	1981	H	77,500	60,000	1
Thompson	California	1981	H	395,000	250,000	0
Vail	Cincinnati	1981	H	225,000	175,000	1
Farmer	Chicago White Sox	1981	P	495,000	300,000	0
Frost	California	1981	P	112,500	95,000	0
Honeycutt	Texas	1981	P	167,500	110,000	0
Minton	San Francisco	1981	P	265,000	180,000	1
Moskau	Cincinnati	1981	P	125,000	90,000	1
Norris	Oakland	1981	P	450,000	300,000	1
Rajsich	Texas	1981	P	65,000	35,000	0
Sutcliffe	Los Angeles	1981	P	110,000	85,000	1

* *Note:* In the column labelled "Award," the numeral "1" indicates that the arbitrator chose the player's final salary offer as the binding award. The numeral "0" indicates that the arbitrator chose the club's final salary demand as the binding award.

Data Sources: New York Times, March 3, 1974; *Business Week,* March 23, 1974; *U.S. News and World Report,* March 24, 1975; *Sports Illustrated,* April 7, 1975; *The Sporting News,* March 31, 1979; *The Sporting News,* March 15, 1980 and March 14, 1981. Summary data for 1978 not reflected in the above table were provided by Mr. Peter Rose, Legal and Administrative Assistant, MLBPA, in a personal correspondence addressed to the author and dated April 19, 1978. Additionally, Mr. C. Raymond Grebey, Director of the Major League Baseball Player Relations Committee, Inc., was kind enough to provide a tabulation of summary data on the use of the final-offer salary arbitration procedure from 1974 through 1979 in a letter addressed to the author and dated May 8, 1979.

APPENDIX IV

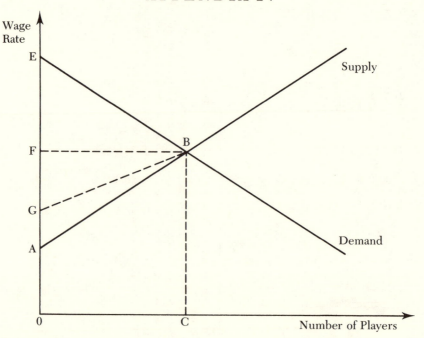

The Labor Market as It Appears to the Team. Players are assumed to be homogeneous in their baseball performance. (*Source:* James R. Chelius and James B. Dworkin, "An Economic Analysis of Final-Offer Arbitration As A Conflict Resolution Device," *Journal of Conflict Resolution*, Vol. 24, 2 [June, 1980], pp. 293–310.)

APPENDIX V

Principal Components Results (Varimax Rotated Factor Matrices)

Hitters

Performance Measures	Factor 1 (Production)	Factor 2 (Power)	Factor 3 (Seniority)
1	.18	.19	.91
2	.02	.10	.93
3	.85	.22	.11
4	.52	.77	.15
5	.58	.23	.55
6	.85	.11	−.04
7	.28	.83	.16
8	.06	.95	.16
9	.70	.24	.28
Eigenvalue	4.51	1.50	1.21
Variance Explained	50.2	16.6	13.5

Pitchers

Performance Measures	Factor 1 (Workload)	Factor 2 (Inefficiency)	Factor 3 (Seniority)
1	.20	−.02	.94
2	.02	−.10	.94
3	.18	−.63	.04
4	.87	−.20	.23
5	.92	−.12	.21
6	.83	−.30	.01
7	.92	−.21	−.01
8	.90	.08	.16
9	.86	.01	−.06
10	−:05	.76	−.07
11	−.06	.86	−.02
Eigenvalue	5.16	1.77	1.64
Variance Explained	46.9	16.1	14.9

Note: Sample sizes equal 563 for hitters and 347 for pitchers. The variables listed above are defined as follows. For both hitters and pitchers, 1 = years in majors and 2 = player age. For hitters, 3 = lifetime batting average, 4 = lifetime slugging average, 5 = lifetime average at-bats per season, 6 = batting average in the previous season, 7 = home runs in the previous season, 8 = lifetime average home runs per season, 9 = at-bats in the previous season. For the pitchers sample, 3 = lifetime strikeout-to-walk ratio, 4 = lifetime average games won per season, 5 = lifetime average innings pitched per season, 6 = games won in the previous season, 7 = innings pitched in the previous season, 8 = lifetime average games lost per season, 9 = games lost in the previous season, 10 = earned run average in the previous season, 11 = lifetime earned run average. Factor score coefficients obtained in the principal components analyses were used to build the composite indices (Seniority, Work Load, etc.) employed to evaluate and explain salary levels.

APPENDIX VI

Regression Results for Models of Real Salary and Performance

Hitters	Constant	Production	Power	Seniority	$\bar{R}^2$	Overall F
Prearbitration	30,140	9,828	8,121	10,682	.65	157
$n = 256$	(1,400)	(149)	(98)	(160)		
Postarbitration	34,897	11,625	10,193	15,118	.69	233
$n = 307$	(1,903)	(214)	(167)	(386)		

Pitchers	Constant	Workload	Inefficiency	Seniority	$\bar{R}^2$	Overall F
Prearbitration	26,466	10,080	−4,541	9,272	.56	71
$n = 164$	(756)	(101)	(23)	(100)		
Postarbitration	33,654	11,365	−6,804	10,941	.65	112
$n = 183$	(1,185)	(152)	(44)	(116)		

Note: The numbers in parentheses below the regression coefficients are *F* values. All of the coefficients are statistically significant at the .01 level. Data includes all players in one league, except rookies and those players with arbitrated salaries in 1974 and 1975.

APPENDIX VII

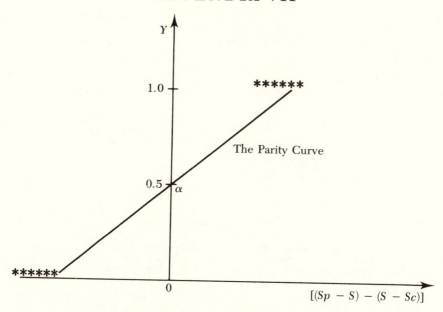

The Final-Offer Arbitrator Decision Making Process. (For a more thorough treatment of this issue, see James B. Dworkin and Mario Bognanno, "A Model of Final-Offer Arbitrator Behavior," unpublished manuscript, 1980.)

APPENDIX VIII

The Probability of Management Winning a Salary Arbitration Case in Professional Baseball

$[(Sp - S) - (S - Sc)]$	*Probability of a Management Win*
−$216,423	.001
− 135,121	.023
− 53,821	.159
0	.366
27,480	.500
68,130	.691
108,780	.841
190,081	.977
271,382	.999

Note: These results stem from a probit probability model specification where $Y = -.338 + .0000123X$ (where $X = [(Sp - S) - (S - Sc)]$). The probability values found in column two can be obtained from any statistics text containing a Standardized Normal Distribution Table.

Chapter 5

THE IMPACTS OF COLLECTIVE BARGAINING: OTHER MONETARY AND NONMONETARY ISSUES

In the previous two chapters we have considered three of the major gains made by the professional baseball players through the process of collective bargaining. The case has been made that while the players have certainly seen other progress through collective bargaining since 1968, free agency, grievance, and salary arbitration represent their most important achievements.

However, it would be very shortsighted simply to make the above statement and then say nothing more about the other changes that have occurred through collective bargaining. The purpose of this chapter is briefly to review and describe other gains the players have made at the bargaining table not covered in Chapters 3 and 4. The collective bargaining contract between the players and the owners contains some twenty-one articles and an additional two attachments, the Uniform Player's Contract and the Rules of Procedure for grievance/arbitration. Both of these attachments have been discussed in previous chapters but we have only comprehensively examined three of this total of twenty-one articles.

We shall now examine the other gains achieved by the players and agreed to by the owners through collective bargaining. In the discussion to follow, these achievements will be divided up into two broad categories, as is often the case in collective bargaining, monetary and nonmonetary issues. This distinction stems from the fact that some items in a collective bargaining contract, such as wages, holidays, pensions, and the like, are in fact easily translated into dollars and cents terms. One can easily cost out a wage increase, holiday package, pension plan, and the like so that both sides will know exactly what the total cost to management will be. On the other hand, there are other items contained in a collective bargaining contract that can not easily be translated into dollars and cents terms. For instance, grievance procedures, recognition clauses, and management rights clauses are extremely difficult to translate into monetary terms, yet these rules of the shop, dealing with the issues of industrial democracy at the workplace, are extremely important aspects of the modern collective bargaining contract. One would be hard pressed to determine exactly how much a grievance/arbitration procedure costs, and this is obviously true for many other types of rules of employment.

Certain issues have elements of both above described qualities, that is, some easily monetarized sections and others that can't be translated into dollars. For instance, the grievance/arbitration procedure that we discussed in Chapter 4 would fall into this mixed category. It is pretty difficult to estimate the cost of granting the overall benefit of being able to file grievances to the union. Yet, for cases that proceed all the way to arbitration, it is a relatively simple matter to estimate cost. The parties are all aware of the normal charge for an arbitration hearing and award, and since they split the cost evenly, they can divide this total by two and add to it any other expenses that they can reasonably anticipate. As another example, the salary arbitration procedure we have discussed in Chapter 4 would definitely be classified as a monetary gain to the players, as costs are readily known (the salary arbitration awards). But even in this procedure, many of the rules and regulations leading up to the actual arbitration hearing must be classified as nonmonetary in nature. For instance, consider the rules about who is eligible to use salary arbitration, the arbitrators' rules for conduct of the hearing, and the timetable for the rendering of decisions. The reader should be able to see by now that the changes made to the reserve system described in Chapter 3 are basically monetary in nature. These changes have led to the current system of free agency and the higher player salaries forthcoming from the new free market system. The costs of this free agency system in terms of losses of star players and the salaries paid to acquired free agents could indeed be estimated. As we have noted in Chapters 3 and 4, both the salary arbitration and the free agency procedures have proven costly to the owners, in that they have been forced through collective bargaining to share some of their previous monopsony/monopoly rents with the players for the first time. However, even this free agency system has certain aspects on which it would be hard to put cost estimates.

While it is useful to categorize bargaining issues into monetary and nonmonetary groupings for pedagogical purposes, bargaining issues will often contain both monetary and nonmonetary components. Hopefully, the reader will keep this in mind as we move through our discussion of the other gains achieved by the players through the process of collective bargaining.

Other Monetary Gains Achieved Through Collective Bargaining

When one speaks of the monetary gains associated with unionism, the first item likely to come to mind is the wage effect of unionism. In economic theory, unions are predicted to have an incremental impact on wages, and in fact, many empirical studies support the prediction of a positive wage effect. While the MLBPA has had a positive wage impact on baseball players' salaries, it has not been through the traditional union method of bargaining collectively on salaries. Recall that in professional baseball (as well as in all of the other sports we shall discuss in Chapter 6), there is *no* collective bargaining over wages. Individual bargaining over salaries continues to be the *modus operandi,* and it is highly unlikely that we will see any changes to this system in the near future. But given that the MLBPA does not bargain collectively with the owners over wages, how has this union been able to secure higher individual wages for today's ballplayers? And besides these wage effects, what other monetary benefits has the MLBPA been successful in attaining in the years since 1968?

The major reasons for these player salary advances in recent years have been the availability of salary arbitration and free agency, as discussed in Chapters 3 and 4. These systems provided individual players with the additional bargaining power necessary to force their club owners to share a larger portion of scarce club resources with the players in the form of higher salaries. In addition to these two mechanisms, the MLBPA has provided today's ballplayer with several other significant monetary gains.

Salaries

First, in the area of salaries, the MLBPA has continuously bargained to increase the minimum salary level that can be paid to a professional baseball player. While individual salary bargaining is the typical method employed in baseball, the owners and the MLBPA do bargain collectively over one aspect of pay, minimum salaries. From humble beginnings, when there was in fact no such thing as a minimum wage in baseball, the union and the clubs have agreed in recent years to several increases in such minimum salary, after the floor was first established. For instance, the minimum wage for 1976 and 1977 was $19,000, and this wage was increased to $21,000 for the 1978 and 1979 seasons. The most recent round of bargaining produced even further increases in the minimum wage. These minimum wages may not sound like very much when compared to the huge sums received by free agents like Dave Winfield and Claudell Washington, but in truth they do represent important gains for the union. Certain rookies and other fringe players will not have the type of bargaining power possessed by a Reggie Jackson or a Pete Rose and need the help of their union in order to insure themselves of receiving some minimally acceptable wage. Remember, the union does not exist only for the superstars and the rich players. It is also the union of the third string first baseman, the rookie outfielders, and the fifth relief pitchers. These players need their union too, and it is much to the credit of the MLBPA and Marvin Miller that they have not been forgotten. The players have won the written right to be represented by an agent in salary bargaining, and when players must attend to regularly scheduled military duty during the regular playing season (such as Reserve or National Guard training camps), they continue to receive their paychecks during such times.

Expense Allowances

The collective bargaining contract also provides for the payment of expenses for ballplayers during the regular season and during any postseason play that teams may become involved in due to winning their division or league championship series. Players are guaranteed all necessary traveling expenses while on the road, including hotel accommodations, meal money, and first-class jet air fare. Players are also provided with jet air fare en route to spring training camps and to their homes after the termination of their team's regular playing season. Players who are traded or assigned to other clubs during spring training or the regular season are also guaranteed first-class jet air fare and meals en route to the new club. Finally, players whose contracts are terminated for whatever reason are provided with a plane ticket to their home city.

During the regular season, players receive a daily meal allowance for each day their club is on the road. Set rules are established to determine the exact number of days of such allowance on any particular road trip. The daily meal allowance for the 1977 season was $25.50, and this figure has gone up since that time according to a formula based upon the Consumer Price Index, which is reported in the collective bargaining contract. Disabled players not traveling on the road with their clubs receive full daily meal allowances if they are residing in a motel in the club's home city, or some portion thereof if residing at an in-season or permanent residence in the metropolitan area of the home club. Hospitalized players and those players living in their homes outside of the club's metropolitan area receive no daily meal allowance while their club is on the road.

Players also receive allowances during the spring training season prior to the beginning of each championship year. The weekly allowance for 1977 to cover training camp expenses was $78. This allowance was also increased in more recent years according to a formula based upon the cost of living. Players not living at the club's spring training headquarters received a daily meal allowance of $22 in 1977, with this figure to be increased in subsequent years by the same cost-of-living formula referred to above. If a player does live at the club's headquarters during spring training, his meals will be provided by the club. However, when the club does not provide meals, the daily meal allowance will be paid. The clubs also must provide either rooms or room allowances to the players during spring training.

Another provision with regard to expenses allows a player to specify that he wishes to occupy a single room during the regular playing season while his team is on the road. Each club must make arrangements for such single rooms for any player who so indicates his desire in this area. However, the club need only pay 50 percent of the cost of the normal double room for this player. The individual ballplayer is responsible for the remaining portion of the hotel bill. Additionally, players selected for their respective league's All-Star teams receive payment for themselves and one guest to and from the city in which the game is played plus hotel accommodations for a maximum of three days for the guest. These expenses, plus all others traditionally covered, are to be paid for by the American and National Leagues.

Moving Allowances

Players who are traded or otherwise have their contracts assigned to another club during the championship season have the right to receive a lump sum expense payment based on the geographic zones in which the two teams are located according to the contractual rules. Such payments are made to the player by the new team and equal $300 if the player remains in the same zone, $600 if he switches from the Eastern to the Central zone (or vice versa), $900 for switches between the Central and Western zones, and $1200 if the contract is assigned between clubs in the Eastern and the Western zones. The zones, as presented in the collective bargaining contract, are reprinted in Table 5.1. Besides this lump sum payment described above, the new club also must reimburse the player for transportation and moving expenses of his family associated with the aforementioned assignment of the player's contract.

Termination Pay

The collective bargaining contract also provides for termination pay to be paid to players whose contracts are cancelled due to the club's

Table 5.1 Zones for Moving Allowance Expenses

Eastern	*Central*	*Western*
Baltimore	Atlanta	California
Boston	Chicago	Los Angeles
Montreal	Cincinnati	Oakland
New York	Cleveland	San Diego
Philadelphia	Detroit	San Francisco
Pittsburgh	Houston	Seattle
Toronto	Kansas City	Texas
	Milwaukee	
	Minnesota	
	St. Louis	

Source: Basic Agreement between the American League of Professional Baseball Clubs and the National League of Professional Baseball Clubs and Major League Baseball Players Association, Effective January 1, 1976, Article VII, A, pp. 14–15.

determination that the player no longer possesses sufficient skill or competitive ability to remain on the roster. If such termination occurs during spring training, the player is entitled to a severance payment equivalent to thirty days of his regular salary as specified in paragraph 2 of his Uniform Player's Contract. If, however, the club waits until the regular playing season to terminate a player for insufficient skill under the terms of paragraph 7(b)(2) of the Uniform Player's Contract, such player is then entitled to receive as termination pay the *unpaid balance* of his full salary as stipulated in paragraph 2 of his contract. The only proviso here is that should the released player refuse to accept a reasonable major league contract offered to him by another club, that player shall then be deemed to have forfeited the portion of the termination pay that would not have been paid to him had he accepted the other contract. In other words, there is an incentive provided for released players to sign new contracts with other clubs, if such offers are forthcoming. If such an alternate offer is forthcoming and reasonable, the player must accept it or forfeit his termination pay from his previous club. Of course, if no such alternate offers are made, the player is guaranteed the termination payment.

Clubs are obligated to pay injured players whose difficulties stem from baseball-related employment the unpaid balance of their regular season's wages, less any workers' compensation benefits received by the player as compensation for loss of income during the period in which the injury prevented the player from pursuing his occupation. The idea is to make the player "whole" during the period of incapacitation.

World Series and League Championship Players' Pool

Players on teams that finish high in the standings during the regular season are guaranteed bonus payments. These bonus payments are higher for better performing clubs, peaking for players on those clubs involved in the annual World Series. The collective bargaining contract specifies that 60 percent of the gate receipts from the first four World Series games and 60 percent of the total gate receipts from the first three games of each League's Championship Series go into the makeup of this player bonus pool. This bonus money is then distributed according to the formula presented in Table 5.2.

Table 5.2   **Distribution of World Series and Championship Playoff Money**

Outcome	Percentage of Pool
World Series Winner	36%
World Series Loser	27%
Championship Series Losers (two teams)	25%
Second Place Division Teams (four teams)	9½%
Third Place Division Teams (four teams)	2½%

Source: Basic Agreement, op. cit., p. 17.

Minimum amounts are guaranteed for this players' pool. For example, the minimum guaranteed amount for the World Series winner is $640,000, the World Series loser $320,000, the Championship Series losers $160,000 each, the second-place division teams $128,000 each, and the third-place Division teams $32,000 each. If the pool fails to achieve these levels, the contract specifies that the pool will automatically be increased to these levels, presumably by the Leagues and/or the club owners. Finally, if the clubs choose to raise World Series ticket prices, the players have the right to reopen negotiations over the issue of player compensation. Thus, higher World Series ticket prices would probably lead to some changes in the distribution formula or, more likely, the minimum guarantees specified above.

Pensions

Although not formally a part of the collective bargaining agreement, certainly another important monetary benefit that the players have been able to achieve relates to their pension benefits. Two separate documents labelled "The Major League Baseball Players Benefit Plan" and "The Agreement *re* Major League Baseball Players Benefit Plan" contain the basic provisions of the plan. It would take far more time and space than we have available here to describe adequately the workings of baseball's pension system. But it should be noted that the baseball player has progressed a long way in this area from the early days of no pensions to what today probably should be considered a very adequate system. It is certainly likely that this tradition of pension progress will be carried on into the future as both sides seek to make improvement in the pension plan through the process of collective bargaining.

Miscellaneous Provisions

There are a few other minor monetary benefits that the players enjoy which are explicitly written into their collective bargaining contract with the owners. For example, players receive free parking at home games and on practice days at their own ballpark. Additionally, the Leagues run a college scholarship plan under which a player may commence or resume work toward a college degree.

Other Nonmonetary Gains Achieved Through Collective Bargaining

The other type of benefit that the players have been able to achieve through collective bargaining is nonmonetary in nature. Nonetheless, these benefits too represent significant progress for the players, even though such progress is not easily measured in dollars and cents terms.

Purpose and Recognition

Prior to the advent of unionism and collective bargaining in baseball, all rules concerning the terms and conditions of employment for professional baseball players were set by the leagues and/or the clubs unilaterally. No meaningful player input was allowed to enter into this process. The adoption of the formal process of collective bargaining changed all of this as we have seen. Specifically, collective bargaining has forced each of the parties in baseball to negotiate in good faith and to respect the legal rights of its opponent. Written agreements covering bilaterally agreed-upon terms and conditions of employment are entered into for the purposes of making these rules explicit in nature and to emphasize the point that both sides are legally bound and agree to discharge their responsibilities under the written terms of the contract. Just as crucial as the contractual purposes described above, the baseball clubs have agreed to recognize the MLBPA as the sole and exclusive bargaining agent for all baseball players for the purposes of negotiations over the rules and regulations of employment. Both sides are legally bound to continue this relationship in good faith until such time as the players might decide to abandon their union or switch to another union, both of which seem to be extremely unlikely events given the current and past record of progress established by the MLBPA.

Uniform Player's Contract

As we have seen in Chapter 3, the important gains the players have achieved in the area of free agency were really made possible by the incorporation of the Uniform Player's Contract into the collective bargaining agreement in 1973. This opened up various controversial areas within the uniform contract, such as the reserve rule, to the process of interpretation through the grievance/arbitration mechanism. As we are all aware, a famous arbitration decision by Peter Seitz with regard to the reserve clause in the Uniform Player's Contract has opened the flood gates for the present free agency system. Were it not for the incorporation of the Uniform Player's Contract into the collective bargaining contract in 1973, which led to the arbitration decision mentioned above, it is quite likely, given baseball's antitrust exemption, that perpetual reservation would still prevail. Therefore, consider how very important these seemingly nonmonetary benefits, such as the inclusion of the Uniform Player's Contract into the collective bargaining contract and the grievance/arbitration procedure, have really been for the players. The Uniform Player's Contract contains many other provisions and rules which will not be repeated here. The interested reader is referred to Appendix I at the conclusion of this chapter where this uniform contract is reprinted in full from the 1976 collective bargaining agreement.

Scheduling

Another area in which players have become involved with regard to determining the terms and conditions of their employment comes under the general heading of scheduling. In order to put some of the following accomplishments into their proper perspective, the reader is reminded that prior to unionism, all scheduling decisions were made exclusively by the leagues and/or clubs. Players had no input whatsoever into decisions regarding the number of games to be played, road and home schedules, times for games, off-days, and the like. With collective bargaining, the players have been able to make their desires known and in some cases, convince management to agree to various constraints on their former unilateral schedule making authority.

For instance, the length of the regular playing season is pegged at 162 games by contractual agreement. Any attempt either to increase or decrease the number of games to be played in any future season has thus become a mandatory subject of bargaining between the players and the clubs. The two sides have also agreed not to schedule day/night doubleheaders, not to schedule one-day road trips except for opening day games and doubleheaders followed by an off-day. The number of exhibition games was limited to three per team during 1976 and has since been reduced to two. The parties have also negotiated rules over the times at which games may start. For instance, teams can not be required to play a night game the evening prior to a day when either of the teams has a doubleheader scheduled. Thus, we see a lot of Saturday afternoon games in the schedule in order to comply with this provision (note that most doubleheaders are played on Sundays). Day games are not allowed to commence prior to 1:00 P.M. except on certain dates (holidays) and if certain other conditions are met. The league president may give approval for the scheduling of a maximum of six games per season per team to start between 10:30 A.M. and noon, if certain conditions are met.

Rules are also prescribed that forbid the playing of a night game on a getaway day if either team has to travel more than 1½ hours for a day game to be played the following afternoon. The contract specifies that off-days are to be just that, and not scheduled for travel. No team is required to play for more than nineteen consecutive days without an open day. Finally, each club is limited to scheduling three twi-night doubleheaders per season. Thus, from this set of rules noted above, it is clear that today's ballplayer has had a real impact into scheduling decisions. In essence, through collective bargaining, rules have been established that have been responsible for eliminating many of the abuses and problems with scheduling that had been in evidence in previous seasons.

Safety and Health

Through collective bargaining, the parties have shown evidence of being interested in establishing and maintaining safe playing conditions for participants in the game. Thus, a bipartisan Safety and Health Advisory Committee has been established comprised of an equal number of player and club representatives. The express purpose of this committee, as stated in the collective bargaining contract, is to deal with emergency safety and health problems as they arise in baseball and to plan for the maintenance of safe and healthful working conditions for the players. The committee must meet at least once annually and can be called into session by any member who feels that an emergency safety or health situation exists. The committee has the power to make only nonbinding recommendations in the areas of safety and health, but is charged with using its best efforts to convince the involved parties to adopt such recommendations. Players retain the rights to pursue safety and health matters either through the grievance/arbitration procedure or under procedures established pursuant to the Occupational Safety and Health Act of 1970.

Spring Training Conditions

Under the collective bargaining agreement, players are guaranteed that they will not have to report to spring training any earlier than March 1 of any particular year. The only exception to this rule is that clubs may invite only pitchers and catchers to report to training camps earlier on a voluntary basis. Married players with 60 or more days on a major league roster or any player with a total of three or more years of major league experience may choose to live *away* from their club's spring training headquarters. Finally, the MLBPA has won the right to hold one union meeting per team during the spring training season. These meetings are to be held during normal spring training work hours and in the team's spring training clubhouse. The MLBPA must notify the team involved of their intent to hold such a meeting at least 10 days prior to its occurrence, and these meetings are to last no longer than 90 minutes. It is in these meetings that representatives of the MLBPA can update the players on various happenings either at the bargaining table or with grievance cases. It can safely be predicted that prior to the start of the 1981 season, these meetings have been the setting for heated discussions over the owners' proposed changes to the free agency system and whether or not the players should exercise their right to strike.

Rule Changes

Prior to unionization, clubs were free to make rule changes whenever they deemed them to be necessary. However, this unilateral power to change the rules of employment or rules pertaining to the playing or scoring of the game no longer exists. Clubs can no longer make employment rule changes without first notifying the MLBPA of their intention to do so and then negotiating over the proposed changes in good faith with the union. Any proposals for changes in playing or scoring rules are usually to be made during the off season. The clubs must notify the MLBPA of such intended rule changes and sit down to discuss only those changes that could significantly affect the terms and conditions of employment. If no agreement can be reached on such rule changes, the clubs may put these rules into effect unilaterally, but only after the completion of the next full championship season.

Assignment of Player Contracts

Before collective bargaining, players pretty much had to go along with any assignment of their contract made by their current club to any other club in either league. The player's alternative in many cases was to retire from the game. Through collective bargaining the players have won several important rights with regard to the assignment of their contract from team to team.

First, many of today's players have won the right to disapprove a trade or other such assignment of their contract to a different team. Essentially, any player with five or more years of major league experience can veto any trade that does not meet with his approval. Prior to trading a five-year veteran to another club, the player's present team must first receive the player's written consent.

Additionally, specific rules governing the assignment of player contracts to minor league teams are provided, and assignments to teams in countries other than the United States and Canada are expressively prohibited.

Major league waiver requests can be withdrawn by the same club only once in a year. That is, if a player is put on waivers and claimed by one or more clubs, the original club may withdraw the player's name from the waiver list one time only. The next time the player is put on waivers, such a move is irrevocable on the part of the original club.

Interleague trading is expressly provided for in the collective bargaining agreement from February 15 through March 15 of every year. Finally, rules are prescribed for the handling of unconditional player releases by their respective clubs.

Management Rights

A rather terse but standard management rights clause is included in the collective bargaining contract, which reserves for the clubs the sole right to manage and direct their operations as they see fit in regard to any decisions not expressly limited by the terms of the collective bargaining contract. That is, as is standard for most collective bargaining contracts in the private and public sectors, any rights not expressly bargained away remain in the sole possession of management.

Miscellaneous Items

There are many other miscellaneous nonmonetary items that the parties have agreed to through bilateral negotiations. Just a few of the more notable of these issues will be reported here so as to give the reader a flavor for their variety and breadth. The interested reader is referred to the collective bargaining contract itself for a complete treatment and listing of all of these miscellaneous items.

Both sides have agreed in writing to apply all the terms of the collective bargaining contract in a nondiscriminatory fashion. Additionally, clubs cannot require players to play Winter League baseball, although they are free to recommend the advisability of such action to any player. The active player limit per club is set at 25 from opening day until August 31. After that time, clubs are allowed to expand their rosters to 40 players until the conclusion of the regular season. Teams engaged in postseason play must adhere to the 25-player roster limit. The minimum number of active players that can be maintained by any club throughout the championship season is 24.

Since several professional ballplayers are of Hispanic descent, the parties have agreed to print copies of the collective bargaining pact in Spanish for distribution to these players. The players also have the right to request the reopening of negotiations upon the giving of ten days' written notice if the clubs propose to expand the number of professional teams beyond the current number of twenty-six. If such a proposal is forthcoming, the MLBPA has the right to bargain with the clubs only over the effects such expansion might have upon the players. Besides the items noted above, the collective bargaining contract contains several attachments regarding the parties' understanding of the meaning of certain provisions in the contract, and a list of regulations attached to the Uniform Player's Contract.

Summary

Collective bargaining in baseball has meant more to today's baseball player than grievance/arbitration, salary arbitration, and free agency. While these benefits, described in Chapters 3 and 4, have been very important, the process of collective bargaining has also been responsible for many other monetary and nonmonetary benefits that the players now enjoy. Some of the most important of these other benefits have been described, and the situation of today's ballplayer has been compared with the lot of the ballplayer of yesteryear. When viewed in this context, the gains made by professional baseball players in search of a more equitable pattern of employment regulations through unionism are truly amazing.

APPENDIX I

SCHEDULE A

UNIFORM PLAYER'S CONTRACT

THE NATIONAL LEAGUE OF
PROFESSIONAL BASEBALL CLUBS

Parties

Between _____ herein called the Club, and _____ of _____, herein called the Player.

Recital

The Club is a member of The National League of Professional Baseball Clubs, a voluntary association of member Clubs which has subscribed to the Major League Rules with The American League of Professional Baseball Clubs and its constituent Clubs and to The Professional Baseball Rules with that League and the National Association of Baseball Leagues.

Agreement

In consideration of the facts above recited and of the promises of each to the other, the parties agree as follows:

Employment

1. The Club hereby employs the Player to render, and the Player agrees to render, skilled services as a baseball player during the year(s) 19_____ including the Club's training season, the Club's exhibition games, the Club's playing season, the League Championship Series and the World Series (or any other official series in which the Club may participate and in any receipts of which the Player may be entitled to share).

Payment

2. For performance of the Player's services and promises hereunder the Club will pay the Player the sum of $ _____
_____, in semi-monthly installments after the commencement

of the playing season covered by this contract except as the schedule of payments may be modified by a special covenant. Payment shall be made on the day the amount becomes due, regardless of whether the Club is "home" or "abroad". If a monthly rate of payment is stipulated above, it shall begin with the commencement of the Club's playing season (or such subsequent date as the Player's services may commence) and end with the termination of the Club's scheduled playing season and shall be payable in semi-monthly installments as above provided.

Nothing herein shall interfere with the right of the Club and the Player by special covenant herein to mutually agree upon a method of payment whereby part of the Player's salary for the above year can be deferred to subsequent years.

If the Player is in the service of the Club for part of the playing season only, he shall receive such proportion of the sum above mentioned, as the number of days of his actual employment in the Club's playing season bears to the number of days in said season.

Notwithstanding the rate of payment stipulated above, the minimum rate of payment to the Player for each day of service on a Major League Club shall be at the rate of $19,000 per year for the 1976 and 1977 playing seasons and $21,000 per year for the 1978 and 1979 playing seasons.

Payment to the Player at the rate stipulated above shall be continued throughout any period in which a Player is required to attend a regularly scheduled military encampment of the Reserve of the Armed Forces or of the National Guard during the Club's playing season.

Loyalty

3. (a) The Player agrees to perform his services hereunder diligently and faithfully, to keep himself in first-class physical condition and to obey the Club's training rules, and pledges himself to the American public and to the Club to conform to high standards of personal conduct, fair play and good sportsmanship.

Baseball Promotion

3. (b) In addition to his services in connection with the actual playing of baseball, the Player agrees to cooperate with the Club and participate in any and all reasonable promotional activities of the Club and its League, which, in the opinion of the Club, will promote the welfare of the Club or professional baseball, and to observe and comply with all reasonable requirements of the Club respecting conduct and service of its team and its players, at all times whether on or off the field.

Pictures and Public Appearances

3. (c) The Player agrees that his picture may be taken for still photographs, motion pictures or television at such times as the Club may designate and agrees that all rights in such pictures shall belong to the Club and may be used by the Club for publicity purposes in any manner it desires. The Player further agrees that during the playing season he will not make public appearances, participate in radio or television programs or permit his picture to be taken or write or sponsor newspaper or magazine articles or sponsor commercial products without the written consent of the Club, which shall not be withheld except in the reasonable interests of the Club or professional baseball.

PLAYER REPRESENTATIONS

Ability

4. (a) The Player represents and agrees that he has exceptional and unique skill and ability as a baseball player; that his services to be rendered hereunder are of a special, unusual and extraordinary character which gives them peculiar value which cannot be reasonably or adequately compensated for in damages at law, and that the Player's breach of this contract will cause the Club great and irreparable injury and damage. The Player agrees that, in addition to other remedies, the Club shall be entitled to injunctive and other equitable relief to prevent a breach of this contract by the Player, including, among others, the right to enjoin the Player from playing baseball for any other person or organization during the term of his contract.

Condition

4. (b) The Player represents that he has no physical or mental defects known to him and unknown to the appropriate representative of the Club which would prevent or impair performance of his services.

Interest in Club

4. (c) The Player represents that he does not, directly or indirectly, own stock or have any financial interest in the ownership or earnings of any Major League Club, except as hereinafter expressly set forth, and covenants that he will not hereafter, while connected with any Major League Club, acquire or hold any such stock or interest except in accordance with Major League Rule 20(e).

Service

5. (a) The Player agrees that, while under contract, and prior to expiration of the Club's right to renew this contract, he will not play baseball otherwise than for the Club, except that the Player may participate in post-season games under the conditions prescribed in the Major League Rules. Major League Rule 18(b) is set forth herein.

Other Sports

5. (b) The Player and the Club recognize and agree that the Player's participation in certain other sports may impair or destroy his ability and skill as a baseball player. Accordingly, the Player agrees that he will not engage in professional boxing or wrestling; and that, except with the written consent of the Club, he will not engage in skiing, auto racing, motorcycle racing, sky diving, or in any game or exhibition of football, soccer, professional league basketball, ice hockey or other sport involving a substantial risk of personal injury.

Assignment

6. (a) The Player agrees that this contract may be assigned by the Club (and reassigned by any assignee Club) to any other Club in accordance with the Major League Rules and the Professional Baseball Rules. The Club and the Player may, without obtaining special approval, agree by special covenant to limit or eliminate the right of the Club to assign this contract.

No Salary Reduction

6. (b) The amount stated in paragraph 2 and in special covenants hereof which is payable to the Player for the period stated in paragraph 1 hereof shall not be diminished by any such assignment, except for failure to report as provided in the next subparagraph (c).

Reporting

6. (c) The Player shall report to the assignee Club promptly (as provided in the Regulation) upon receipt of written notice from the Club of the assignment of this contract. If the Player fails so to report, he shall not be entitled to any payment for the period from the date he receives written notice of assignment until he reports to the assignee Club.

Obligations of Assignor and Assignee Clubs

6. (d) Upon and after such assignment, all rights and obligations of the assignor Club hereunder shall become the rights and obligations of the assignee Club; provided, however, that

(1) The assignee Club shall be liable to the Player for payments accruing only from the date of assignment and shall not be liable (but the assignor Club shall remain liable) for payments accrued prior to that date.

(2) If at any time the assignee is a Major League Club, it shall be liable to pay the Player at the full rate stipulated in paragraph 2 hereof for the remainder of the period stated in paragraph 1 hereof and all prior assignors and assignees shall be relieved of liability for any payment for such period.

(3) Unless the assignor and assignee Clubs agree otherwise, if the assignee Club is a National Association Club, the assignee Club shall be liable only to pay the Player at the rate usually paid by said assignee Club to other Players of similar skill and ability in its classification and the assignor Club shall be liable to pay the difference for the remainder of the period stated in paragraph 1 hereof between an amount computed at the rate stipulated in paragraph 2 hereof and the amount so payable by the assignee Club.

Moving Allowances

6. (e) The Player shall be entitled to moving allowances under the circumstances and in the amounts set forth in Article VII of the Basic Agreement between the Major League Clubs and the Major League Baseball Players Association, effective January 1, 1976.

"Club"

6. (f) All references in other paragraphs of this contract to "the Club" shall be deemed to mean and include any assignee of this contract.

TERMINATION

By Player

7. (a) The Player may terminate this contract, upon written notice to the Club, if the Club shall default in the payments to the Player provided for in paragraph 2 hereof or shall fail to perform any other obligation agreed to be performed by the Club hereunder and if the Club shall fail to remedy such default within ten (10) days after the receipt by the Club of written notice of such default. The Player may also terminate this contract as provided in subparagraph (d)(4) of this paragraph 7.

By Club

7. (b) The Club may terminate this contract upon written notice to the Player (but only after requesting and obtaining waivers of this contract from all other Major League Clubs) if the Player shall at any time:

(1) fail, refuse or neglect to conform his personal conduct to the standards of good citizenship and good sportsmanship or to keep himself in first-class physical condition or to obey the Club's training rules; or

(2) fail, in the opinion of the Club's management, to exhibit sufficient skill or competitive ability to qualify or continue as a member of the Club's team; or

(3) fail, refuse or neglect to render his services hereunder or in any other manner materially breach this contract.

7. (c) If this contract is terminated by the Club, the Player shall be entitled to termination pay under the circumstances and in the amounts set forth in Article VIII of the Basic Agreement between the Major League Clubs and the Major League Baseball Players Association, effective January 1, 1976. In addition, the Player shall be entitled to receive an amount equal to the reasonable traveling expenses of the Player, including first-class jet air fare and meals en route, to his home city.

Procedure

7. (d) If the Club proposes to terminate this contract in accordance with subparagraph (b) of this paragraph 7, the procedure shall be as follows:

(1) The Club shall request waivers from all other Major League Clubs. Such waivers shall be good for six (6) days only. Such waiver request must state that it is for the purpose of terminating this contract and it may not be withdrawn.

(2) Upon receipt of waiver request, any other Major League Club may claim assignment of this contract at a waiver price of $1.00, the priority of claims to be determined in accordance with the Major League Rules.

(3) If this contract is so claimed, the Club shall, promptly and before any assignment, notify the Player that it had requested waivers for the purpose of terminating this contract and that the contract had been claimed.

(4) Within 5 days after receipt of notice of such claim, the Player shall be entitled, by written notice to the Club, to terminate this contract on the date of his notice of termination. If the Player fails so to notify the Club, this contract shall be assigned to the claiming Club.

(5) If the contract is not claimed, the Club shall promptly deliver written notice of termination to the Player at the expiration of the waiver period.

7. (e) Upon any termination of this contract by the Player, all obligations of both Parties hereunder shall cease on the date of termination, except the obligation of the Club to pay the Player's compensation to said date.

Regulations

8. The Player accepts as part of this contract the Regulations set forth herein.

Rules

9. (a) The Club and the Player agree to accept, abide by and comply with all provisions of the Major League Agreement, the Major League Rules, the Rules or Regulations of the League of which the Club is a member, and the Professional Baseball Rules, in effect on the date of this Uniform Player's Contract, which are not inconsistent with the provisions of this contract or the provisions of any agreement between the Major League Clubs and the Major League Baseball Players Association, provided that the Club, together with the other clubs of the American and National Leagues and the National Association, reserves the right to modify, supplement or repeal any provision of said Agreement, Rules and/or Regulations in a manner not inconsistent with this contract or the provisions of any then existing agreement between the Major League Clubs and the Major League Baseball Players Association.

Disputes

9. (b) All disputes between the Player and the Club which are covered by the Grievance Procedure as set forth in the Basic Agreement, effective January 1, 1976, shall be resolved in accordance with such Grievance Procedure.

Publication

9. (c) The Club, the League President and the Commissioner, or any of them, may make public the findings, decision and record of any inquiry, investigation or hearing held or conducted, including in such record all evidence or information, given, received, or obtained in connection therewith.

Renewal

10. (a) Unless the Player has exercised his right to become a free agent as set forth in the Basic Agreement between the Major League Clubs and the Major League Baseball Players Association, effective January 1, 1976, the Club may, on or before December 20 (or if a Sunday, then the next pre-

ceding business day) in the year of the last playing season covered by this contract, tender to the Player a contract for the term of the next year by mailing the same to the Player at his address following his signature hereto, or if none be given, then at his last address of record with the Club. If prior to the March 1 next succeeding said December 20, the Player and the Club have not agreed upon the terms of such contract, then on or before 10 days after said March 1, the Club shall have the right by written notice to the Player at said address to renew this contract for the period of one year on the same terms, except that the amount payable to the Player shall be such as the Club shall fix in said notice; provided, however, that said amount, if fixed by a Major League Club, shall be an amount payable at a rate not less than as specified in Article V, Section B, of the Basic Agreement. Subject to the Player's rights as set forth in the Basic Agreement, effective January 1, 1976, the Club may renew this contract from year to year.

10. (b) The Club's right to renew this contract, as provided in subparagraph (a) of this paragraph 10, and the promise of the Player not to play otherwise than with the Club have been taken into consideration in determining the amount payable under paragraph 2 hereof.

Governmental Regulation—National Emergency

11. This contract is subject to federal or state legislation, regulations, executive or other official orders or other governmental action, now or hereafter in effect respecting military, naval, air or other governmental service, which may directly or indirectly affect the Player, Club or the League and subject also to the right of the Commissioner to suspend the operation of this contract during any national emergency during which Major League Baseball is not played.

Commissioner

12. The term "Commissioner" wherever used in this contract shall be deemed to mean the Commissioner designated under the Major League Agreement, or in the case of a vacancy in the office of Commissioner, the Executive Council or such other body or person or persons as shall be designated in the Major League Agreement to exercise the powers and duties of the Commissioner during such vacancy.

Supplemental Agreements

The Club and the Player covenant that this contract, the Basic Agreement effective January 1, 1976 and the Agreement Re Major League Baseball Players Benefit Plan effective April 1, 1976 fully set forth all understandings and agreements between them, and agree that no other understandings or agreements, whether heretofore or hereafter made, shall be valid, recognizable, or of any effect whatsoever, unless expressly set forth in a new or supplemental contract executed by the Player and the Club (acting by its President or such other officer as shall have been thereunto duly authorized by the President or Board of Directors as evidenced by a certificate filed of record with the League President and Commissioner) and complying with the Major League Rules and the Professional Baseball Rules.

Special Covenants

Approval

This contract or any supplement hereto shall not be valid or effective unless and until approved by the League President.

Signed in duplicate this _____ day of _____, A.D. 197___

_____   _____
                    (Player)   (Club)

_____   By _____
     (Home address of Player)   (Authorized Signature)

Social Security No. _____

Approved _____, 197___

_____

President, The National League of Professional Baseball Clubs

REGULATIONS

1.   The Club's playing season for each year covered by this contract and all renewals hereof shall be as fixed by The National League of Professional Baseball Clubs, or if this contract shall be assigned to a Club in another League, then by the League of which such assignee is a member.

2.   The Player, when requested by the Club, must submit to a complete physical examination at the expense of the Club, and if necessary to treatment by a regular physician or dentist in good standing. Upon refusal of the Player to submit to a complete medical or dental examination the Club may consider such refusal a violation of this regulation and may take such action as it deems advisable under Regulation 5 of this contract. Disability directly resulting from injury sustained in the course and within the scope of his employment under this contract shall not impair the right of the Player to receive his full salary for the period of such disability or for the season in which the injury was sustained (whichever period is shorter), together with the reasonable medical and hospital expenses incurred by reason of the injury and during the term of this contract; but only upon the express prerequisite conditions that (a) written notice of such injury, including the time, place, cause and nature of the injury, is served upon and received by the Club within twenty days of the sustaining of said injury and (b) the Club shall have the right to designate the doctors and hospitals furnishing such medical and hospital services. Failure to give such notice shall not impair the rights of the Player, as herein set forth, if the Club has actual knowledge of such injury. All workmen's compensation payments received by the Player as compensation for loss of income for a specific period during which the Club is paying him in full, shall be paid over by the Player to the Club. Any other disability may be ground for suspending or terminating this contract at the discretion of the Club.

3.   The Club will furnish the Player with two complete uniforms, exclusive of shoes, unless the Club requires the Player to wear nonstandard shoes in which case the Club will furnish the shoes. The uniforms will be surrendered by the Player to the Club at the end of the season or upon termination of this contract.

4.   The Player shall be entitled to expense allowances under the circumstances and in the amounts set forth in Article VI of the Basic Agreement between the Major League Clubs and the Major League Baseball Players Association, effective January 1, 1976.

Source: Basic Agreement between The American League of Professional Baseball Clubs and The National League of Professional Baseball Clubs and the Major League Baseball Players Association, effective January 1, 1976.

5.   For violation by the Player of any regulation or other provision of this contract, the Club may impose a reasonable fine and deduct the amount thereof from the Player's salary or may suspend the Player without salary for a period not exceeding thirty days or both. Written notice of the fine or suspension or both and the reason therefor shall in every case be given to the Player.

6.   In order to enable the Player to fit himself for his duties under this contract, the Club may require the Player to report for practice at such places as the Club may designate and to participate in such exhibition contests as may be arranged by the Club, without any other compensation than that herein elsewhere provided, for a period beginning not earlier than March 1 or ten days prior to the second Saturday in March, whichever is earlier, provided, however, that the Club may invite pitchers and catchers to report at an earlier date on a voluntary basis. The Club will pay the necessary traveling expenses, including the first-class jet air fare and meals en route of the Player from his home city to the training place of the Club, whether he be ordered to go there directly or by way of the home city of the Club. In the event of the failure of the Player to report for practice or to participate in the exhibition games, as required and provided for, he shall be required to get into playing condition to the satisfaction of the Club's team manager, and at the Player's own expense, before his salary shall commence.

7.   In case of assignment of this contract the Player shall report promptly to the assignee Club within 72 hours from the date he receives written notice from the Club of such assignment, if the Player is then not more than 1,600 miles by most direct available railroad route from the assignee Club, plus an additional 24 hours for each additional 800 miles.

Post-Season Exhibition Games. Major League Rule 18(b) provides:

(b) EXHIBITION GAMES.   No player shall participate in any exhibition game during the period between the close of the Major League championship season and the following training season, except that, with the consent of his club and permission of the Commissioner, a player may participate in exhibition games for a period of not less than thirty (30) days, such period to be designated annually by the Commissioner. Players who participate in barnstorming during this period cannot engage in any Winter League activities. Player conduct, on and off the field, in connection with such post-season exhibition games shall be subject to the discipline of the Commissioner. The Commissioner shall not approve of more than three (3) players of any one club on the same team. The Commissioner shall not approve of more than three (3) players from the joint membership of the World Series participants playing in the same game. No player shall participate in any exhibition game with or against any team which, during the current season or within one year, has had any ineligible player or which is or has been during the current season or within one (1) year, managed and controlled by an ineligible player or by any person who has listed an ineligible player under an assumed name or who otherwise has violated, or attempted to violate, any exhibition game contract; or with or against any team which, during said season or within one (1) year, has played against teams containing such ineligible players, or so managed or controlled. Any player violating this Rule shall be fined not less than Fifty Dollars ($50.00) nor more than Five Hundred Dollars ($500.00), except that in no event shall such fine be less than the consideration received by such player for participating in such game.

Chapter 6

LABOR RELATIONS IN OTHER PROFESSIONAL SPORTS: A BRIEF OVERVIEW

Earlier chapters of this book have been entirely concerned with unionism in professional baseball. We have now concluded our discussion of both the history and impacts of unionism in baseball from 1885 to the present. While the baseball industry represents the most mature example of labor-management relations in the realm of professional sports, and certainly is the area in which the vast majority of research and writing has been conducted, it is nonetheless just one example out of many. Thus, in order to present a better-rounded viewpoint of the infiltration of the union movement into the professional sports industry, this chapter will briefly review the experiences of several other sports with unionism.

The choice of which other sports to review is in a sense somewhat arbitrary. For athletes in almost every sport in America today (and in many foreign countries as well), be the sport popular or unpopular, large or small, individual or team based, have either flirted with or actually chosen to adopt unionism as a method of negotiating wages, hours, and conditions of employment. Given the broad range of alternatives from which to choose, two basic decision rules were employed in arriving at the subject matter for this chapter. First, it was felt that for comparative purposes with baseball, this chapter should properly focus on major team sports. Thus, the three sports of professional basketball, football, and hockey were chosen as being consistent with the above goal of comparability. Secondly, it was felt that some mention needed to be made of nonplayer attempts at unionization within the professional sports industry. Of course, the most obvious example of this trend in recent years is the unionization of professional baseball umpires and professional basketball referees. A brief review of the happenings in this area will be presented to alert the reader that the players have not been the only group that has turned to unionism in an attempt to achieve better employment conditions. The treatment of all of these issues will be necessarily brief, but the reader should gain at least some appreciation for the comparative aspects of labor relations in these other sports and realize that the same sets of employment problems that have faced baseball players have also been endemic to other professional athletes.

We will then discuss several aspects of unionism among athletes in basketball, football, and hockey. Finally, our focus will shift to a discussion of the unionization attempts among officials in baseball and basketball. Some attention will be paid to the fact that while these officials have unionized, their counterparts in football and hockey remain nonunionized. A concluding section will briefly address the future of labor-management relations in professional sports other than baseball.

One way to compare the union movement in various other professional team sports with that in baseball would be to go through an extensive item-by-item review of the respective collective bargaining contracts and thereby, come up with some composite contract score that would reflect the favorableness of the contract to either labor or management. This is a rather tedious exercise; and so it was decided to concentrate on a smaller set of crucial issues for comparative purposes. Based on what we have covered most extensively in the realm of baseball, it would seem that for comparative purposes the four issues that should be covered in some detail in each sport are:

1. The history of unionism in each sport.
2. Grievance/arbitration.
3. Salary arbitration.
4. The reserve clause and free agency.

However, there are several problems with this design. First, none of the other sports to be discussed has had an extensive history of previous unionization attempts by the players, as was the case in baseball; so the history of unionization in each area can be covered very rapidly. Secondly, with the exception of hockey, no other sport has adopted any form of salary arbitration; there is really no basis for making comparative statements in this area. Finally, while a griev-ance/arbitration procedure has been adopted in each of the other team sports referred to above, the procedure in no case has taken on the extreme role of importance that we witnessed in the game of baseball.

Thus, for all of these reasons, the major thrust of the following paragraphs will be in the area of collective bargaining over what was referred to in baseball as the reserve system. The exact name of the system may differ from sport to sport, but the underlying nature of the fundamental employment problems brought on by this type of a system has been remarkably constant across all of the sports to be covered. In every case, one of the key issues which has led players to turn to unionism has in fact been the lack of freedom of movement from team to team and the correspondingly lower salaries that such lack of freedom makes inevitable.

Unionism in Basketball

In professional basketball, player attempts at unionization have begun only rather recently. Bob Cousy, a star player for the Boston Celtics for many years, is usually given credit for helping to establish the then-informal National Basketball Players Association (NBPA) back in the early 1950s. As was the case with the MLBPA in its early years, the NBPA really didn't accomplish too much until the hiring of an Exectuive Director (Lawrence Fleisher) in 1962. The National Basketball Association was forced to recognize this union shortly thereafter as threats of strikes and other concerted actions by the players became common.[1] Since that time, the players have won many gains in the areas of pensions, minimum salaries, scheduling, and many other aspects of the formerly unilaterally controlled rules of employment. Just as in baseball, the club owners in basketball were forced to share a good portion of their decision-making powers in the realm of employment relationships with the players for the first time. Two of the major gains won by the players through unionization, grievance/arbitration and free agency, will be dis-cussed in the paragraphs that follow.

Salary Arbitration

It has already been noted that professional basketball players have yet to acquire the right to use any kind of arbitration to resolve their

salary disputes with their respective clubs. Salary bargaining is conducted much as in the baseball industry (described in Chapter 4),
with the exception that neither side can invoke arbitration. However, several other factors that existed in basketball, such as a rival
league (American Basketball Association) and the lack of antitrust
law exemption, served to put the players in a much stronger bargaining position than were their counterparts in baseball. While the
balance of bargaining power did lie with the owners, the players
possessed several options not available in baseball, and salary arbitration was not a high-priority item for bargaining.

Grievance/Arbitration

While the players have never achieved the right to use salary arbitration, their collective bargaining contract does provide for a strong
system of grievance/arbitration in Article XV.[2] As is the case in
baseball, this provision provides for the amicable resolution of all
disputes arising over the interpretation, application, or compliance
with the terms of the collective bargaining contract and the Uniform
Player Contract. Also as is true in baseball, a few items are precluded from consideration through this impartial grievance/arbitra-
tion procedure, including disputes involving fines or suspensions
imposed by the commissioner, disputes involving actions taken by
the commissioner in preserving the integrity of the game, and,
finally, disputes over Article XVI of the collective bargaining contract, which deals with Free Agency. These latter types of disputes
are handled through a separate procedure, which will be described
shortly.

The principle of providing a forum for the airing of player and club
employment grievances and the possibility of using impartial arbitration to resolve the toughest of these disputes has a firm rooting in
professional basketball. As is typical in most grievance procedures,
an initial attempt is made to resolve such disputes bilaterally, at the
lower stages of the grievance process. However, where this option
fails, either side may press for an impartial, binding solution to the
issue at hand. The 1976 contract specifies Peter Seitz as the permanent umpire in basketball grievance cases that proceed all the way to
arbitration. As in baseball, either side may signify its intention of
replacing the arbitrator with a new person by giving thirty days'
notice to the other party. The contract specifies the exact procedures
to be employed if the choosing of a new arbitrator becomes neces-

sary. Finally, with regard to a wide variety of disputes that may arise over Article XVI dealing with free agency, the players and the clubs have agreed to use arbitration to resolve their differences. Examples of these types of potential disputes will be discussed in the context of our description of the free agency process in basketball.

Player Reservation in Professional Basketball

For many years, the professional basketball player found himself in virtually the same position as his counterparts in baseball, unable to exercise any type of freedom of movement from team to team. The Uniform Player Contract in Basketball contained a paragraph number 22, which management argued made the employment relationship perpetual in nature. That is, if a player failed to sign a contract for the upcoming season, his contract could be renewed by his club for the following season at a wage no lower than that he was paid in the previous season. And then the player's new contract also contained clause 22, which reserved the player to the club for the following season as well. As the reader can see, this process of reserving players to one team had the potential for some amount of abuse. The exact wording of paragraph 22 is reproduced below.[3] Instead of referring to this as a reserve clause, as was the case in baseball, in basketball this short paragraph was named the option clause. Players who failed to sign a contract for the upcoming season and whose salaries therefore came under the provisions of paragraph 22, were said to be playing out their options.[4]

> *On or before August 1 next following the last playing season covered by this contract and renewals and extensions thereof, the Club may tender to the Player a contract for the next succeeding season by mailing the same to the Player at his address shown below, or if none is shown, then at his address last known to the Club. If the Player fails, neglects or omits to sign and return such contract to the Club so that the Club receives it on or before September 1st next succeeding, then his contract shall be deemed renewed and extended for the period of one year, upon the same terms and conditions in all respects as are provided herein, except that the compensation payable to the Player shall be the sum provided in the contract tendered to the Player pursuant to the provisions hereof, which compensation shall in no event be less than the compensation payable to the Player for the last playing season covered by this contract and renewals and extensions thereof.*

The provisions are very similar to those described in Chapter 3 with regard to professional baseball's perpetual reserve clause. A player first tries to get the best possible salary through bilateral negotiations, and, of course, the club attempts to do the same thing. If the agreement can't be reached, the club's ultimate weapon is paragraph 22. Under this procedure, an unsigned player can be reserved to his original team for the upcoming season at no less than the salary paid to him in the previous year. Thus, if the player wished to remain in the NBA, he would have to play for his original team. Of course, as in baseball, other options such as retirement, attempting to get traded, and attempting to be released outright were available to these basketball players. Additionally, for a number of years, basketball players could jump leagues to the rival American Basketball Association, whose clubs did not honor the NBA's no-tampering rules nor the NBA provisions of paragraph 22 in the NBA Uniform Player Contract. While the professional basketball player had one additional weapon, which certainly enhanced the bargaining power and salaries of several players over a number of years, the basic situation of club domination over the rules of the shop prevailed just as in baseball. Basketball players quickly tired of the notion of perpetual ownership of their services by the clubs, and it was only a matter of time before they rose up in protest over this option rule, which they believed to be so unfair.

Compensation

While the option rule seemed in theory to grant the player a bit more opportunity to choose where he would play, compared to baseball's former reserve system (recall the language of paragraph 22 restricting clubs to a one-time usage of such an option procedure), in practice there was very little difference between an option and a reserve system. The basic problem in basketball was the so-called compensation rule. In baseball, there has never been much of a history of compensation for teams losing free agents. In the early history of the game, there was not much of a possibility of becoming a free agent and so the issue of compensation was moot. The initial modification made to this perpetual reserve system through collective bargaining in 1976 provided for minimal levels of compensation, as described in Chapter 3. Thus, a club losing a superstar player might receive a player of only high school caliber in return for the loss of the established star. The team picking up the star player clearly comes out of the deal way ahead. Because of this lack of meaningful compensation, teams continue to bid up free agent player's salaries in an attempt to sign one or two superstars who might lead their team to a pennant. Also recall the great number of players in baseball who have successfully changed teams under this system. The single issue threatening to precipitate a strike prior to or during the 1981 baseball season has been the nature of *compensation* to teams who have lost players through the free agency route. The players like the situation just the way it is, while the owners want to impose stringent compensation rules that would probably hold down the rapid escalation of free agent players' salaries and drastically reduce the amount of player movement from team to team through the usage of the free agency route.

But in basketball, the situation had been quite a bit different from the start. As noted above, compensation for teams losing free agent players was an integral part of the game's employment relationships. In essence, the commissioner of the NBA was empowered, but not required, to award compensation to the team losing a player or players. The typical compensation procedure was for the two involved teams to try to reach a negotiated settlement prior to any involvement on the part of the commissioner. Where these attempts proved to be successful, there was little need for the commissioner to take any action. If the two teams failed to reach an agreement, the commissioner did have the power to award cash, players, and/or draft choices to the team that had lost a player to the free agency route. The great uncertainty involved, as to (a) whether the commissioner would indeed award compensation and (b) if he chose to do so, what the exact nature of this award would be, put most teams in the position of being extremely afraid of going after free agents. Essentially, teams could never be exactly sure of the price they might have to pay for obtaining the services of a particular player. From the players' standpoint, this compensation rule was very unpopular, as it basically destroyed any freedom of movement in their labor market. Clubs were just too intimidated by the uncertainty factor, and it was the players who were forced to bear the brunt of the compensation rule in the form of lower salaries and limited opportunities for mobility.

While the players did have legitimate gripes over the option and compensation rules, which essentially bound them to their teams in perpetuity, much the same as the reserve clause did for professional baseball players, these basketball players did have a number of weapons to enable them to fight back. Thus, growing player resentment over the control systems referred to above led to the eventual unionization of professional basketball players and several changes to the option/compensation system. These changes will be reported in detail below; but prior to that, a brief recounting of these player weapons seems in order. Recall that in baseball in recent years, the players really had only collective bargaining on which to rely if they sought to bring about changes in the rules of employment.

Besides collective bargaining and the use of grievance/arbitration, professional basketball players have had two additional routes through which to force their club owners to effectuate changes in the option compensation system. These two additional factors are the possibility of antitrust law prosecution of the teams and the possibility of jumping leagues made available through the formation of the ABA. For instance, players like Rick Barry[5] and Dick Barnett[6] were able to jump leagues to the ABA after having served out their option seasons in the NBA. These players successfully challenged the perpetual nature of the NBA's option clause, and the league relented to accept the position that, in fact, the option clause is usable only once. Thus, whether a player sat out for an entire year or actually played out the option season, the result was the same. After such season was over, the player became free to negotiate with any team in the other league (ABA). Of course, no compensation was provided to teams in the NBA losing players to the ABA and so the NBA owners were quite interested in rectifying this situation, which they felt was quite intolerable. Thus, both the factors of the possibility of legal action by the players under U.S. antitrust laws and league jumping to achieve higher wages and escape from the provisions of paragraph 22 of the uniform player contract put the owners in the frame of mind where they were ready to compromise over the option-compensation system. This compromise was to come through the process of collective bargaining and was to be incorporated into the game's employment rules in the form of Article XVI of the basic agreement between the players and the clubs.[7]

The Robertson Case and Collective Bargaining

The final judicial setback the club owners suffered in this area stemmed from the 1970 Oscar Robertson suit.[8] Basically, the players liked the idea of having rival leagues, as this enabled them to bargain for higher salaries with the threat of jumping leagues in the back of the owners' minds. The club owners wanted to end this rivalry, and so a merger between the two leagues was finally negotiated. Once the merger was successfully pulled off, the players' options would be limited to salary bargaining with one team in just one league. The Robertson action accused the leagues of violating the Sherman Antitrust Act of 1890 by conspiring to merge and thereby form a monopoly. Thus, one purpose of the suit was to block the proposed merger. In addition, the suit attempted to ban the further usage of the option-compensation system that the NBA had used for some time. The argument of the players was that this option system restrained trade in violation of the Sherman Act and unduly restricted their freedom of movement from team to team.

The Robertson suit was eventually settled out of court, but not before the owners had attempted to receive summary judgment and approval for both the draft and reserve systems. This motion was rejected in harsh wording that left very little doubt in the minds of the owners that they would in fact lose their case if it was decided in court. The combination of all of these various factors put the owners in the mood to reach a negotiated compromise over the issue of the option system with the players.

In essence, in exchange for dismissal of the Robertson lawsuit, a new collective bargaining pact was signed in which the parties agreed to the concept of the merger of the two leagues in exchange for several modifications of the former reservation or option system.[9] Major changes were also made to the college draft system. The most significant of these collectively bargained changes are highlighted below.

First, it ought to be noted that Section 1 of Article XVI states that the purpose of these negotiated changes is ". . . to increase the number of Teams in the NBA with which present and future NBA players may negotiate and sign Player Contracts during their careers . . ."[10] Thus, both sides made the purpose of these changes quite clear: to increase player bargaining power through a more liberal system of player movement from team to team during his career. Compare this newer attitude with the former position of the clubs on perpetual reservation, and one can see that quite a change had taken place indeed!

The old NBA player draft was established such that once a team drafted a college player, this player could negotiate only with that one team. There were no time limitations on the duration of this exclusive negotiating right on the part of the drafting team. Thus, a player who was drafted by Philadelphia in 1970 and remained unsigned for five years still remained the property of the same club for purposes of negotiations over salary and the like. Both sides realized the inequities in the former system and so, commencing with the college draft of June 1976, several important changes were made. First, the team that initially drafts a player no longer has an unlimited time period in which to sign the drafted player. In fact, the team has one year to do so, after which time the player is eligible to be redrafted by any team in the subsequent college draft. The new team drafting the player has a similar period of time (one year) of exclusive negotiating rights. After such time, if no contract has been signed, the player becomes a free agent and can negotiate with any team in the league.

With respect to the option system, the parties agreed to the following changes. First, it was agreed that rookies could continue to have option clauses in their contracts, but only if the contract was for a period of one year, and only where the option could be exercised for one year beyond the stated term of the contract. The perpetual nature of basketball's option clause was put to rest forever under this new agreement. Secondly, any other player signing a contract of any length may agree to a one-year option clause to be included in the contract. This is quite a bit different from the previous system where option clauses (paragraph 22) were automatically included in all contracts. The newer system allows such clauses to be used only where both sides specifically agree to include such a provision in the uniform player contract through negotiations.

Perhaps the most interesting and far-reaching change agreed to in the 1976 collective bargaining contract had to do with the issue of compensation for teams losing free agents. Recall that under the former system, where the two clubs could not come to terms on compensation, the commissioner was empowered to make awards (but not required to do so) of cash, draft choices, or players to the team having lost the free agent. Remember the great deal of uncertainty with which clubs approached free agent players, because of their fears of some sort of unfair compensation from the commissioner's office. Evidence does indicate that the fear of just what the compensation might be has drastically reduced the options available to players for movement from team to team; and in those few cases where a player has been able to switch teams, the worst fears of the club owners seem to have been borne out. For instance, when the Seattle Supersonics lost Marvin Webster in 1978 to the New York Knicks, Commissioner Larry O'Brien awarded them Lonnie Shelton, a first-round draft pick in 1979, and $450,000 in cash. As might be expected, the reactions of the two teams to this decision were markedly different. While Seattle was quite satisfied, New York club officials seemed shocked and dismayed by the severity of the compensation award. In defense of O'Brien, this was probably the toughest compensation case he has yet to decide, in terms of the magnitude of the loss to the Seattle team from New York's signing of 7'1" Webster. Other cases on which he has ruled have included Houston's signing of Rick Barry in 1978 and New Orleans's acquisition of Truck Robinson in 1977. In any case, the system of using the Commissioner to resolve issues of compensation does have several problems.

The First-Refusal System

Nonetheless, in the 1976 negotiations, the players and clubs agreed to continue operating under the commissioner system through the end of the 1980–1981 playing season. However, following the last NBA playoff game of the 1980–1981 season, and up until the last day of the 1986–1987 season, the two sides agreed to eliminate this commissioner system altogether in favor of a first-refusal system. In essence, the new system, when implemented at the end of the 1980–1981 season, will do away with compensation altogether. A free agent is free to negotiate the best possible contract he can get with any club, subject only to the right of first refusal from his original club. Assume that a player from Boston becomes a free agent and decides that the best deal he can get in the open market is from Seattle. He is then obligated under the collective bargaining contract to obtain an "offer sheet" from Seattle which contains the principal terms of his new agreement. This offer sheet must be signed by both the player and the Seattle club and must be presented by the player to the original club (Boston) to enable them to exercise their right to first refusal.

When the original team receives the offer sheet, it has fifteen days in which to take action. This action can take one of two forms. First, the original club may simply not wish to match the offer made to the player by the Seattle club. After the expiration of the fifteen-day period with no response from the original team, the player and Seattle will be deemed to have entered into a binding contract based on the terms stipulated in the offer sheet. However, if the original club wishes to retain the player's services, it must present to the free agent a "First Refusal Exercise Notice" within the fifteen-day period. In so doing, the former club has agreed to match all of the terms that the player and the new club set forth in writing on the offer sheet. If the former club does decide to match this offer, the player and his former club are bound to enter into a written agreement stipulating said terms. Thus, where the former club chooses to match a player's best offer, that player must sign with his former club, but at the higher salary offered by the other team. In essence, basketball has adopted a completely free player movement mechanism. The player goes out and gets his best offer, and the only question becomes for whom will he play, the new team or his former club? Where the former club fails to exercise its right of first refusal, no compensation whatsoever is involved. In essence, the original club is provided with one last chance to retain the player's service. Failing to exercise this option, both sides have agreed that no compensation should be necessary.

It is too soon to review the impacts of this new system; but one can certainly speculate that things will look a lot different during the period of this five-year experiment with first refusal. For one thing, the currently high NBA salaries can be expected to go even higher as teams seek to protect their rights to their star players and seek to steal dissatisfied players away from other teams. We can also predict that the current trend toward longer-term contracts will continue to be in evidence. Teams that can lock players into longer pacts need not worry about these players becoming free agents at least until the expiration date of these longer contracts. Finally, it can be predicted that many more players will test the free agent waters and actually be able to change teams under this new system. Since no compensation from teams acquiring a free agent player will be required, the former reluctance on the part of the owners to negotiate with free agents based on the uncertainties of what the commissioner might do should be removed. Players should enjoy much more freedom of movement under this newer system.

Even though this new procedure would seem to be quite fair and workable in nature, there are several potential problems that could arise with it. First, the exact meaning of the principal terms specified on the offer sheet may cause some problems. The collective bargaining contract specifies that these principal terms shall include:

- The money to be paid, current and/or deferred, and the method of calculation of this payment if salary is variable.
- A description of any property to be made available to the player.

- A description of any investment opportunities to be made available to the player.
- Any modifications to the Uniform Player Contract referring to noncompensation terms of employment.
- Any other payments of any kind to be made to the player by the team for his services other than as a basketball player.[11]

From the listing above, it seems pretty obvious that it may indeed be hard to determine what exactly is involved in the matching of an offer. What sort of value shall be placed on property, investment opportunities, and the like? How do the players and/or the clubs really know if two offers are essentially equivalent in value or not? The negotiators anticipated just such a problem, and so they set up a procedure referred to as "valuation arbitration" to resolve such disputes. Essentially, this means that when an offer sheet contains items of property or investment opportunities whose fair market value is difficult to ascertain, prior to presenting such offer sheet to the former team, the player and/or the new club must seek valuation arbitration to determine the worth of these assets. The arbitrator in such proceedings is called upon only to render a judgment regarding the fair market value of such items. This determination is final and binding and becomes part of the record attached to the offer sheet.

In addition, it may be the case that certain unique terms provided by one team in the principal terms can't possibly be duplicated by the prior team in exact form. The collective bargaining contract provides that the former team must make an effort to provide substantially equivalent terms to the player to replace these unique terms. However, the prior team does not have to provide substantial equivalents for (a) the intangible benefits a player might accrue by playing and living in a certain geographic area of the new team, or (b) promises by the new team of auditions, try-outs, and the like for the possibility of performing services other than as a basketball player.[12]

A prior club that exercises its right of first refusal has ten days afterwards in which to notify the free agent player of any terms which it deems to be unique. If no such notice is given, the prior team is assumed to have waived its right to contend that any unique terms exist. Where the prior team does contend that unique terms exist, it seems obvious that disputes may easily arise. Again, in anticipation of such potential problems, the parties have agreed to impartial arbitration to determine whether a particular item is a unique term or not.[13]

Where such disputes do arise, the impartial arbitrator has no power to terminate an agreement between a free agent player and his prior team as evidenced by the rendering to the player by the former team of the first refusal exercise notice. Thus, once a team exercises its right of first refusal, it is assured of retaining the services of the player. The major question for the arbitrator in this type of a procedure then becomes to determine the exact nature of the bargain to be struck between said player and his former team.

In this regard, the arbitrator really has three options at his disposal. First, if the arbitrator rules that there are no unique items involved in the offer sheet, he may simply order the prior club to match the terms on the offer sheet in kind. Or, if a unique item *is* determined to be included on the offer sheet, the arbitrator may force the prior club to substitute a substantially equivalent item for this unique term. In such situations, the arbitrator is the one to determine what the nature of such a substantially equivalent item will be. Finally, situations may arise where the unique term(s) in the offer sheet cannot be replaced by a substantially equivalent item through a reasonable effort or expense on the part of the prior team. In such cases, the impartial arbitrator may award the player the cash equivalent of the unique item(s). The fair market value of such unique items can either be arrived at through the valuation arbitration procedure described above, or if this procedure has not been used, through a determination by the arbitrator in the particular case. A few other uses for arbitration are prescribed in the 1976 contract, all of which deal with other potential problems with the first refusal system. The interested reader is referred to the contract for a further treatment of these items.[14]

Summary

We have seen how professional basketball players turned to unionism for many of the same reasons which prompted baseball players to do so several years earlier. We have noted how the NBA and the NBA Players Association have been able to resolve major differences over the merger with the ABA, the player draft, the option paragraph 22 in the Uniform Player Contract, and the former compensation rule through the process of good faith collective bargaining. Also important in bringing the parties together in these areas have been the threats of league jumping and antitrust prosecution by the players, two options *not* available to the baseball players during the reign of Marvin Miller as the executive director of the MLBPA. We have described the major changes brought forth in many of the areas denoted above. Of particular interest was the first refusal system, a five-year experiment which will begin after the last playoff game of the 1980–1981 season. During the five-year period, ending after the 1986–1987 season, the former option-compensation system will be replaced by a system providing players with much easier access to the free agency route. Additionally, while former clubs can retain free agent players by matching the best offer the player receives in the open market, the failure to do so will allow the player to sign with the new club making him the best offer. No compensation for the team losing the player through this free agency system will be provided. One thing for certain is that the outcomes of this rather bold experiment agreed to by the players and the clubs will be watched by many persons over the next five years. Several predictions as to the effects of this new system have been made, but the true test will not come until after the procedure has been in operation for some time. Basketball's new free agency system is much different than the one described for baseball in Chapter 3. These differences and the variance in outcomes of these two systems will most probably be the subject for much speculation and scholarly research and writing in the years to come. For now, one is left with the feeling that this new procedure probably will work quite well. And even if it does not, the players and owners have demonstrated previously a positive climate for labor-management relations that will probably extend at least through the end of this decade. Any and all problems that might arise in the context of the employment relationship would seem to be able to be resolved amicably through the process of collective bargaining. Both sides seem to believe that their differences can be worked out at the bargaining table, and hopefully this philosophy will continue into the future.

Unionism in Football

When we speak of the unionization of professional football players and the impacts that collective bargaining has had on the employment relationships in the game, it is extremely interesting to compare the important issues in football to the cases of baseball and basketball, discussed earlier in this chapter and in Chapters 3 through 5. As in basketball, the history of player attempts at organizing into unions is rather short in professional football. The first and only players' union in professional football, the National Football League Players Association (NFLPA) was formed in the year 1956.[15] While this new association was initially more of a social organization, many players were concerned with issues such as their lack of bargaining power, low salaries, and the option system employed in football (that is, a clause in every player's contract that allowed the team for which the player had played in the previous season to renew the player's contract for one extra year at not less than 90 percent of last season's pay). These concerns and others led the players to consider unionism as an alternative to the strict managerial control of all aspects of the game's employment relationships that had existed up to that time.

Shortly after this union was formed, an important Supreme Court ruling was handed down that in essence stated that the National Football League, unlike baseball, was subject to our nation's antitrust laws.[16] As we shall see in short order, the ruling in the Radovich case became the basis for several later challenges to the legality of the option and compensation rules that had been established in football over time.

The Radovich ruling led the owners to seek legislation in order to achieve the same type of protected status enjoyed by baseball.[17] Such legislation was never passed, but the hearings held in Congress on this issue had a big impact on the fledgling NFLPA. The NFL commissioner at the time, Bert Bell, testified before a House subcommittee that in fact, the NFL players did not require antitrust protection as they were already covered under the National Labor Relations Act for the purposes of collective bargaining. When asked by the chairperson of the subcommittee as to whether the NFL had recognized this players' union, Commissioner Bell was forced to reply yes. Thus the NFLPA initially gained informal recognition from the National Football League.[18]

This informal recognition proved rather meaningless as the owners continued acting as they had in the past, with the one exception being that they acquiesced to several of the player demands in the areas of minimum wages and injury pay in exchange for the players' dropping a threatened antitrust suit. As noted above, the NFLPA existed mainly as a "loose knit social organization"[19] from its inception until 1968.

Things started to heat up during the latter part of the 1960s when a football player named Bernard Parrish attempted to form a rival union. Parrish was dissatisfied with the NFLPA and was determined to organize a new union, which he called the American Federation of Professional Athletes (AFPA), to better represent the players' interests.[20] Interestingly, Parrish intended to have his union affiliate with the International Brotherhood of Teamsters in an effort to obtain the bargaining power associated with a strong national union. Although his efforts to convince the players to turn to the AFPA proved to be in vain, nonetheless, the mere threat of having to face the power of the Teamsters in collective bargaining with the players caused the owners suddenly to rethink their position on formal recognition of the NFLPA. It is reported that almost immediately upon hearing of this threat by the AFPA, the club owners officially recognized the NFLPA for the first time.[21] The Teamsters then withdrew from the fray,[22] and the time was set for an authorization card check. The idea behind such a card check is to make a formal National Labor Relations Board election unnecessary where only one union seeks to represent the workers in question and where a large majority of such workers have already indicated their interest in being represented by that union for the purposes of collective bargaining by signing authorization cards. As predicted, the card check went smoothly, and in March 1968 the owners formally recognized the NFLPA and the process of collective bargaining began.

Since the formal recognition in 1968, the owners and players have agreed to three collective bargaining pacts, the latest of which still remains in effect today. However, this period has been marked by a fairly hostile climate for labor-management relations as compared to that in the other major professional team sports. The signing of each of these contracts was prefaced with some type of concerted activity on the part of either the owners or the players. Prior to signing the initial contract in 1968, a ten-day strike and lockout occurred before the two sides were able to come to terms over a two-year contract. Essentially, this contract reduced to writing the unilateral changes that the clubs had made during the interleague war years.[23] The union had not made much progress except in placing these terms in writing in the first formal collective bargaining contract.

The first contract expired at the end of January 1970. Again, the players struck, and it took approximately seventeen months before the next contract was signed in June 1971. This contract was for a four-year period, and was back-dated to February 1970. Soon after the new contract was signed, the players hired Edward Garvey, a lawyer from the firm that represented the NFLPA in the 1970 negotiations, to be their executive director. Garvey's bargaining talents were to be severely tested in the years to come, especially in the next round of negotiations, which began in February of 1974. Despite a heavy bargaining schedule and direct intervention from William Usery, then director of the Federal Mediation and Conciliation Service, a third player strike could not be avoided. The strike began on July 1, 1974, and was to last for some forty-two days before both sides agreed to a two-week cooling-off period in an effort to make one last-ditch attempt to resolve the dispute. No resolution was accomplished, but the NFLPA voted to continue the cooling-off period indefinitely so that the 1974 playing season could be continued. In fact, a settlement on the third collective bargaining pact was not reached until March 1, 1977, a full three years after the earlier pact had expired. Thus, it took the players and owners three full years to hammer out the terms of a new, five-year pact, which expires at the conclusion of the 1981 season. These three years were marked by a turbulence heretofore unknown in labor relations in professional team sports. Besides the strike alluded to above, numerous unfair labor practice and antitrust law violation charges were filed by the players against the owners in an attempt to force them to bargain in good faith over wages, hours, and the like. It would take an entire book to review all of these charges and counter-charges and the eventual outcomes of the various issues through the process of collective bargaining. However, it is possible to review some of the major events so the reader can compare what has happened in football with what we have already observed in other sports.

Salary Arbitration

Salary arbitration has never been employed in professional football. From time to time, there has been some talk about switching over from the individual salary bargaining that is practiced today to some sort of a salary schedule determined by position. That is, all guards with five years of experience would earn a certain fixed dollar amount, and so on. To date, there has not been much player sentiment in favor of such a system, and so, individual salary bargaining prevails. Players in football have very few options available to them if they cannot come to salary terms with their respective teams. In essence, the lot of the professional football player has not been much different than that of his counterparts in baseball and basketball, discussed earlier. Players were bound to one team and were more or less forced to sign on the terms proposed by that team if they intended to continue playing football. One additional option the players did possess was the threat of league-jumping (to the American Football League up until 1966 and more recently to the now-defunct World Football League), which had a major impact in professional basketball labor-management relations. As was the case for basketball, these extra powers were important in furthering the causes of the professional football player for justice and fairness in many aspects of the employment relationship.

Grievance/Arbitration

In the realm of grievance/arbitration, football players for a long time lagged far behind players in other major team sports. In both baseball and basketball, impartial grievance/arbitration has been provided for through the process of collective bargaining. While some issues do remain outside of the scope of the grievance process, and therefore certain types of disputes are ultimately settled by the commissioner in each of these respective sports, the basic right of players to file grievances and in most instances to have them settled by an impartial third party has been firmly established. This was not so for the professional football player up until 1977. While earlier collective bargaining contracts in football did include a grievance/arbitration procedure, it was closely akin to the original system employed in baseball. That is, the "impartial" arbitrator for most cases was none other than the commissioner of the National Football League, Pete Rozelle. The argument of the team owners in football in favor of this nonneutral arbitration system was that the NFL requires a "strong" commissioner system in order to enable the league to avoid a scandal such as the one that plagued baseball in 1919. (The owners were referring to the Chicago "Black Sox" alleged fixing of the 1919 World Series with Cincinnati.) Why or how employing the commissioner as the arbitrator of grievance disputes would prevent such a scandal to occur in football remained somewhat of a mystery. The deficiencies with such a contrived system of neutrality have already been discussed in some detail. Suffice it to note here that this grievance procedure remained the source of a good deal of dissatisfaction among the players and the executive director of their union, Edward Garvey. It could safely have been predicted that this item would continue to be the subject of much heated discussion in future negotiation sessions between the club owners and the players.[24]

Prior to 1977 the football players had been able to achieve the right to use impartial arbitration in just one area, that of injury grievances. In this area a neutral third party could be called upon to render a final and binding decision as to whether an injury was in fact football-related or not. Management representatives were quick to point out that this type of grievance was far and away the most common type of dispute to arise in football, and thus the lot of the player might not be as bad as it would first appear. The impartial arbitrators in this type of injury grievance could rule on one and only one issue, whether a player's injury was football-related, which entitled him to continue receiving his full salary and benefit package, or due to, say, falling off a ladder while painting his home. In the latter case, the player would not continue to receive his customary salary payments. Even given their rights to use impartial arbitration to resolve injury disputes, it can readily be seen that the professional football player trailed his counterparts in both baseball and basketball in regard to the much broader interpretation of the sorts of issues that could be submitted to final and binding arbitration in these other sports. Only time will tell if football players will ever catch up. If they did, they would have the process of collective bargaining and the good faith negotiating efforts of both their union and the clubs to be thankful for.

The football players' lot in the realm of grievance dispute resolution improved drastically with the signing of the 1977 collective bargaining pact on March 1, 1977. Although they were quite a few years behind other athletes, they had achieved for the first time in the 1977 negotiations the right to use impartial arbitration to resolve player or club grievances. This system replaced the commissioner-arbitrator system described above. As in the other major sports, the new contract reaffirmed the commissioner's final and binding authority with regard to matters pertaining to discipline for conduct on the playing field and other matters relating to the integrity of the game. Thus, the professional football player too now has the protected right to file grievances and if necessary to have these grievances decided on their merits by an impartial person. We have seen how important such a provision has been in baseball and basketball, and there is no reason to believe that this newly won right will not take on a similar importance in professional football. The players had truly gained an important new right through the process of collective bargaining.

The Option-Compensation System and Free Agency

While the foregoing issues have been important, the single most crucial issue in the minds of most football players most certainly has been the option-compensation system employed in their sport. As we shall see, the players have been quite successful in bringing about several major changes to this system, which they deemed to be unfair and capricious. But before we can discuss the nature of these changes, a short history of the development and usage of the option-compensation system in football must be presented.

It all started in the early years of the game when a perpetual reservation clause similar to that found in baseball was included in each and every contract signed between a professional football player and a team in the National Football League. In 1947, this perpetual clause was replaced with a one-year option rule, which has appeared as paragraph 10 of the Standard Player Contract ever since.[25] This paragraph reads as follows:[26]

> *The Club may, by sending notice in writing to the Player, on or before the first day of May following the football season . . . , renew this contract for a further term of one (1) year on the same terms as are provided by this contract, except that (1) the Club may fix the rate of compensation to be paid by the Club to the Player during said further term, which rate of compensation shall not be less than ninety percent (90 percent) of the sum set forth in paragraph 3 hereof and shall be payable in installments during the football season in such further term as provided in paragraph 3; and (2) after such renewal this contract shall not include a further option to the Club to renew the contract. The phrase "rate of compensation" as above used shall not include bonus payments or payments of any nature whatsoever and shall be limited to the precise sum set forth in paragraph 3 hereof.*

Up until 1947, players could not become free agents, as they were owned in perpetuity by their teams. The option clause reprinted above and adopted in 1946 clearly limited this renewal period to one additional year after the expiration of the player's contract. This system operated for sixteen years. Under it, a player who had been reserved to his team for the one-year period became a free agent with no strings attached immediately after the completion of the option year. No compensation was provided for teams losing players through this process.

The Rozelle Rule

The owners received a sudden jolt in 1962 when R. C. Owens actually played out his option and switched teams from San Francisco to Baltimore.[27] This action set the fearful owners in motion to adopt some form of protective device for their precious player assets, and the result was the adoption of the so-called "Rozelle rule" in 1963. This provision stated that[28]

> Any player, whose contract with a League Club has expired, shall thereupon become a free agent and shall no longer be considered a member of the team of that club following the expiration date of such contract. Whenever a player, becoming a free agent in such manner, thereafter signed a contract with a different club in the league, then unless mutually satisfactory arrangements have been concluded between the two League clubs, the Commissioner may name and then award to the former club one or more players from the Active, Reserve or Selection List (including future selection choices) of the acquiring club as the Commissioner in his sole discretion deems fair and equitable; any such decisions by the Commissioner shall be final and conclusive.

Through the Rozelle rule the owners sought to protect their clubs from the potentially damaging loss of one or more star or otherwise free agent players. Owners could not prevent players from changing teams as the standard player contract clearly allowed the owners but one usage of the option clause. However, if a player did change teams, the owners were now guaranteed compensation for their losses. As in basketball, the first step in assigning compensation was to be an attempt on the part of the two involved teams to reach some mutually satisfactory arrangement. Barring this, the commissioner was empowered to assign current players or future draft choices to the former team in repayment for the loss of the free agent. As in basketball, the commissioner's decision as to the proper compensation due was final and binding. And, as we have seen was the case in basketball, in football the incredible amount of uncertainty surrounding the compensation award that the Commissioner might decide upon in any particular case caused most clubs to be very wary about bargaining with free agent players. As was the case in basketball, the one-year option system, with the uncertainty of the exact nature of the compensation that would be due to the former club, led to a situation where players had very little freedom of movement from team to team. Growing player resentment over this seemingly perpetual reserve system and the uncertainties of the Rozelle rule led to increased activity geared toward changing these rules. This activity took the form of collective bargaining, unionism, and legal challenges to the option-compensation system. While the ultimate changes did come through the collective bargaining process, the importance of several legal battles that served as a catalyst for this change process should not be minimized. Recall that the Radovich case had established that professional football was subject to antitrust prosecution. Thus it was that several players, dissatisfied with the inequities of the option-compensation system, took it upon themselves to go to court to challenge the legality of these provisions. Two of the most important cases in this area were brought forward by players Joe Kapp and John Mackey.

Joe Kapp was a star quarterback for the Minnesota Vikings who was dissatisfied with the salary he was being paid and decided to play out his option in 1969. Despite a fine season with Minnesota, no teams seemed particularly interested in signing him for the 1970 season, probably because of the uncertain compensation penalty that would face the signing team. Eventually, Kapp was signed by New England for the 1970 season after Minnesota and New England had come to terms over just compensation for the Vikings, a procedure provided for by the Rozelle rule. Since the two teams were able to agree on the exact nature of the compensation due the Vikings, no ruling from the Commissioner's office was necessary. But the case didn't end here. In fact, it was just beginning. Kapp was to be paid a very high salary for 1970 ($600,000), and he asked permission from the commissioner's office to delay signing of the standard player contract until such time as he could further study the tax implications of his higher salary. Such permission was granted and Kapp played the entire 1970 season with New England without having signed a standard contract. In 1971 Kapp again decided against signing a standard player contract. This time, Commissioner Rozelle ordered him to either sign a contract or refrain from playing the game. Kapp refused to sign and was ordered to leave New England's training camp.

It was at this juncture that Joe Kapp filed suit against the NFL for conspiring to restrain trade and monopolize football in direct violation of the federal antitrust laws.[29] Judge William Sweigert agreed in principle with Kapp's argument about the unfairness of the option-compensation system and stated that, "We conclude that such a rule imposing restraint virtually unlimited in time and extent, goes far beyond any possible need for fair protection of the interests of the club-employers or the purposes of the NFL and that it imposed upon the player-employees such undue hardship as to be unreasonable restraint . . ."[30]

For their part, the NFL club owners had argued that Joe Kapp's case should not be supported by the courts because of the so-called "labor exemption" to the antitrust laws. The NFL noted that it had entered into a good faith collective bargaining agreement with the NFLPA, and in that contract both sides agreed to the provision that all players must sign standard player contracts. Thus, Kapp was clearly violating the labor agreement and should have been forced by his union to sign a standard contract. Furthermore, the owners noted that the standard player contract was made part and parcel of the collective bargaining agreement (as we saw was the case in baseball, in Chapter 3) and thus, all of the rules challenged by Kapp were essentially agreed to by his union through collective bargaining. As such, they could potentially be revised through future rounds of negotiations. But since both sides agreed to these rules, the owners argued that the court should respect the labor exemption to the antitrust laws. Judge Sweigert disagreed with the owners on this point and noted that[31]

> . . . *even if the NFL Standard Player Contract requirement had been accepted through collective bargaining, there would still remain the question, well put by Marshall, J. in Flood . . . , as to what are "the limits to the antitrust violations to which labor and management can agree." We are of the opinion that however broad may be the exemption from antitrust laws of collective bargaining agreements dealing with wages, hours and other conditions of employment, that exemption does not and should not go so far as to permit immunized combinations to enforce employer-employee agreements which, being unreasonable restrictions on an employee's right to freely seek and choose his employment, have been held illegal on grounds of public policy long before and entirely apart from the antitrust laws.*

Thus, the Judge ruled that the option clause by itself was not unreasonable, but that in combination with the Rozelle rule, it did have the effect of perpetually restraining a player from pursuing his occupation.

Court Cases

In a similar case, U.S. District Judge Warren Ferguson issued a temporary restraining order barring the NFL from requiring Cullen Bryant of the Los Angeles Rams to report to the Detroit Lions. Commissioner Rozelle had ordered Bryant to report to the Lions as compensation to them for their loss of free agent Ron Jessie to the Rams. The Commissioner went along with this injunction and revised his compensation award to include two future draft choices instead of Bryant. At the time of this decision, Rozelle noted[32]

> *That trial (the Mackey case), for the first time in NFL history, produced a complete record of all relevant facts and arguments, both in support of and in opposition to the legality of the Rule. We believe a legal decision on an issue of this importance should be made only on the basis of a record of that nature. We are advised by counsel that it would be impossible to develop such a complete record in a prelimi- nary injunction hearing involving Bryant.*

Thus, Rozelle gave in on the Bryant case so that the final determina- tion of the legality of the Rozelle rule might be determined in yet another trial, involving player John Mackey.[33] In the Mackey case, the District Court was able to review the origins and history of the usage of the Rozelle Rule in the NFL. It was noted that through the time of the completion of the Mackey trial, there had only been four previous instances where Commissioner Rozelle had awarded some form of compensation to a team losing a free agent player to another team in the NFL. These four cases were:

1. *Pat Fischer*. Fischer played out his option year with St. Louis in 1967 and signed with Washington in 1968. Rozelle awarded St. Louis a second-round draft choice in 1969 and a third- round choice in 1970 as compensation.
2. *David Parks*. Parks played out his option with San Francisco in 1967 and signed with New Orleans in 1968. Rozelle awarded San Francisco player Kevin Hardy from the New Orleans ros- ter plus first-round draft choices in both 1968 and 1969 as compensation.
3. *Phil Olson*. Olson was declared to be a free agent because his former team, the New England Patriots, did not exercise their option for his services for the 1972 season in a timely fashion. Olson signed with Los Angeles and Rozelle awarded New En- gland a first-round draft pick in 1972, $35,000 in bonus and other expenses, and a third-round draft pick.
4. *Dick Gordon*. Gordon played out his option with Chicago in 1971 and was a free agent for 1972. However, intimidated by the uncertain nature of the compensation that would be re- quired should they sign Gordon, no team was willing to offer him a contract. In an unprecedented move, Commissioner Rozelle announced the compensation for Gordon in advance, after which he was immediately signed by Los Angeles. The

Chicago Bears received a first-round draft choice in 1973 in exchange for the loss of Gordon's services.

The court ruled that the Rozelle rule did in fact constitute a *per se* violation of our nation's antitrust laws. The NFL and all of its member clubs were enjoined from continuing to enforce the provisions of said rule. In effect, the rule had prevented players from having the freedom to move from team to team by imposing an uncertain penalty in the form of compensation decided by the commissioner upon the acquiring team. Evidence in favor of the strong anticompetitive nature of the Rozelle rule was found in the fact that since its inception, only four players had been able to switch teams. In all other cases, the player who thought he was a free agent was forced to re-sign with his prior club if he intended to continue to play football. The court ruled that the requirement of bilateral agreement between the two involved clubs over the nature of the compensation to be paid was in fact nothing more than a trade. Therefore, while the option-compensation system in football seemed to provide players with more liberal possibilities for movement from team to team, in practice it was really not better nor any different than baseball's perpetual reservation system. Based on these arguments, the United States District Court, Fourth Division for the District of Minnesota, ruled that the labor exemption that the owners had hoped for would not be granted and that the Rozelle rule was *per se* illegal. The NFL immediately announced their decision to appeal this ruling but a higher court affirmed the earlier decision. It is interesting to note that this decision from the Eighth U.S. Circuit Court of Appeals went so far as to offer the suggestion that[34]

> It may be that some reasonable restrictions relating to player transfers are necessary for the successful operation of the NFL. The protection of mutual interests of both the players and the clubs may indeed require this. We encourage the participants to resolve this question through collective bargaining. The parties are far better situated to agreeably resolve what rules governing player transfers are best suited for their mutual interests than are the courts.

The courts had made several things perfectly clear. First, the Rozelle rule as it stood was illegal and could not be forced upon the players by the NFL. The players had never had the chance seriously to bargain collectively over such a rule. It had been imposed upon them by the club owners to discourage player transfers from team to team, and it constituted a *per se* violation of the antitrust laws.

However, the Courts made no judgment as to the desirability of some form of restriction on player movement from team to team, where such procedure was negotiated in good faith and accepted by both sides at the bargaining table. Therefore, the way was left open for the players and the owners to resolve their differences over the free agency/compensation issue through the process of collective bargaining. And as we have seen in the above quotation from the Eighth Circuit Court of Appeals, the three-judge panel went so far as to strongly suggest that the process of collective bargaining and *not* the court system was the proper forum for the negotiated modification of the Rozelle rule. Rather than imposing some legally determined compromise, the judges offered to let the parties use the process of collective bargaining to work things out for themselves. And that is just what they did.

The Negotiated Compromise

A new five-year agreement was reached on March 1, 1977. Prominent among the issues contained in this new settlement was a negotiated option-compensation system to govern player transfers from team to team, which totally replaced the former compensation rules of the Rozelle era. The most dramatic of these negotiated changes included:[35]

1. The use of the former option clause was severely limited in future Standard Player Contracts to be signed between players and league clubs. This one-year renewal clause could still appear in all contracts of players who had three or fewer years of NFL experience. As in the past, the club was limited to a single exercise of this option for a single period of one year, after which time the player was to become a free agent.
2. All players with four or more years of experience could have the option clause removed from their standard contracts. It would only remain in their contracts where both sides agreed to keep it there. In essence, this meant that for veteran players, free agency could be achieved as soon as their current contract expired. No longer would they have to wait for the additional option year before they could test the free agency market.
3. The Rozelle rule was completely eliminated. No longer would the commissioner determine compensation for teams losing free agent players.

4. To replace the system of uncertain compensation and limited player freedom of movement, the NFL and the NFLPA adopted two new ideas, first refusal and an explicit compensation formula.

5. The idea of first refusal was pretty much the same as in the case of basketball. A former club was to receive one last chance to match a free agent player's best salary offer. If they did, they retained the player for the next season. If they did not match the offer, unlike basketball, they were not to be left empty-handed. Some compensation would still be provided.

6. The players and clubs decided not to abandon completely the idea of compensation for teams losing free agents. But rather than have to put up with the uncertainties that were prominent under the Rozelle rule, they decided to negotiate a specific compensation formula based upon the free agent player's salary in the forthcoming season. In this manner, every club thinking about signing a free agent would know exactly what penalty it would face. Compensation was to be provided in the form of future draft choices only. For instance, if the free agent's salary were in excess of $200,000, the new team signing this player would have to compensate the player's former team with two first-round draft picks. The compensation to be paid for other players was fixed on a sliding scale; for instance, the signing of a $55,000-a-year free agent would cost the acquiring club only one third-round draft pick. Heavier compensation was set for the loss of more highly paid and presumably better players than for average or journeymen ballplayers.

The players and the owners seemed to have accomplished exactly what the courts meant for them to do in negotiating a compromise set of rules to govern player movements from team to team to replace the former, unfair option system coupled with the Rozelle rule. The former system had been just as bad as baseball's perpetual reservation clause in that very few players could every truly become free agents and find out what their real market value was. Now, the stage was set through collective bargaining for an onslaught of free agents similar to that witnessed in baseball and expected in basketball beginning in 1981. Or was it?

While we only have observations for a limited number of players and years on which to base any preliminary conclusions, it is interesting to review briefly what has occurred in professional football since the adoption of the new option-compensation system in 1977. To say the least, player movement in professional football has been nowhere near as spectacular as that which we have witnessed and commented on in Chapter 3 with regard to professional baseball. But why should this be the case? What is it about football's system of free agency that has made its results so different from those in baseball? After all, weren't both systems agreed to through collective bargaining?

About the *only* similarity between the free agency systems in baseball and football is that both were the results of collective bargaining. After that, major differences arise in many aspects of the procedures themselves and the impacts these negotiated procedures have had on the players' freedom of movement. Since basketball's newer free agency system is not in operation yet, and therefore we have no comparative data on that sport, this discussion will be limited to a comparison of only baseball and football. The impact of the free agency system employed in hockey will be taken up in the next section of this chapter.

Compensation

The biggest single difference in the 1977 football free agency system as compared to the 1976 baseball system is in the area of compensation. Recall that baseball's contract specified a very minimal compensation award for teams losing free agents, a high school draft pick. These high school players rarely made it to the big leagues and even if they did, usually required a number of years of minor league training before they were ready to play professional ball. Thus, a professional baseball team signing a free agent player risked very little in terms of what it stood to lose in exchange, one player from the Amateur Draft. Compare this situation with what we have just described for football. Here, both sides agreed to a rather stiff system of compensation for teams losing free agent players. A team not willing to match a player's best offer was not out of luck, as we saw was the case in basketball. Rather, they were to be given, at worst, a third-round draft pick and, at best, two first-round draft choices from the acquiring club, depending on how much money the free agent player was to be paid for the upcoming season by the new team. These draft choices are in no way similar to those referred to in regard to the baseball case. Instead of seventeen- and eighteen-

year-olds fresh out of high school, players drafted in professional
football have usually completed their college education and, more
importantly, have had as much as four years of playing experience in
big-time collegiate football. Many are ready to step right into the
NFL and assume crucial starting or back-up assignments. Thus,
teams thinking about signing free agents must consider the losses
that they will incur. First of all, they must have the necessary draft
choices even to be able to sign a free agent player. For example, if a
team has already traded away all of its first-round draft choices for
the next three years, they will not be allowed to sign any free agents
for over $75,000 until that three-year period is over and they again
have a first-round draft pick. But even if a team does have all of its
draft picks remaining, the compensation formula and the potential
value of these first-, second-, and third-round picks will tend to
make teams very cautious in their dealing with free agents.

The evidence tends to support the theory of the cautious approach
to the signing of free agents in professional football. Some would go
so far as to suggest that things are worse now than they were under
the old Rozelle rule. However, it must be pointed out that no matter
how bad things appear to be at present, these rules, unlike the
former set of provisions collectively referred to as the Rozelle rule,
were agreed to by both parties through head-to-head negotiations.
As such, both sides are bound to live by these terms until the
current contract expires (after the end of the 1981 season). Only then
can the parties seek to renegotiate aspects of this new compensation
formula or other items in the collective bargaining contract that have
not proven to be satisfactory.

The evidence to date has shown that very few NFL players have
been able to switch teams under the new first-refusal/compensation
formula hammered out in the 1977 negotiations. First, it is true that
many players are playing out their options in order to become free
agents under the 1977 agreement. In each of the first two years
under the new system, there were over 100 free agents. Many of
these players received qualifying offers from their respective former
clubs (110 percent of the previous season's salary) and thus were
eligible for free agency under the first-refusal/compensation system.
However, only a very small fraction of this total number of players
were able to actually switch teams (four players in 1977). As noted
above, player movement is not much different than it was in the
Rozelle rule days. As in basketball, the element of compensation in
the football free agency package has inhibited player movement

from team to team. It is obvious that the baseball club owners would love to emulate the situation now existing in basketball and football; witness their recent proposals to add much stiffer compensation into the free agency formula in that sport. With the evidence now accumulated for basketball and football, it seems likely that such a move in baseball would severely limit player movement in what up to now has been a fast-paced open market.

Edward Garvey, executive director of the NFLPA, has accused the football team owners of conspiring not to sign free agents, an action that he claims is yet another violation of U.S. antitrust laws. Legal action was filed by Garvey on behalf of the NFLPA, but it does seem that since the players and their union agreed to the above described system through collective bargaining in and of their own free will, the system will be allowed to stand on its own merits at least until the expiration of the current collective bargaining contract following the end of the 1981 season. It is true that players are not moving from team to team, but the culprit seems to be excessive compensation rather than any conspiracy on the part of the owners. In baseball, where compensation is almost nonexistent, owners are in keen competition with one another to sign free agent players. Thus, although the football players do have a procedure for obtaining free agent status, it seems that their bargaining power has been severely limited by their willingness to agree to a compensation system that seems to have many of the trappings of the former Rozelle rule. Instead of the owners being uncertain as to the amount of compensation they will have to endure after signing a free agent player, as was the case under the Rozelle rule, today's owner knows exactly what the price tag will be; no uncertainty whatsoever is involved. However, certain or uncertain, the owners still realize that the signing of a free agent player will cost them a lot, both for the player and for the compensation for that player's old team. And thus, the players feel that same sort of disdain for the collectively bargained compensation system that they felt for the older Rozelle system. The outcome under both of these arrangements has been almost exactly the same, very little ability on the part of the players to transfer from team to team through the free agency route. This is not to suggest that their salaries have not gone up in response to the possibility of being able to change teams. Indeed, NFL salaries have increased, but whether because of the new option-compensation system or other factors is very difficult to assess. It does seem clear that salaries would have increased more had the players obtained the ability to switch clubs easily without harsh compensation provisions, as is the case in baseball.

Summary

We have seen how the professional football player has struggled to obtain rights similar to those enjoyed by other athletes. Only recently has he obtained a grievance procedure with impartial arbitration to replace the former system where the commissioner, an employee of the owners, served as the arbitrator. Additionally, the football player has never enjoyed the privilege of using salary arbitration as have his counterparts in professional baseball. Finally, we have seen how the football player has had to struggle through three strikes, numerous unfair labor practices, the Rozelle rule days, and more in order to achieve a modified option-compensation system through collective bargaining. Several teams were accused of firing star players on account of their unionization activity in this regard. These unfair labor practice charges were sustained and several players were made whole, but how can a court ruling ever be able to replace several prime years in an athlete's career in which he was unable to participate on account of such managerial actions? But the courageous actions of a few players seemed to have paid off in 1977 when a new contract replaced the Rozelle rule with a newer option-compensation system. However, at least for the time being, the high hopes of the players seem to have been for naught. Possibly because of an excessive amount of compensation provided for in the contract to teams losing free agent players, very few players have been able to change teams under the new procedure. Some attention has been given to the charge of a conspiracy among the owners to avoid signing free agents, but this theory would be very hard to prove. In fact, it does seem likely that the basic factor inhibiting the development of a much more brisk free agent market in football, like the one witnessed in professional baseball, is the high payment in terms of compensation that teams signing a free agent player must render to the player's former team. Such high compensation scares most potential bidders out of the market.

Thus, it does seem a bit ironic but true that the very system which the players won through collective bargaining and which was supposed to emancipate them has in fact proven not to be much more to the players' liking than the old Rozelle rule. But that is the nature of collective bargaining: sometimes you gain a little more, other times you gain a little less. While in football it seems to be clear that in the 1977 negotiations the latter was the case, at least the two sides were able to reach an agreement that at the time was agreeable to both parties. Even though the relations between the players and the owners in professional football have been far from amicable and trusting in nature, at least the two sides have been able to get together and somehow work out their differences through collective bargaining. No one is predicting that future negotiations or relations between the parties will be easy. Overnight changes simply can not be made in a relationship filled with some hostility and bitterness on both sides. Collective negotiations and labor relations in professional football can be expected to retain many of the features of open hostility and warfare that have been hallmarks of the past. But all is not gloomy. At least, the parties are talking, and hopefully, through the process of collective bargaining will be able once again to solve their major employment differences and perhaps, cement a better relationship for all times. Only time will tell. For now, the fan of professional football can only wait and watch to see what will occur in the negotiations that will ensue following the Superbowl in January of 1982. It should be interesting.

Unionism in Hockey

The final sport that we will consider in this chapter will be professional hockey. Players in professional hockey first turned to unionism in the late 1950s in order to obtain funding for player pensions from league television revenues. The owners at first refused to meet with players and their union, claiming that since they dealt with teams in two countries (the United States and Canada), negotiations with a players association would be impossible. For their part, the players hired attorney J. Norman Lewis to represent them (the same attorney who had successfully represented baseball players in their attempts to have World Series and All-Star game revenues contributed to their pension plans). Lewis filed an antitrust suit in 1957 in order to force the National Hockey League (NHL) to meet with representatives of the new players union, the National Hockey League Players Association (NHLPA).[36]

Formal recognition of the NHLPA did not come until ten years later, in June 1967. As was the case in the other sports we have discussed, hockey players came to be represented by a union for the purposes of collective negotiations over several aspects of their employment relations that were unsatisfactory to them. The very same issues that were at the root of employer-employee relations problems in the sports of baseball, basketball, and football were also to be in the limelight in professional hockey.[37]

Grievance/Arbitration

Professional hockey players today have a grievance/arbitration system very similar to those we have already described with respect to baseball, basketball, and football. As in these other sports, players did not always have the right to file grievances and have them decided by an impartial neutral. In fact, for many years after the founding of the NHL in 1917, the final arbiter of all disputes was none other than the president of the NHL.

This situation by now sounds all too familiar to the reader. Since the president was and is an employee of the club owners, the crucial aspect of neutrality was missing in grievance handling for many years. Why would a player ever bother to file a grievance when he knew that the final decision would always come from management? Apparently most hockey players realized what the answer to this question was; very few complaints were ever filed.

All of this changed with the advent of unionism and the signing of a formal collective bargaining pact in 1976. Formal procedures for the orderly handling of player and club grievances were provided, which included binding arbitration as a final step.[38] This grievance/arbitration process is quite similar to those described for baseball, basketball, and football in that two basic types of disputes are considered. One type deals with the question of the severity of any discipline or penalty meted out to a player by his club or any dispute over the interpretation of the Standard Player Contract, the NHL constitution or bylaws, or any league rule. In these cases, while grievances certainly may be filed, the president of the National Hockey League is empowered to make a final and binding decision on all such items at dispute. This is very similar to the commissioner-arbitrator procedure used in baseball, basketball, and football to resolve issues involving the integrity of the game and the like. In each sport, some issues were always reserved to managerial rights, and even with unionism, a grievance procedure with impartial arbitration over all issues of contract interpretation and the like has yet to be achieved.

The second type of grievance in hockey can be filed over any other dispute as to the interpretation of the provisions of the collective agreement (with a few minor exceptions such as medical arbitration and salary arbitration, each of which proceeds under a separate arrangement). For these disputes, impartial arbitration is provided for upon the demand of either party. The collective bargaining contract specifies provisions for timely filing of grievances, selection and payment of arbitrators, and time frameworks for the various steps in the grievance procedure, and imposes standard limitations on the arbitrators in the sense that they are prohibited from adding to, subtracting from, or otherwise altering the provisions of the Standard Player Contract, NHL bylaws, collective bargaining contract, and so forth.

Salary Arbitration

In and of itself, the right to file grievances and have them determined by an impartial arbitrator constituted a substantial gain for the players through collective bargaining. But this was not to be the only usage for arbitration that the players were to gain. Since the 1969 season, players in the NHL have also had the right to demand salary arbitration, much the same as their counterparts in baseball. Thus, of the four major sports that we have considered, only players in professional hockey and baseball have enjoyed the right to demand salary arbitration. Recall that the right to employ salary arbitration in baseball was in a significant manner responsible for the salary gains that the players made for the years 1974 and 1975, and most likely, ever since as well. With the positive impact that we have witnessed in baseball, is it safe to assume that the same has been true in the realm of professional hockey? Has the hockey player benefited in a similar fashion from the implementation of salary arbitration?

These questions are particularly hard to answer because of the lack of pre- and postarbitration salary data in hockey coupled with the fact that to date, no one has performed a study that answers or even begins to address such a set of questions. Nonetheless, it is instructive briefly to review the history of hockey's salary arbitration procedure and the mechanics of the process so as to be able to make some comparisons with baseball. The lack of salary data prevents us from presenting any empirical estimates as to the impacts of the availability of salary arbitration in hockey. Hopefully, this issue will be addressed in the near future by someone well trained in scientific inquiry. For now, our discussion must by necessity be institutional in nature.

The first mention of the possibility of using arbitration to resolve salary disputes in professional hockey came back in 1969. In this case and in all other instances hereafter, salary arbitration was contemplated only for those players who were subject to the provisions of the reserve rule in the standard player contract, which ever since the year 1958 had stated that[39]

> *The player hereby undertakes that he will at the request of the club enter into a contract for the following playing season upon the same terms and conditions as this contract save as to salary which shall be determined by mutual agreement . . . .*

A 1969 Task Force on Sports in Canada reported unfavorably on several aspects of this reserve clause and in effect recommended that it be abolished in that the clause tended to force players to give their services indefinitely to the club that first signed them to a professional contract. Of course, the players were very much in favor of this recommendation; while the owners, understandably, were reluctant to make any major changes to the system.

Impartial Arbitration

Finally, in an effort partially to offset the wave of criticism that was encircling the reserve rule as encompassed in paragraph 17 of the Standard Player Contract, the NHL and the NHLPA agreed in June 1969 to allow salary arbitration over the exact amount of compensation due to a player under paragraph 17. Players in their option or reserve year could have their salaries determined by an impartial arbitrator. After that year, they would be free to sign with any team in the NHL for the best salary they could negotiate. This, the first salary arbitration procedure, provided that each party to the dispute could choose an arbitrator, and that if these two persons could not resolve the dispute, the two arbitrators could then choose a mutually agreeable third arbitrator who would render a final and binding salary award.

After this system had been in operation for two years, the owners and players agreed in 1971 to a modified salary arbitration system to be instituted for a two-year trial period. The major difference between this system and the earlier one was that a single arbitrator, Edward J. Houston, was chosen to hear all salary disputes arising under paragraph 17 of the Standard Player Contract. The players and owners agreed to let the president of the NHL (Clarence

Campbell at that time) and the executive director of the NHLPA (Alan Eagleson) choose the arbitrator to employ to resolve such disputes.[40] This second procedure (referred to as the 1971 Arbitration Agreement) was extended with minor modifications in 1972 for a period of three additional years. The same arbitrator, Edward J. Houston, was retained during the life of the so-called 1972 Arbitration Agreement. Finally, the idea of salary arbitration was formally incorporated into the 1975 collective bargaining pact between the parties in the form of Article X.[41] As a procedure to help resolve salary disputes that might arise concerning paragraph 17 of the Standard Player Contract, salary arbitration has been available in hockey for some eleven years. The courts have ruled that this salary arbitration procedure was negotiated in a *bona fide*, good faith manner. However, the courts have also ruled that this procedure encompasses but one sentence in the entire reserve clause found in paragraph 17. Thus, just because salary arbitration was the subject of good faith negotiations from the beginning does not imply that the entire reserve clause was subject to the same type of *bona fide*, good faith negotiations.[42] As we shall see shortly, this became one of the bases upon which hockey's reserve rule was to be challenged by several players attempting to jump to the World Hockey Association.

The salary arbitration procedure contained in the 1975 collective bargaining agreement is in many ways similar to that employed in baseball and described in detail in Chapter 4. Either a player or a club may invoke salary arbitration and the case is heard before a single arbitrator, Gary E. Schreider, who has the final and binding authority to specify the player's salary for the option year. The decision of the arbitrator is binding on both parties. The contract clearly lists permissible evidence at the hearing (overall performance, number of games played, length of service, and the like) and also specifies that the financial position of the club involved in the case shall not be taken into account in determining the compensation of the player. Parties share the expenses of arbitration equally and the contract specifies provisions for replacing Mr. Schreider should this become necessary.

Comparison to Baseball

The two major differences in this procedure from that we have discussed for baseball players revolve around the issues of who is eligible for arbitration and how the arbitrator makes his decisions.

Recall that in baseball's current contract, players with between two and six years of experience are eligible to invoke arbitration. Clubs may also invoke salary arbitration. Players with over six years in professional baseball may use salary arbitration only if their clubs agree to such usage. In essence, salary arbitration is basically reserved to those players who have not yet accrued enough seniority to allow them to take advantage of baseball's free agency system. In hockey, only players who are in the option year of their contract may invoke salary arbitration. There seems to be no limit to the number of times any particular player or club can invoke the procedure so long as in each case the player is in his option year. Recall that this notion of salary arbitration was invented in response to the Task Force's criticisms of the unfairness of salary bargaining which took place under paragraph 17 in the option year. It was hoped that by allowing a neutral person to determine the player's salary in his option year instead of doing it by executive fiat as in the past, some semblance of fairness could be restored to the system.

The second major difference between baseball and hockey's salary arbitration schemes lies in the flexibility granted to the arbitrator in rendering the final awards. In baseball, the arbitrator is bound to pick only one or the other of the two final positions presented to him, either the club's final offer or the player's final demand, as the salary award. This system leads to good faith negotiations by both sides in an attempt to avoid having to use arbitration. The bargaining incentives associated with final-offer arbitration have been shown to be important in the empirical results presented in Chapter 4. The salary arbitration system employed in hockey is a more conventional arbitration procedure, as opposed to final-offer arbitration. The arbitrator in a conventional system usually has a large amount of flexibility at his disposal in the award-making process. If presented with final positions of a club and one of its players that were, say, $80,000 and $110,000, respectively, the arbitrator could decide on either of these two positions, or any wage in between these two. In fact, if the arbitrator felt the player was really worth $120,000, nothing would prevent him from making that figure the final award. Compare this system with final-offer arbitration where the neutral would have been restricted to choosing only between $80,000 or $110,000. In Chapter 4, several advantages and disadvantages of each of these systems were discussed, and such efforts need not be repeated here. However, it should be pointed out that in theory, conventional arbitration should lead to a higher impasse rate (more usage of the procedure) as both sides inflate (deflate) their true positions in order to leave the arbitrator with positions from which he can compromise. The lack of true bargaining incentives associated with conventional arbitration, when compared with final-offer arbitration, would lead one to predict that in hockey, salary arbitration should be quite common.

Having said this, we should briefly note that there are several problems associated with trying to test the above hypothesis. First is the problem of data nonavailability. One first needs access to data such as the total number of players eligible to use arbitration, the number of players actually using arbitration, salary awards, and the like before any meaningful testing can be done. And then, even if the data is available, the problem of comparability crops up. If we know the impasse rate in hockey (number of players using salary arbitration/number of players eligible to use arbitration), just what does that tell us? Is an impasse rate of .31 high, low, or medium? And compared to what? Just because we have an impasse rate of .31, is that necessarily due to the nature of conventional arbitration or could other factors have just as equally well accounted for this observed phenomenon? How do we go about controlling for these other factors?

It seems that we should compare hockey's impasse rate with that of baseball or other domains using final-offer arbitration. But even if we do, we can never be sure that we have controlled for the myriad of other factors which may be partially responsible for any observed differences. Because all field studies in this area have suffered from this same set of problems, several authors have turned their attention to laboratory research. In order to answer the above questions, a focus is needed on *programmatic research,* where both field and laboratory methods are employed. For now, about all we can say is that we know very little about the impacts of professional hockey's salary arbitration procedure on either the process or outcomes of salary bargaining. Comparatively speaking, professional baseball's final-offer salary arbitration procedure has been fairly well studied to date. It is not clear exactly why this great disparity exists in the research literature. Hopefully, in the next few years researchers will provide us with the careful kinds of analyses of the impacts of hockey's salary arbitration procedure that we currently have available for baseball. When that occurs, we will have proceeded a long way toward our goal of answering many of the complex questions posted above.

The Reserve System and Free Agency

The final major change brought about through the process of collective bargaining in professional hockey to be discussed in this section is in the area of player reservation and free agency. To begin with, the scenario is very similar to what we have become familiar with in the three other major professional team sports. The NHL initially forced every player in the league to sign a Standard Player Contract which contained a perpetual reservation clause similar to those employed in other sports. Prior to the year 1973, every player's contract had such a provision in it. Part of this provision from paragraph 17 of the Standard Player Contract was reprinted earlier in this chapter. The reader will note the perpetual nature of the wording in this clause. If a player and club could not agree to terms over salary through bilateral negotiations, the club had the right to invoke the paragraph 17 procedure, year after year if necessary. Recall that one of the early changes to this procedure occurred in 1969 when both sides agreed to insert a few extra words at the conclusion of paragraph 17, which in essence allowed either side to request salary arbitration to resolve such a dispute. Thus, step one was the club's notification to the player that because of a salary bargaining impasse, they were invoking the reserve clause (paragraph 17) in the player's Standard Contract, which required that player to play for the same club in the next season, if he were to play hockey at all. Prior to 1969, salary bargaining ensued and the player could only hope to get the best possible wage outcome. In truth, the only real choice the player had was to accept his club's last best offer and continue to play hockey or retire. Ever since 1969, step two has involved the added possibility of invoking the salary arbitration procedure, in which case an outside party will determine the exact salary to be paid to the player for the upcoming season. In either case, the clubs argued that the player, once reserved for a particular year, again had a signed contract that contained a paragraph 17 provision and could be reserved for another year, and another, ad infinitum.

As in the other major team sports, professional hockey players soon grew tired and suspicious of this system, contrived by the owners to limit player mobility and hold their salaries below what they would have been in a competitive market. Dissatisfaction with the perpetual reserve rule was a major factor that led to the unionization of professional hockey players. As in basketball and football, players in hockey had several other aces up their sleeves besides unionism and collective bargaining. Specifically, in 1971 a rival league known as the World Hockey Association (WHA) came into existence. The coming of this new league brought with it inter-league player bargaining wars similar to those witnessed in football and basketball. Players attempted to jump leagues in an effort to increase their salaries. When they did, the owners in the NHL attempted to strike back by claiming that such player actions violated the provisions of the Standard Player Contracts each player in the NHL had signed. But here is where the players used their other ace, as several of them proceeded to go to the courts and charge the NHL with violation of U.S. antitrust laws through the usage of the aforementioned paragraph 17 language. As we shall see shortly, both of these actions were to prove extremely successful for the players.

As soon as the WHA got organized, a high-priority item on their list of things to do in order to achieve success and stability was to raid the NHL. Owners in the WHA sought to lure NHL players over to their newer league with much higher salary offers than these players were accustomed to receiving for playing hockey in the NHL. Several star players took the bait. One early case involved Boston players Gerry Cheevers and Derek Sanderson, who decided to forego playing with Boston in favor of signing with the Cleveland Crusaders of the WHA. The NHL owners in general, and the Boston Bruins management in particular, were not willing to take the loss of two such reputable players lying down. Instead, they decided to take the matter to court and hoped that a judge would uphold the binding nature of the paragraph 17 language. In essence, they were looking for a ruling that would bar NHL players from jumping to the WHA based on the perpetual nature of the reservation system in the NHL Standard Player Contract. What they got instead was a ruling that hinted that professional hockey's reserve clause, in conjunction with other agreements such as the NHL bylaws, in fact violated the antitrust laws.[43] Thus, Cheevers and Sanderson were permitted to jump leagues in complete disregard of their NHL player contracts. A second ruling permitted Edward Hampson to change leagues from the NHL's New York Islanders to the WHA's Minnesota Fighting Saints.[44]

Finally, the crucial blow was struck when Judge Higginbotham erased the NHL reserve clause from player contracts altogether by ruling that it was clearly in violation of the Sherman Antitrust Act.[45] In this ruling, the judge noted that the perpetual reserve clause had never been the subject of good faith collective bargaining. Rather, it was imposed upon the players by the club owners and as such, it did not qualify under the labor exemption to the antitrust laws. Furthermore, the judge noted that the clause, in conjunction with NHL bylaws and minor league rules, enabled the NHL to monopolize professional hockey and severely limit free trade. Thus, the perpetual reserve rule was struck down for all time.

But the owners were not through yet. Based on these unfavorable decisions, the club owners announced in late 1973 that henceforth the perpetual reservation system was to be replaced by a one-year option clause in all standard player contracts, quite similar to that used in professional football. Teams could no longer reserve players into perpetuity but instead, for only one added year after their contract had expired. This new rule was incorporated as part of the collective bargaining agreement of 1975 referred to earlier. Thus, both sides had put their seal of approval on the newer, more flexible reserve rule. Players who wished to play out their option year must sign a Player's Option Contract, while clubs no longer desiring a player's services may tender them the so-called Player's Termination Contract. Both of these contracts must be for a period of one year, and salary is fixed at the previous season's wage. If neither party takes the action noted above, the two sides may enter into a new Standard Player Contract by mutual agreement or, failing such agreement, they may enter into a new one-year Standard Player Contract where the salary to be paid to the player is determined through the salary arbitration procedure discussed earlier.

Compensation

One other important aspect of the 1975 collective bargaining pact was the incorporation into it of the National Hockey League bylaw Section 9A, dealing with *Free Agents and Equalization*.[46] This provision was adopted on November 27, 1973, by the club owners and was incorporated into the collective bargaining agreement in 1975 by mutual consent of the owners and the players. In essence, this bylaw reasserted the right of NHL players to become free agents able to bargain with any team in the NHL after having played out their option season. However, the club owners were of the opinion that even if free agency was allowed to occur, such a system should not be allowed to cause irreparable harm to the various NHL clubs. Thus, a system was devised for equalization or compensation (as we have referred to it before) for teams losing free agent players. In part, this provision governing equalization reads as follows:[47]

> *Each time that a player becomes a free agent and the right to his services is subsequently acquired by any Member Club other than the club with which he was last under contract or by any club owned or controlled by any such Member Club, the Member Club first acquiring the right to his services, or owning or controlling the club first acquiring that right, shall make an equalization payment to the Member Club with which such player was previously under contract, as prescribed by subsection 8 of this By-Law. Each Member Club may acquire the right to the services of as many free agents as it wishes, subject to the provisions of subsection 9 of this By-Law.*

As in other sports we have examined, an attempt must first be made between the two involved clubs to settle on some agreeable amount of compensation for the club losing the free agent. If the two clubs cannot arrange a settlement within three days of the signing of the free agent, the whole matter of equalization then goes to an arbitrator. Interestingly, in this situation, the parties have chosen to adopt the final-offer arbitration procedure. That is, each side must submit to the arbitrator what it considers to be the fairest compensation award in the particular case. The arbitrator must then select, without change, one of the two final proposals submitted to him as the equalization award. The bylaws specify that the parties' final positions and the arbitrator's award can consist of players, draft choices, and, as a last resort, cash. As was the case for salary arbitration, no data is currently available from which to evaluate the effectiveness of this equalization/arbitration system. Hopefully, it will be the subject of future research in the realm of labor relations in professional sports.

While there is not much to report in the way of theoretical or statistical analyses of the impacts of this equalization procedure, there have been several interesting legal developments in this area since 1975, the most crucial of which involved a player named Dale McCourt. The problem began when the Detroit Red Wings signed free agent goaltender Rogie Vachon from the Los Angeles Kings in 1978. The teams could not come to terms on equalization, and the matter went before an arbitrator, as specified in the bylaws of the NHL. The Red Wings offered Los Angeles William Lochead and

James Rutherford as their final position before the arbitrator. But the Kings demanded Dale McCourt as compensation. Unfortunately for McCourt and the Detroit Red Wings, the arbitrator sided with the Los Angeles Kings and awarded McCourt to them as compensation for their loss of Vachon. However, McCourt filed an appeal of the arbitrator's ruling in court, arguing that the NHL rules governing compensation for free agents constituted illegal restraint of trade under the Sherman Act. In what was believed to be a landmark ruling at the time, U.S. District Judge Robert DeMascio agreed with McCourt and issued a temporary restraining order allowing McCourt to stay in Detroit instead of reporting to Los Angeles.

Interestingly, the suit filed by McCourt was against the Los Angeles Kings, the Detroit Red Wings, and the NHLPA. McCourt contended that the procedures that labor and management had agreed to through collective bargaining for free agency and equalization were unfair and in violation of the antitrust laws. Apparently, Judge DeMascio agreed in substance with these claims. Thus, as of September 1978, the NHL's free agency/compensation system seemed to be in a state of limbo.

But then, some eight months later, a federal appeals court in Cincinnati reversed the lower court's decision and ruled that McCourt would have to report to the Los Angeles Kings as the arbitrator originally had prescribed. In a two-to-one decision, the Sixth U.S. Circuit Court of Appeals ruled that the NHL reserve clause did not violate the antitrust laws. While the former court had argued that the reserve rule was never the subject of good faith negotiations, the Appeals Court emphasized the principle that nothing in our nation's labor laws requires either party in negotiations to yield on its original position. This court found that the reserve clause had been the subject of good faith negotiations and was, as such, placed into the collective bargaining contract between the NHL and the NHLPA. It was thus immune from the antitrust laws.

Obviously, McCourt and the NHLPA were very upset by this decision. McCourt had to report to Los Angeles and all other players in the NHL were to be bound by the provisions of paragraph 17 and bylaw 9A for the foreseeable future. This simply meant that free agency in the NHL would not be quite as free as that variety practiced in baseball. Rather, more like football and basketball, the hockey free agency market was to continue to be marked by the uncertainty of just which final position the arbitrator would pick as the fairest equalization payment. As in football and basketball, we can predict that this uncertainty factor will dampen the free agency market in hockey quite a bit, as compared to what we have witnessed for baseball. We can also predict that the hockey players and the NHLPA will continue to try to attain a free agency system that does away with equalization while the NHL owners will react in just the opposite manner. For it is to their advantage to maintain the current system in that it clearly limits player mobility and holds down salaries from what they might have been, given a completely free system.

Summary

The major gains professional hockey players have made through unionization and collective bargaining have been extensive. In many respects, hockey players today enjoy the same benefits that are by now customary in baseball, basketball, and football. Grievances can be filed and in many cases submitted to impartial arbitration for final adjudication. Additionally, players and clubs involved in a paragraph 17 salary dispute may seek to have this issue resolved through salary arbitration. Finally, hockey players have been able to force the NHL and its member clubs to revise the former perpetual reservation system into a one-year option procedure. From the players' standpoint, a problem still remaining with this system is the method of equalization, described above, which tends to limit player movement from team to team because of the uncertain penalties involved for teams signing free agent players. This uncertainty causes many teams to stay out of the free agent market altogether and, therefore, salaries have not gone up as much as might have been expected. But all in all, hockey players have fared quite well through collective bargaining. Both sides have problems with the current collective bargaining pact and would like to be able to change certain aspects of it. And that is what collective bargaining is all about, the give and take that occurs between two parties over various issues on which initially, at least, they have diametrically opposing interests. The two sides in hockey have shown that the process of collective bargaining has in fact worked for them in the past and it can be predicted that the same will probably hold true for future disputes over various aspects of the employer-employee relationship.

The Unionization of Officials

So far in this chapter, we have discussed the unionization attempts, successes, and failures of professional basketball, football, and hockey players. Previous chapters in this book have been devoted solely to the inroads made by the professional baseball player through unionization and the process of collective bargaining. While it is certainly true that the actions of these various player groups have been spectacular and quite noteworthy, it would be shortsighted on our part simply to end our story here. For other groups in professional sports have also heard the rally cry of unionism. One of the groups of employees that has received by far the most attention in recent times has been the professional sports official. A brief review of the activities of sports officials in regard to unionization and collective bargaining will be presented at this time. The two groups of officials to be discussed here include baseball umpires and basketball referees, the only two such groups to have adopted unionism and collective bargaining in recent years. For the time being at least, football and hockey officials have not attempted to unionize. The football situation is fairly easy to understand. Most football officials have full-time jobs elsewhere as doctors, lawyers, judges, and the like, and spend only one afternoon per week for approximately sixteen weeks in the capacity of an official; they are truly part-time employees of the NFL. Historically, part-time employees have been very difficult for unions to organize, and the case is no different in football. These officials are fairly well treated by the NFL and moreover, since all of them have other full-time jobs at which they presumably earn respectable salaries and derive many other fringe benefits, there really is no perceived need for a union of officials. Thus, it can be predicted that no matter what gains the baseball umpires or basketball referees might achieve through unionism, these football referees will be in no hurry to follow in the footsteps of their counterparts and adopt unionism and collective bargaining.

The case of the professional hockey referee is a bit harder to explain. These referees are more akin to the baseball umpire and the basketball referee in that they are employed as officials on essentially a full-time basis for at least six months out of every year. Yet, to date hockey officials have not chosen to unionize. One can only speculate as to the reasons for this phenomenon. Perhaps hockey officials are paid so well and treated so fairly in all aspects of their dealings with the NHL that they perceive no great need for or advantages from unionization. In any event, a fertile area for future research would be to look at the differences among the employment relationships enjoyed by officials in the four sports treated in this book and thereby try to explain the various patterns of interest in unionization among them. Until such research is conducted, the best we can do is to describe what has occurred to date in those professional sports where officials have turned to unionization.

Baseball Umpires

Not long after the professional baseball players had entered into their initial collective bargaining contract with the National and American Leagues, umpires in professional baseball also tried to get into the act. After having viewed the gains made by the players through collective bargaining, the umpires decided that maybe they too could profit from associating with a union for the purposes of collective bargaining over wages, hours, and other terms of employment. A major test came in December 1969 when a unit of American League umpires filed a petition under section 9(c) of the National Labor Relations Act, asking the National Labor Relations Board (NLRB) to assert jurisdiction over them and hold a certification election to determine the desires of the umpires with regard to the question of unionization. If such an election were to be held, each umpire would have the choice of indicating whether or not he wished to be represented for purposes of collective bargaining over wages, hours, and the like by a union. If a majority of the participating umpires voted in favor of unionization, the NLRB would then certify their union as the exclusive bargaining agent for all umpires in the unit. Management (the leagues) would then be legally bound to sit down and negotiate wages, hours, and conditions of employment in good faith with this union. Whereas the leagues had previously set all such terms on a unilateral basis, unionization of the professional umpires would mean that henceforth, such terms would have to be bilaterally agreed to through the process of collective bargaining.

The owners were not willing simply to capitulate to the demands of their umpire/employees for recognition. Instead, in the hopes of retaining their unilateral decision-making powers, the owners contested the right of the umpires to bargain collectively on several grounds. For instance, the owners argued that because of baseball's internal self-regulation through a system of rules interpreted by the commissioner of baseball, a labor dispute in baseball was not likely to have much of an effect on interstate commerce. Additionally, they felt the NLRB should decline to assert jurisdiction over the baseball umpires based on the 1922 Federal Baseball Club decision discussed in Chapter 3. It was also argued that the umpires' association was not a true labor organization within the meaning contemplated under the National Labor Relations Act, section 2(5), and finally, that the umpires were not covered under the law in any event because they were supervisors and not employees. Despite this impressive array of arguments, the NLRB found merit in none of them and ordered an election to be held. It should be noted that one member of the NLRB dissented from the opinion of his colleagues and would have dismissed the petition for an election on the grounds that professional baseball had only a very minimal impact on interstate commerce.[48]

The First Strike

Since the umpires were found to be covered under the National Labor Relations Act and their union, the Association of Major League Umpires (AMLU), had been chosen as the exclusive bargaining agent for these umpires in a formal NLRB certification election, collective bargaining between representatives of the two sides soon began. Early relations between the parties were marked by some degree of hostility, and in fact, the first strike by baseball umpires occurred on the opening day of the 1970 league playoffs in Pittsburgh and Minneapolis, and was triggered by the umpires disgust over not having won a contract. The work stoppage lasted but one day, yet neither was it to be responsible for the elimination of all of the umpires' complaints nor was it to be the last usage of the strike weapon by umpires in professional baseball.

Relations between the parties seemed to be in a state of limbo until March 1977 when representatives of the AMLU and both the National and American Leagues agreed to a formal collective bargaining contract. The agreement was negotiated by attorney John L. Cifelli for the umpires, and it was to be in effect until the last day of 1981. About one year into the contract, the umpires replaced Cifelli with Richie Phillips, who had quite a bit of experience in this area, as he was the founder of the National Basketball Association Referees Association, which will be discussed shortly.

The Second Strike and Its Aftermath

Upon taking over in baseball, Phillips found that the umpires were very unhappy with the five-year contract negotiated by Cifelli. Many of the umpires felt that they had been deceived, and that the contract was silent on many important issues that should at least have been addressed through face-to-face collective bargaining. The mounting uneasiness and anger on the part of the umpires led them to stage their second strike, a one-day walkout on August 25, 1978. Every one of the fifty-two major-league umpires participated in this brief strike, the purpose of which was to focus attention on some thirty issues that the umpires felt should have been the subject of collective negotiations. In essence, these umpires wanted to re-negotiate a collective bargaining pact that still had some three years to run. This was not very likely to occur, but the umpires sincerely felt that the contract had been signed by Cifelli without their approval.

The presidents of the American and National Leagues, Lee McPhail and Charles Feeney, respectively, reacted to the strike by seeking a court order forcing the umpires to return to work. This order was granted and by August 27, 1978, all fifty-two umpires were back at their jobs. Both sides continued hurling charges and countercharges during the remainder of the 1978 season, but in truth, the season ended without much additional fanfare. The court had ordered the umpires back to work based on the fact that they all had signed contracts at the start of the season and were bound by the rules of the collective agreement as signed by Cifelli.

But things were just starting to heat up. In December 1978, all major league umpires received a copy of their contract for the 1979 playing season. Usual protocol was for each league to grant its umpires some minor increases in pay as represented by the terms of the mailed contract. Each contract was for a one-year period, and salaries were derived from minimum salary schedules contained in the Basic Agreement and were supplemented by any merit increases the leagues wanted to offer.[49] What the two leagues were soon to find out was that about a month earlier, in November 1978, all of the major league umpires agreed not to sign these individual contracts.

Rather, all of these contracts were sent unsigned to Phillips, who was to represent all of the umpires in salary negotiations. By February 2, 1979, not a single contract had been returned to the leagues. With the spring training season just weeks ahead, both leagues sent a second contract to each umpire along with a fairly strongly worded statement to the effect of "sign this contract or lose your job." Both leagues stressed that the failure on the part of the umpires to sign these individual contracts was in fact a violation of their collective bargaining contract.

In mid-March, the two major leagues decided to take this matter to court, hoping that the judge would reinstitute the injunction from the previous fall, which barred the umpires from striking. After all, the beginning of the season was only days away, and a strike was starting to look more and more like a real possibility. Substitute umpires were already being used during spring training, and contingency plans were being drawn up in case of a strike. But it was hoped that through court action a last-minute ban against a regular-season strike could be obtained.

U.S. District Court Judge Joseph McGlynn ruled on March 27, 1979, that he lacked any authority to order the umpires back to work for a second time. In the previous fall, each umpire was working under a signed individual contract and, as an employee of baseball, was bound by the no-strike terms of the collective bargaining agreement. But all that was different for the time being. The 51 umpires in question in March of 1979 (one umpire had previously signed a two-year contract and was bound to report to work) were no longer employees of baseball, as they had not signed their individual contracts for the 1979 season. Thus, there was no way in which they could be ordered back to work at the present time.

As the regular major-league season began on April 4, 1979, only two of the total number of 52 umpires had signed contracts. One umpire, Ted Hendry, had signed a two-year pact much earlier and returned to work under this contractual obligation. Additionally, Paul Pryor decided to sign his contract on April 2, 1979, and he also returned to work, criticized by his fellow umpires as being a "scab" to their cause. The two leagues had to hire a mixture of minor league and other amateur umpires to work the regular-season games while the regular umpires were forming picket lines outside many ball parks, attempting to bring their situation to the attention of the baseball fan. In essence, the umpires demanded higher salaries, higher *per diem* expense allowances, grievance/arbitration in their collective bargaining contract, a five-man umpiring crew, and a three-week vacation sometime during the regular season. As might have been expected, these proposals received a rather cool reception from the two league presidents.

The position of the umpires was strengthened somewhat on April 7, 1979, when Paul Pryor decided to join his fellow umpires on the picket lines. He was forced to return to work for ten days to fulfill the termination period specified in his contract, but after that, he too joined the ranks of the strikers. And to make it unanimous, Ted Hendry, the only remaining regular umpire, also served his ten-day notice on the league. When he joined the picket lines shortly thereafter, not a single regular umpire was working regular-season games. This was quite a show of solidarity on the part of the umpires and certainly had to be noticed by both the American and National Leagues. It seemed that their choices were either to continue the season with amateur umpires or to renegotiate the 1977 collective bargaining pact with their regular umpires. The leagues wisely chose the latter route.

Negotiations with the striking umpires proceeded for over a month during the regular season. During this time, there was much criticism of the replacement umpires who were, after all, doing the best jobs they could under the trying circumstances. And this criticism was just the type of publicity the striking umpires wanted to see. Nothing could further their cause more than a lot of controversy by fans, players, and the media over the poor umpiring that was going on down on the playing field. A settlement was finally announced on a new three-year contract on May 19, 1979, after the strike had lasted for a full month and a half during the regular season of play. The umpires were able to secure higher salaries and higher *per diem* payments, as well as increased contributions to their pension fund and, finally, an in-season vacation. All in all, both sides left the negotiations feeling that they had a good contract. Even though an older contract had not yet expired, the umpires had been able to force the leagues to renegotiate with them and were able to secure this new, much improved contract. The major problem under this new contract to date has been the treatment of the strike-breaking umpires. During the strike, the leagues hired several top-notch minor-league umpires through promises of higher salaries and no-cut contracts. These umpires remain on the job to date and, to say the least, are not well regarded by the regular umpires, each of whom worked his way up to the big leagues through effort and fine umpiring. The strike-breakers, on the other hand, reached the major leagues only because of the regular umpires' strike. Each umpiring crew contains one of these newer umpires, and hard feelings still abound. While the umpires seem to work together effectively on the field, off the field it is entirely another matter. The regular umpires refuse to have any contacts with the strike-breakers, whether it be at meal time, in pregame locker room conversation, or the like. It certainly looks as though the situation described above will not be resolved quickly or easily. Both sides have lingering feelings of hostility toward one another, and the group of strike-breaking umpires will continue to bear the burden of this hostility. Only time will tell how this situation will eventually work itself out. Aside from this one problem, the umpires and leagues seem to have been able, for now at least, to resolve the most serious of their employment disputes through collective bargaining. Once again, collective bargaining is seen to have been an effective tool for resolving disputes over wages, hours, and the like in the realm of professional team sports.

Basketball Referees

Even earlier than their counterparts in baseball, basketball referees began thinking about the possible benefits they might accrue from unionization. Many years of frustration seemed to come to a head toward the conclusion of the 1976–1977 regular playing season. It was at this time that the referees decided to play their trump card. With the NBA playoffs scheduled to begin on April 12, 1977, the 26 NBA referees decided to test their bargaining power by demanding more money, better pensions, multiyear contracts, grievance/arbitration, and the like. Representing the referees in the presentation of these demands was the same Richie Phillips who we have seen was responsible for the successes the umpires were able to attain through collective bargaining.

Phillips and his union decided to take action at just the right time, when their bargaining power was at its peak. The NBA could hardly afford to cancel the most exciting part of their season, the playoffs. Or could they? And if they chose to run the playoffs as usual, they would have to use regular referees. Or would they? Wouldn't substitute, minor league referees officiating in the playoff games cause many potential problems? Could these substitutes keep control of the games? The world was awaiting the answers to these questions, and they were soon to be provided. The playoffs were scheduled to begin on April 12, 1977.

Prior to the start of the playoffs, the referees decided to take their case to the National Labor Relations Board (NLRB), charging that the NBA had committed an unfair labor practice by refusing to bargain collectively with them over salaries and the like. Remember that the referees brought up the subject of bargaining in late March of 1977. The position of the NBA was that they first wanted the referees to participate in a formal NLRB certification election to see if the majority of the officials did indeed wish to unionize. Only then would they bargain with these referees as a group. Of course, this bargaining would take place after the regular season and playoffs had been concluded. It does seem likely that this was a bit of a stalling tactic on the part of the NBA as they already were aware of the fact that 24 of their 26 officials (a majority indeed) were not going to work the playoffs if negotiations didn't commence in short order. The two veteran officials who wanted no part of the union and were willing to work in the playoffs as usual were Richie Powers and Earl Strom.

The owners' strategy proved to be ineffective as the referees voted 24–0 in favor of a strike. Meanwhile, the NBA made arrangements to have the playoffs officiated by Powers, Strom, and a fleet of Eastern League officials. Both sides continued to hurl verbal jabs at each other while waiting on an NLRB ruling in their case. However, a formal NLRB ruling was never to come.

The strike began on April 10, 1977, two days prior to the start of the playoffs, with neither side seeming to be too interested in making any sort of concessions. The NBA held steadfastly to its position of not being willing voluntarily to recognize the referees' union, the National Association for Basketball Referees (NABR). Many persons thought this stance to be rather curious as the NBA had previously agreed voluntarily to recognize the union representing its players, the NBA Players Association.

The NABR was banking on the prospect of the televised playoff games getting out of control under the handling of the amateur referees. If this occurred, tremendous pressure would be placed on the NBA to settle with their regular referees in order to get them back to work for the remainder of the playoffs. This strategy did seem to work as several games were extremely rough, and fights did break out on the playing floor. NBA management representatives were quick to point out that these fights were not the fault of the amateur referees, and that pressure-packed playoff games often led to fights even with the regular referees. Additionally, there had been fighting during the regular season as well, all of which games were worked by members of the NABR. But mounting player, coach, and fan resentment seemed to be turning the tide in favor of the referees. At one point during the strike, the accusation was made that the NBA had tried to lure several of their senior officials back to work with promises of big money contracts. The NBA denied that they had undertaken any such action, but whether this really occurred or not, the bad publicity they received from this alleged incident further added to the players' bargaining power.

Negotiations proceeded, and after a sixteen-day strike, a settlement was announced by the NBA and the NABR on April 26, 1977. Everyone, including the officials, seemed to be very happy that the strike was officially over and that the remaining playoff games would now be worked by veteran NBA officials. For their part, the officials had won recognition of the NABR as their exclusive bargaining agent and the provision that all NBA referees had to pay dues to the NABR. Additionally, they achieved a $150 across-the-board wage increase for all games worked. In exchange, the referees agreed to a no-strike pledge, and both sides dropped all pending legal actions against one another. This interim agreement was to serve as the basis for the continuation of negotiations on a formal collective bargaining pact to begin after the playoffs had ended. Such bargaining was conducted in good faith by both sides and today, as is the case in baseball, the NABR has a formal collective bargaining arrangement with the NBA. It is expected that this relationship will grow and mature as the parties realize that instead of trying to resolve their problems through open warfare and legal actions, bilateral negotiations conducted through the process of collective bargaining are much to be preferred. Given this type of an attitude on both sides, it can be predicted that we are just seeing the beginning chapter of a rather long-standing, and hopefully amicable and productive, relationship between the NBA and the NABR.

Conclusions

In this chapter, we have turned our attention away from the baseball player to consider momentarily the unionization attempts of players in other major team sports such as basketball, football, and hockey. Additionally, we have briefly touched upon the recent unionization of baseball umpires and basketball referees.

For players in basketball, football, and hockey, we have seen how unionism came about through resentment over and dissatisfaction with many of the same aspects of their employer-employee relations that led baseball players to turn to unionism many years ago. In each case, perhaps the single most compelling issue was that of player reservation. After creating the history of unionization in each sport, an attempt was made to review the history and current status of three issues, grievance/arbitration, salary arbitration, and free agency. Similarities and differences among the various sports with regard to these three issues were discussed. All of the sports currently have similar grievance/arbitration procedures, though arrived at in different manners and at different times. Additionally, it was noted that only baseball and hockey currently employ salary arbitration; but even these two systems are very dissimilar in nature. Finally, it was noted that all of these sports moved from an earlier position of perpetual reservation of players to much easier access to free agency through collective bargaining, legal battles, and the like. Although these newer free agency systems are very different in many ways, perhaps the most crucial distinguishing characteristic is the compensation required to be paid to teams losing free agents. Only baseball requires minimal or no compensation, and only in baseball have free agents enjoyed the type of mobility and much higher salaries that in theory such a system should bring forth. In each of the other sports, compensation is required for teams losing free agents. The nature of such compensation has been either so heavy or so uncertain as to preclude many teams from entering the bidding for free agent players. Thus, in basketball, football, and hockey, while players can obtain free agency rights, in practice they aren't all that much better off as new teams are afraid to sign them because of the threat of excessive compensation. Players in these other sports have not really benefited all that much from free agency, and it can safely be predicted that future negotiations will focus squarely on attempts to rectify this situation. In this vein, it will be particularly interesting to watch for the impacts of basketball's new free agency system with no compensation, to be instituted after the 1981 season.

Finally, we traced the history and current events surrounding the unionization of baseball umpires and basketball referees. Each group now has a formal collective bargaining pact in which many former unilateral decisions on the part of the respective leagues are handled through a joint decision-making process known as collective bargaining. Each group has had to employ the strike tactic to achieve its goals, but hopefully in the future, the parties will be able to resolve their differences through less spectacular means.

Thus, it can be safely concluded that unionism and collective bargaining are not unique to professional baseball among the various team sports. Unionism has spread to basketball, football, hockey, and many other team and individual sports. These unionization attempts often are on the part of the players of these sports, but as we have seen, are just as likely to involve officials or other types of employees in the professional sports industry. All in all, collective bargaining has come a long way in professional team sports, and many would argue that it still has a long way to go.

Endnotes

1. Erwin Krasnow and Herman Levy, "Unionization and Professional Sports," *Georgetown Law Journal*, 51 (Spring 1963), pp. 749–764.
2. *National Basketball Players Association Agreement*, entered into April 29, 1976, between the National Basketball Association and the National Basketball Players Association, pp. 16–20.
3. *National Basketball Association Uniform Player Contract*, paragraph 22, in Martin E. Blackman, *Representing the Professional Athlete*, New York City, Practicing Law Institute, 1976, pp. 205–211.
4. James B. Dworkin and Thomas J. Bergmann, "Collective Bargaining and the Player Reservation/Compensation System in Professional Sports," *Employee Relations Law Journal*, 4 (Autumn, 1978), pp. 241–256.
5. *Lemat Corp.* v. *Barry*, 275 Cal. App. 2d 671, 80 Cal. Rptr. 240 (1969).
6. *Central New York Basketball* v. *Barnett*, 19 Ohio Op. 2d 130, 181 N.E. 2d 506 (Ct. of Common Pleas, 1961).
7. *National Basketball Players Association Agreement, op. cit.*, pp. 28–46.
8. *Robertson* v. *National Basketball Association*, 389 F. Supp. 867 (S.D.N.Y., 1975).
9. For a review of the events leading up to this compromise see Lionel S. Sobel, *Professional Sports and the Law* (New York: Meilen Press, Inc., 1977), p. 839; also consult Lionel S. Sobel, "The Emancipation of Professional Athletes," *Western State University Law Review*, 3 (Winter, 1976), reprinted in Martin E. Blackman, *Representing the Professional Athlete* (New York City, Practicing Law Institute, 1976), pp. 9–46.
10. *Agreement, op. cit.*, p. 28.
11. *Ibid.*, pp. 38–39.
12. *Ibid.*, pp. 39–40.
13. *Ibid.*, p. 40.
14. *Ibid.*, pp. 40–41.
15. Note that players in the now defunct American Football League (AFL) were also unionized.
16. *Radovich* v. *National Football League*, 352 U.S. 445 (1957).

17. Sobel, *op. cit.*, p. 275.
18. *Ibid.* The interested reader might also enjoy reading through the transcripts of the Hearings on H.R. 5307 before the Antitrust Subcommittee of the House Committee on the Judiciary, 85th Congress, 1st Session (1957).
19. D. S. Shulman and B. M. Baum, "Collective Bargaining in Professional Athletics—The NFL Money Bowl," *Chicago Bar Record*, 50 (January 1969), p. 175.
20. Bernard Parrish, *They Call It a Game* (New York: Signet, 1971), p. 230.
21. *Ibid.*, p. 262.
22. Shulman and Baum, *op. cit.*, p. 175.
23. Thomas J. Bergmann and James B. Dworkin, "Collective Bargaining vs. the Rozelle Rule: An Analysis of Labor-Management Relations in Professional Football," *Akron Business and Economic Review*, 9 (Summer, 1978), pp. 35–40.
24. Barbara D. Dennis and Gerald G. Somers, eds., *Arbitration of Interest Disputes*, Proceedings of the Twenty-Sixth Annual Meeting, National Academy of Arbitrators (Washington, D.C.: The Bureau of National Affairs, Inc., 1974), pp. 119–137.
25. Bergmann and Dworkin, *op. cit.*, p. 36.
26. *Standard Player Contract for The National Football League, op. cit.* Blackman, pp. 212–218.
27. Bergmann and Dworkin, *op. cit.*, p. 36.
28. *Constitution and By-Laws for the National Football League*, 1975, Article 12, Section 1(H).
29. *Kapp v. National Football League*, 390 F. Supp. 73 (ND. Cal. 1974).
30. *Ibid.*
31. Sobel, *op. cit.*, p. 319.
32. *Los Angeles Times*, August 2, 1975, Part 3.
33. *Mackey v. National Football League*, 407 F. Supp. 1000–1007 (D. Minn. 1975).
34. John Mackey et al. v. National Football League et al., No. 76-1184, United States Court of Appeals, Eighth Circuit (October 18, 1976).
35. See the *Collective Bargaining Contract Between the National Football League and the National Football League Players Association, effective March 1, 1977*, Article XV. The exact compensation formula is as follows:

Player Signed For	*Compensation to Previous Team*
$ 50,000– 64,999	Third-round draft choice
$ 65,000– 74,999	Second-round draft choice
$ 75,000–124,999	First-round draft choice
$ 125,000–199,999	First-round *and* second-round draft choices
$ 200,000 and up	Two first-round draft choices

36. Dan Parker, "The Hockey Rebellion," *Sports Illustrated*, October 28, 1957, p. 19.
37. Sobel, *op cit.*, pp. 274–275.
38. *National Hockey League–National Hockey League Players Association Collective Bargaining Agreement, effective September 15, 1975*, Article IV, entitled, "Grievance Procedure and Arbitration," pp. 3–5.

39. *Philadelphia World Hockey Club, Inc.* v. *Philadelphia Hockey Club, Inc.*, 351 F. Supp. 462 (E.D. Pa. 1972), p. 479. It was also noted herein that some sort of a reserve clause has been in effect in the NHL ever since 1952 (p. 474).
40. *Ibid.*, p. 480.
41. *Collective Bargaining Agreement, op. cit.*, Article X, pp. 12–14.
42. *Philadelphia World Hockey Club, op. cit.*, p. 482.
43. *Boston Professional Hockey Association* v. *Cheevers*, 348 F. Supp. 261 (D. Mass.), remanded, 472 F. 2d 127 (1st Cir. 1972).
44. *Nassau Sports* v. *Hampson*, 355 F. Supp. 733 (D. Minn. 1972).
45. *Philadelphia World Hockey Club, op. cit.*, p. 518.
46. *Collective Bargaining Agreement, op. cit.*, pp. 34–37.
47. *Ibid.*, p. 35.
48. See *The American League of Professional Baseball Clubs and Association of National Baseball League Umpires*, Petitioner, 180 NLRB 190 (December 15, 1969).
49. *Agreement Between the National League of Professional Baseball Clubs and the American League of Professional Baseball Clubs and the Association of Major League Umpires, effective March 1, 1977*, pp. 5–6.

Chapter 7

SUMMARY, CONCLUSIONS, AND FUTURE PROSPECTS

This book has traced the development of unionism in professional baseball from the late nineteenth century until the present, stressing both the accomplishments and failures that occurred along the way. The first two chapters dealt extensively with the historical aspects of the union movement in baseball; surprisingly, it was found that unionism has had long roots in the game of baseball. Also somewhat surprisingly, it was noted that many of the very same problems that led ballplayers to form the MLBPA in the year 1954 were crucially responsible for many of the earlier attempts at unionization. In Chapter 1, after a theoretical and empirical discussion of why workers join unions, we focused in on four early and unsuccessful attempts at unionization in baseball, beginning with the formation of the National Brotherhood of Professional Baseball Players in 1885 and ending with the rather rapid demise of the American Baseball Guild in 1946. But the demise of this latter union did not signal the end of the modern day baseball players' interest in unionization and bettering his employment conditions; the so-called "representation plan" dreamed up by the owners did little to smother the mounting flames of resentment the players had regarding the reserve system, salary bargaining, and other aspects of the employment relationship within the game of baseball. Thus, a fifth union was established in 1954. This union, formally known as the Major League Baseball Players Association, was the topic of the second chapter of this book. In this chapter, the history and formation of the MLBPA were discussed, along with a treatment of the significance of the leaders of this union to its ultimate success. Several reasons were suggested to explain why the MLBPA achieved long-lasting success whereas its predecessors had all been doomed to a less than successful fate. Unionism had finally arrived in professional baseball for good, and our attention was then turned to the impacts of unionism on the employment relationship in the game of baseball.

The farthest-reaching change, the modification of the reserve system that had been a hallmark in baseball since the late nineteenth century, was the subject of Chapter 3. Baseball's antitrust exemption had rendered futile many attempts by the players to have this system modified through the courts. It was only through collective bargaining that the players were finally able partially to dismantle the long-standing reserve system and mold instead the modified reserve system that is in effect today. The implementation of a grievance procedure with impartial and binding arbitration has been crucial in this area. Had it not been the right of players such as Andy Messersmith and Dave McNally formally to challenge the perpetual nature of baseball's reserve clause through the grievance procedure, it is quite likely that the former reserve system would still be in existence today. The Seitz decision of December 1975 changed all that. The players had won their cases and were declared to be free agents. Rather quickly, labor and management representatives were able to negotiate a compromise six-year reserve plan, with features such as the reentry draft and free agency status, as described in detail in Chapter 3. Some of the impacts of the new system of free agency in such areas as player salaries and player performance were also discussed. The single most important change brought about through collective bargaining in baseball was the modification of the reserve rule that had existed for some 90 years.

But that was not the only major change to occur. In Chapter 4, we reviewed the history of the implementation of grievance and salary arbitration schemes in professional baseball. The players didn't have much of a grievance procedure under the representation plan, where they had no voting privileges and all final decisions were left up to the commissioner of baseball, an employee of the owners. A more traditional grievance procedure was accepted by both sides in 1968, with one major unconventional element. The owners insisted on using the commissioner of baseball (William Eckert) as the arbitrator for those cases that could not be resolved bilaterally. The players, realizing that they had made many other gains in the negotiations, decided to go along with the owners' proposal and accept this as a foot-in-the-door philosophy. They would then actively pursue cases all the way to arbitration to make their point clear about the nonneutrality of this supposedly impartial arbitrator. In any event, impartial arbitration was not a strike issue in 1968. After just a few cases, the owners fired Eckert (for reasons other than his arbitration performance), and both sides agreed to hire their first truly neutral arbitrator. A succession of neutrals have served baseball, with perhaps the farthest-reaching decision being rendered in the Messersmith/McNally cases decided by Peter Seitz. Several other cases were discussed in Chapter 4, and the importance of a grievance/arbitration procedure was stressed. It is only through this procedure that the players have both the right to challenge decisions made by their clubs that they feel are unfair and the potential to have these disputes adjudicated by a neutral person.

Grievance/arbitration was but one form of arbitration adopted by the parties through the process of collective bargaining. Perhaps equally important was the adoption of final-offer arbitration to resolve interest disputes over salaries beginning with the 1974 season. While this type of a procedure had been discussed earlier in baseball, as a potential cure for the inequality of bargaining power between players and clubs due to the reserve rule, it wasn't until 1973 that the owners formally placed this proposal on the table. The parties agreed upon a variety of arbitration known as final-offer arbitration. Chapter 4 described the procedure and presented a thorough look at the participants since its inception. Finally, the impacts of the threat of final-offer salary arbitration both on the process and outcomes of bargaining were discussed. Theoretical issues were backed up with empirical evidence, which in most cases tended to support our original hypotheses regarding the effects of final-offer arbitration. Also, a theoretical treatment of how arbitrators in baseball make their decisions was presented along with empirical evidence supportive of the so-called parity theory and the predictability of outcomes of these awards. In both Chapters 3 and 4, recent events in the collective negotiations of 1980 were highlighted insofar as they impacted upon the several key issues discussed in these chapters. In the case of compensation as we have seen, key decisions have been delayed and hands are yet to be played out, with a strike deadline of May 29, 1981 staring both sides in the face.

Chapter 5 discussed the other changes in the employment relationship in the game of baseball brought about through collective bargaining. These issues are usually broken down into monetary and nonmonetary benefits. While the argument has been made that changes in the reserve rule and the implementation of grievance and salary arbitration were the three most important player gains through collective bargaining, one must not lose sight of the many other significant gains achieved through bargaining. While none of these was discussed in great detail, the most prominent of these items were called to the readers' attention: significant changes in the employment relationship in the areas of pensions, minimum wages, scheduling, expenses and expense allowances, moving allowances, termination pay, allocation of World Series and League Championship Series pools, spring training conditions, and the like. In each case, an attempt was made to stress the importance and nature of these changes following upon the heels of collective bargaining.

In Chapter 6, our attention was momentarily turned away from the setting of professional baseball to consider the employment conditions and unionization attempts of professional athletes in other major team sports. While one could speak of unionization in sports such as golf, bowling, soccer, auto racing, and the like, our concern was focused strictly on players in professional basketball, football, and hockey.

While none of these sports was treated in any great depth (indeed, each sport's bout with unionism could be the topic of a book by itself), we did highlight the major events leading up to unionism in each area and reviewed some of the major union-won gains. Similarities and differences between negotiated provisions in these other sports and professional baseball were noted where appropriate. One of the striking findings was that each sport has had very similar problems with its handling of employment relations over time and in each case, these problems to a great extent precipitated the drive among the players to unionize. For example, some type of a player control system was employed in each of these sports, and as player resentment grew over time in opposition to this lack of freedom of movement and bargaining power, they turned to unionism as one means of solving these problems. A comparison of the relationships that have evolved in these major sports has led us to conclude that, at least for now, the most mature labor-management situation that has evolved is in professional baseball.

Finally, some mention was made of the growing trend toward the unionization of umpires and other persons employed to officiate these sporting events. While hockey and football officials have not moved to unionize, baseball umpires and basketball referees both now have collective bargaining contracts with their respective leagues and have had to resort to the strike tactic (much as the players have done) to convince management of their seriousness about their demands for changes in the employment conditions that affected them. Some mention was made of the reasons why some officials (baseball and basketball) have unionized while others have not, and some ideas for future research on this subject were presented.

All in all, much material has been covered in a rather small number of pages. Hopefully, by now the reader will have gained an appreciation for the major role that unionism has played in professional sports, and in professional baseball in particular, in the last fifteen years. Given this brief overview of the major issues discussed in the body of the text, it seems appropriate that we now draw several tentative conclusions about the nature of the labor-management relationship in professional baseball that we have witnessed evolving in the past several chapters.

Conclusions

One important thing to remember is that unionism in baseball is not a new phenomenon, introduced to the world by Marvin Miller and the Major League Baseball Players Association in the middle 1960s. The only real new thing about the MLBPA is that they have been successful in bringing about changes in the game's employment relationship, whereas their predecessors had no such good fortune. But, and this is an important point, the seeds of discord in baseball have been visible for a very long time. The early unions were concerned in some cases with the very same issues that have concerned the MLBPA in recent years. However, they simply lacked the power and/or legal basis to pull off significant changes. But management should have been aware for a very long time that a large number of players were dissatisfied with some of the rules of employment in the baseball game.

Secondly, it should be remembered that the successful nature of the MLBPA was due to a combination of factors noted in Chapter 2, including good leadership, favorable legal climate, and mounting player resentment. Any attempt at framing a simple, unicausal explanation for the phenomenal success the players have had at the bargaining table is doomed to fail.

Third, in the opinion of this author, the three most crucial gains won by the players have been in the implementation of grievance and salary arbitration and in the modification of the reserve rule that had plagued the players for many years. While we do not want to belittle the many other bargaining gains achieved, these three items seem to represent the central core of crucial employment changes. The reader is reminded to consider the fact that none of these changes would have been achievable without the give-and-take negotiations made possible through the process of collective bargaining.

Fourth, as we have seen in Chapters 3 and 4, all of these major changes brought about through collective bargaining have had major impacts on the bargaining power relationship between the club owners and the players (through their union). Simply put, collective bargaining in baseball has greatly enhanced the bargaining power position of the players of the game. As noted in an earlier chapter, Congress affirmed in the enactment of the National Labor Relations Act of 1935, and reaffirmed in the Labor Management Relations Act of 1947, the importance of the principle of equalized bargaining power to promote stable and healthy employment relationships in industry. One of the major conclusions of this book is that unionism in baseball has been responsible for redressing a situation where power was terribly skewed in favor of the owners and thus has been able to bring about the much more mature, healthy, and stable employment relationship that exists in the game today. Problems still remain that will need to be worked out, but the same can be said for any bargaining situation. The crucial point is that the parties have now evolved into a functioning labor-management relationship within which any and all such issues can be dealt with.

Fifth and finally, we have noted that unionism is not unique in professional sports to baseball players, nor is it limited to the participants in these various professional team sports. Parallel developments in the unionization of basketball, football, and hockey players have been witnessed in recent years. Additionally, baseball and basketball referees are represented by unions for the purpose of collectively negotiating contracts dealing with issues such as wages, hours, and conditions of employment. Thus, while the baseball experience with unionism was the primary concern of this book, one should be aware that this phenomenon has not occurred in a vacuum.

Given these conclusions, what might one expect for the future of labor-management relations in professional baseball? Are the teams doomed by the higher salaries and greater bargaining power brought on by the many changes in employment conditions due to collective bargaining? Can the sport survive the test of fan loyalty when superstar players regularly are able to become free agents and change their stripes in the pursuit of more money? Are there any significant gains left for the union to seek? Will the club owners seek to negotiate so-called buy-backs, that is, attempt to regain some of their former powers by returning to the rules of a previous era through thoughtful and skillful negotiations?

These and many other questions regularly pop up in newspaper accounts and in fan discussions centering on the game's employment relationship. While it would certainly require a good crystal ball to foretell accurately exactly what might happen in the years to come, one can at least hazard to make some tentative predictions about the likely state of affairs in the future.

The Future

Unionism in baseball has accounted for several significant changes in the game's employment relationship over time. Undoubtedly, further changes will be forthcoming as the parties' relationship continues to grow and mature. It would be pure speculation to try 'to address the areas in which these changes might take place; however, neither the players nor the clubs seem to be perfectly happy with the reserve and free agency system as it now exists. As noted, the players desire even more liberal free agency rights with little or no compensation provided to clubs losing players through this route, while the owners would prefer to tighten up the requirements for free agency and make compensation mandatory. As we have seen in other sports, heavy or excessive compensation dulls the appetite of teams considering whether to bid for a free agent player's services as they can never be quite certain just what player or monetary penalty (or both) might be imposed upon them. Thus, in both basketball and football, where compensation exists and can be quite heavy, we have witnessed very little player movement from team to team. Compare this situation with the robust free agent market now existing in baseball (described in Chapter 3) and it is easy to realize why baseball players reject the notion of compensation. And it is just as easy to see why the club owners would prefer to enact more stringent rules for the acquisition of free agency rights and at the same time mandate substantial compensation for teams losing a player to another club through the free agency mechanism. While many issues will continue to receive high priority in future bargaining discussions, none would seem so likely a candidate for first place on the list than the free agency system. Indeed, as of the writing of this book, negotiations between the players and clubs continue on this issue alone, and the fate of the 1981 championship season may well depend on the outcome of these talks. No matter what the resolution may be in 1981, it seems clear that this issue will be one of prime concern for both sides into the forseeable future.

As noted above, unionism in baseball is here to stay. It has become an institution in the game of baseball, and any attempt by the owners to break the union or by the players to decertify their union seems highly unlikely; and even if such an event would occur, the probability of its success seems very low. The players in baseball have simply benefited too much from their union to be willing to let management destroy it or destroy their union themselves. Industrial relations theory tells us that workers join unions when they perceive a need or a set of needs that a union might be able to fulfill. Players in baseball long ago felt this need, and the MLBPA has stood alone in its successful negotiation of provisions that have served to better the players' lot in a variety of contexts. It would seem highly unlikely that the players would ever consider a return to the pre-MLBPA days of league president and commissioner domination of their sport. The days of unilateral decision-making power on the part of the club owners in the areas of wages, hours, and conditions of employment are gone forever. They have been replaced by a system of bilateral negotiations covering all issues in this broad area, and one can reasonably predict that this tradition of bargaining out differences between club owners and players in these areas will continue for some time to come.

One might note that the mere institutionalization of the process of collective bargaining in baseball, or in any industrial setting for that matter, will not necessarily imply that the parties enjoy a particularly harmonious and productive relationship. Much of the determination of the usefulness of collective bargaining is necessarily due to the way management responds to the union challenge. If management fights the union at every step of the way and essentially refuses

to accept its legitimate role, one type of a rather acrimonious relationship will develop. On the other hand, where management is
willing to accept the union as a full and equal partner in the business
of handling the employment relationship, a much different and more
positive type of relationship will evolve. It is much to the credit of
the baseball club owners that they have collectively chosen to engage in the latter type of response to unionism. The owners realized
that the MLBPA was chosen by the players to represent them in
collective bargaining negotiations over wages, hours, and the like.
Given this understanding, each side will naturally have their own
positions and desires with respect to the various items that are
brought up at the bargaining table. However, the differences of opinions over matters related to employment are at the very heart of
the process which we refer to as collective bargaining. For all time,
this adversarial principle has been a prominent feature of collective
negotiations between unions and firms. However, in the best of
these relationships, both sides also realize the collective gain that
can be achieved through the successful negotiation of difficult contractual matters. And this is really where the nature of labor-
management relations lies in the game of baseball today. Both sides
recognize the legitimacy of the other party, but at the same time,
each side has certain demands for which it will press that are not
popular with the opponent. Both sides also recognize the importance of compromise and concession to the viability of their ongoing
relationship. Thus, even the toughest of issues are negotiated in
good faith by both sides in an honest and sincere attempt to reach
compromise solutions. Certainly, the toughest of these issues may
be intractable and precipitate job actions such as strikes or lockouts.
But these types of job actions, while not really common, do occur
once in a while even in the most cooperative of labor-management
relationships. The main point is that both sides realize that once
their major employment differences are settled, they will both go
back to their respective businesses of running ball clubs and playing
the game; and that is a healthy relationship indeed. Minor differences that come up during the life of the contract are handled
peacefully through the grievance/arbitration procedure, while more
major disputes over future contract terms are reserved for future
rounds of collective bargaining talks.

In recent years, there has been much talk about how unions in
general and the MLBPA in particular have ruined our economy and
indeed, our national pastime as well. The evidence presented in

this book strongly contradicts the above notion. While it is true that unionism in baseball has had major impacts on the business aspects of the sport (as reported in Chapters 3, 4, 5), it is not fair to conclude that the baseball industry is doomed to either a slow or sudden death due to unionism and the advent of collective bargaining. First, if it was meant to be a quick demise, why hasn't this holocaust already happened? After all, unions in baseball have been around for nearly 100 years, and the MLBPA itself is some 26 years old. Baseball seems to have survived quite nicely with unionization.

Others would argue that these devastating effects will not be seen as quickly, but nonetheless, this same result of financial ruin will ensue over a longer period of years. Evidence usually cited in support of this theory is the phenomenal increase in salaries that players have enjoyed in recent years, with the thought being that the clubs can't afford to pay these higher salaries and still stay in business. If that is really the case, that is, that the clubs simply can't afford these higher player price tags, one must necessarily ask, why do they pay their players so much? Economic theory would suggest that rational firms (teams) will never pay a person a salary that exceeds his worth to the organization. To argue that firms pay players more than their worth is to say that the club owners are poor businessmen. But, as we have seen, they certainly are not! Just the opposite seems to be the case.

When we think about the rising salaries of professional baseball players, we need to keep in mind the labor and product market contexts in which the clubs operated before and since unionism. As was shown in Chapter 4, the club's monopoly position in the product market (the only seller of tickets in a particular area) coupled with their monopsony position in the labor market (the only purchaser of player services because of the reserve rule) allowed the club owners to generate a set of economic rents, or excess profits, that they would not have had if their industry had been more competitive in nature. The club owners were used to exploiting players and fans (in the economic sense of the word) and would clearly resist any attempts by the players to lessen their excessive product and labor market powers. For these attempts, if successful, would necessarily mean a reduction in the operating standards to which they had become accustomed over the years.

When viewed in this light, the real impact of unionism was not to break the teams and force them into financial disruption, but instead to force the owners to share some of these excess profits with the players for once and for all. And this is exactly what typically occurs where a union is introduced into a labor market that was previously characterized as monopsonistic in nature. Bargaining ensues! The union was able to force management to share precious resources with the players more than had ever been the case in the past. The total pie of available resources was not increased or decreased by unionism. Rather, the way in which the pie was traditionally split up was radically changed. In a nutshell, the players received a bigger piece than they had been getting in the past. Rather than an increase in resources, unionism in baseball has simply led to a redistribution of the pie of resources that was already available.

It seems predictable that a person who is accustomed to receiving a very large piece of pie would react vociferously to a sudden change in the distribution of resources that would force him to take a severely trimmed-down piece. And that is exactly the way the owners reacted in the press. However, in bargaining, the owners to this day continue to refuse to argue their case on the grounds of inability to pay. If they did, under a well-known policy of the National Labor Relations Board, they would be forced to back up these statements with hard financial data. The owners are reluctant to do this, and why they are reluctant is an issue that can be debated *ad infinitum.* The clubs, for the most part, are closely held corporations and do not have to reveal their financial status to the players. It is extremely difficult to tell what type of financial shape these ball clubs are in because of data unavailability. Given a lack of data, all we have to go on are impassioned pleas made by the respective parties. And the owners' public claims of poverty are made in spite of continued ticket price increases and local and national television packages, which contribute significantly to the revenue side of the equation. One must tentatively label the owners' and fans' claims of ruination of the game due to unionization as premature and made without the benefit of hard data. The fans continue to attend games in record numbers and the owners continue to engage in the process of bargaining for free agent players. Instead of doom, one might say that these were all signs of a healthy and thriving industry within the American economy. The mere institution of unionism in baseball has not to date, and is not likely in the future, to cause the ruin of America's national pastime, the game of baseball.

In conclusion, it does appear that both sides have come a long way since the secret meeting of club owners back in the late nineteenth century when the process of revolving was dealt a severe blow. The players have been able to rise up against the reserve system and other aspects of their employment relationship that they felt were unfair through the process of collective bargaining. Many real gains have been made at the bargaining table. Much to the credit of the club owners, they have responded to this unionization on the part of their employees in a mature and responsible fashion. This positive management response to a great extent has helped to shape the relationship between the parties into what it is today, one of mutual acceptance and the willingness to sit down and negotiate differences over both major and minor issues of concern. Hopefully, this trend will continue. In any event, the evolving relations between professional baseball players and their club owners should continue to provide a fertile ground for research for many persons interested in the field of industrial and labor relations. In fact, nothing could be more gratifying to the author of this book than if these pages provide the spark necessary for the generation of further interest and research into labor-management relations in the game of baseball. For it is only through scientific research that we can really contribute to the advancement of our knowledge in any particular area.

INDEX

Notes

Chapter 3

1. Dostoevsky to Anna Grigorievna, 7 June 1880, in *Selected Letters of Fyodor Dostoevsky,* ed. Joseph Frank and David I. Goldstein, trans. Andrew R. MacAndrew (New Brunswick, N.J.: Rutgers University Press, 1987), 504, 506; hereafter cited in text as *Letters.*

2. Nicholas Berdyaev, *Dostoevsky,* trans. Donald Attwater (New York: New American Library, 1974), 227. Berdyaev's original work, *The World View of Dostoevsky* (1923), was translated into French by Lucienne Julien Cain with modifications proposed by Berdyaev himself. The English translation is based on this French version.

3. D. H. Lawrence, "On Dostoevsky and Rozanov" (a 1936 review of V. V. Rozanov's *Solitaria*) reprinted in *Russian Literature and Modern English Fiction,* ed. Donald Davie (Chicago: University of Chicago Press, 1965), 99–100; and his preface to *The Grand Inquisitor,* trans. S. S. Koteliansky (London, 1930), reprinted in Fyodor Dostoevsky, *The Brothers Karamazov: A Norton Critical Edition* (with backgrounds, sources, and essays in criticism), trans. Constance Garnett, ed. and trans. revised by Ralph E. Matlaw (New York: W. W. Norton, 1976), 829; quotations from the novel will hereafter be cited in text as *BK.*

Chapter 4

1. This idea of rhymes was first developed by J. M. Meijer in "Situation Rhyme in a Novel of Dostoevsky," in *Dutch Contributions to the Fourth International Congress of Slavists, Moscow, September 1958,* Slavistic Printings and Reprintings no. 20 (the Hague: Mouton, 1958), 115–228, and Meijer and J. Van Der Eng, *"The Brothers Karamazov" by F. M. Dostoevskij,* Dutch Studies in Russian Literature no. 2 (The Hague: Mouton, 1971).

2. Leonid Grossman, *Put' Dostoevskogo* (The [creative] path of Dostoevsky) (Leningrad: N.p., 1924), 10.

3. Robert L. Belknap, *The Structure of "The Brothers Karamazov"* (The Hague: Mouton, 1967; reprint, Evanston, Ill.: Northwestern University Press, 1989), [39–42, et passim:] hereafter cited in text as Belknap.

4. Mikhail Bakhtin, *Problems of Dostoevsky's Poetics,* trans. and ed. Caryl Emerson (Minneapolis: University of Minnesota Press, 1984), 6, 39–40, 285, et passim. hereafter cited in text as Bakhtin.

5. The notion of plagiarism will become increasingly important as the novel continues. For a fine discussion of plagiarism as a form of quotation see

Nina Perlina, *Varieties of Poetic Utterance: Quotation in "The Brothers Karamazov"* (Lanham, N.Y.: University Press of America, 1985), 46–48.

6. Victor Terras, *A Karamazov Companion: Commentary on the Genesis, Language, and Style of Dostoevsky's Novel* (Madison: University of Wisconsin Press, 1981), 12; hereafter cited in text as Terras, *Karamazov Companion.*

7. Fyodor Dostoevsky, *Notes from the House of the Dead,* trans. Jessie Coulson (Oxford: Oxford University Press, 1983), chap. 1. For the translation of this passage and an extended analysis of this prototype for Mitya see L. M. Reynus, "Prototypes and Heroes of *The Brothers Karamazov," BK,* 747–51; see also Belknap's forthcoming *The Genesis of "The Brothers Karamazov"* (Evanston, Ill.: Northwestern University Press), as well as his "The Origins of Mitja Karamazov," *American Contributions to the Seventh International Congress of Slavists, Warsaw, 21–27 August 1973,* vol. 2, in *Literature and Folklore,* ed. Victor Terras (The Hague: Mouton, 1973), 39–51.

8. *Pochva* means "soil," although it can also mean "foundation" or "support." Dostoevsky's journal *Time,* which announced the formation of the *pochvenniki* ("men of the soil"), proclaimed that the Russian intelligentsia had become cut off from its roots, from the Russian soil. The *pochvenniki* proposed to heal the breach between the Westerners and the Slavophiles by forming a synthesis out of their ideas with those of the people. Their most important aim was to improve the situation of the peasantry. See Joseph Frank, "A New Movement: *Pochvennichestvo,"* in *The Stir of Liberation, 1860–1865* (Princeton, N.J.: Princeton University Press, 1986), 34–47, 77–78. See also Ellen Chances, *Conformity's Children: An Approach to the Superfluous Man in Russian Literature* (Columbus, Ohio: Slavica, 1978), 93–104.

9. See *BK,* 756. In this brief letter of 16 May 1878 Dostoevsky tells his brother Nikolai of Alyosha's death and informs him of the day of the funeral.

10. Gary Saul Morson, "Verbal Pollution in *The Brothers Karamazov"* (1978), reprinted in *Critical Essays on Dostoevsky,* ed. Robin Feuer Miller (Boston: G. K. Hall, 1986), 235.

11. See Dostoevsky's own account of this true incident in "Foma Danilov: The Russian Hero Tortured to Death" (1877), in *The Diary of a Writer,* trans. Boris Brasol (Santa Barbara, Calif.: P. Smith, 1979), 569–574, third entry for January 1877.

Chapter 5

1. I explore the question of Ivan's possible conversion at length in "Adventures in Time and Space: Dostoevsky, William James, and the Perilous

Journey to Conversion" (manuscript in preparation, to be part of my forthcoming *Dostoevsky: Transformations and Conversions*).

2. Quoted in William James, *The Varieties of Religious Experience: A Study in Human Nature,* intro. by Reinhold Niebuhr (1902; reprint, New York: Collier Books, 1970), 307.

3. "A Gentle Creature," trans. David Magarshack, in *Great Short Works of Fyodor Dostoevsky* (New York: Harper and Row, 1968), 714.

4. Honoré de Balzac, *Old Goriot,* trans. M. A. Crawford (Harmondsworth, Eng.: Penguin Books, 1951), 157. While working on *Crime and Punishment* and the riddle of Raskolnikov's motivations for his crime, Dostoevsky had also grappled in his notebooks with what he called this "Rastignac idea."

5. Terras notes that this was one of the central ideas of the 1850s and 1860s, and that Dostoevsky may be paraphrasing, through his Grand Inquisitor's words, the section in Aleksandr Herzen's *My Past and Thoughts* (1852–55) (part 6, chap. 9) that is devoted to Robert Owen (Terras, *Karamazov Companion,* 232).

6. *Letters,* 477. He repeats the same idea and the same fraction two months later in another letter (480).

7. All the main characters of *The Brothers Karamazov* grapple with the problem of evil, and it is the Book of Job that "confuted for all time the claim that the evils men suffer are their just chastisement by God for the sins they have indubitably perpetrated." Instead, this book of the Bible refutes "utterly the theology of guilt that the prophets [had] advocated" (Lewis S. Feuer, "The Book of Job: The Wisdom of Hebraic Stoicism," in *Biblical and Secular Ethics: The Conflict,* ed. R. Joseph Hoffmann and Gerald A. Larue [Buffalo, N.Y.: Prometheus Books, 1988], 79).

Chapter 6

1. *BK,* 762–63. In another letter Dostoevsky observed that by the end of Book VII, "the *spirit* and *meaning* of the novel had been fulfilled" (*Letters,* 478). In *Letters* Joseph Frank points out that the story of the onion had in fact already appeared in two different versions of A. N. Afanaseva's 1859 collection of Russian legends. For a fascinating account of this legend and its role in the novel see Sarah Smyth, "The 'Lukovka' Legend in *The Brothers Karamazov,*" *Irish Slavonic Studies* 7 (1986): 41–53.

2. Robin Feuer Miller, *Dostoevsky and "The Idiot": Author, Narrator, and Reader* (Cambridge, Mass.: Harvard University Press, 1981), 153–58.

3. Miller, *Dostoevsky and The Idiot,* 273.

Chapter 7

1. For a fuller discussion of Strakhov's critique and Dostoevsky's response see Miller, *Dostoevsky and "The Idiot,"* 19–20, 27–28, 43–44.

2. For a compelling discussion of the vital tension between image and its disfiguring (*obraz* and *bezobrazie*) that operates in both Dostoevsky's aesthetic and moral thinking see Robert Louis Jackson, *The Art of Dostoevsky: Deliriums and Nocturnes* (Princeton, N.J.: Princeton University Press, 1981), 18–19, 95–96, 304–5.

3. Ya. E. Golosovker, "The Words 'Secret' and 'Mystery,' " trans. Ralph E. Matlaw, in *BK,* 857.

4. For an extended discussion of this little frame tale of the drunken peasant see my essay "Adventures in Time and Space," in which I also examine in more detail the question of the devil as a practitioner of homeopathy.

5. Homeopathy is directly opposed to the "allopathic" practices of mainstream medicine. Allopathic medicine seeks remedies that produce effects different from those of the disease, whereas the practitioners of homeopathy— who were discredited yet popular in the nineteenth century—maintained that illness was best cured by giving medicines that mimicked rather than masked the symptoms of disease. The motto of homeopathic wisdom was, "Let likes be cured with likes." See Stephen Cummings, F.N.P., and Dana Ullman, M.P.H., *Everybody's Guide to Homeopathic Medicines* (Los Angeles: Jeremy P. Tarcher, n.d.), 8. Samuel Hahnemann, the eighteenth-century founder of homeopathy, coined the phrase *similia similibus currentur.*

6. I use the term "fantastic" as it has been defined by Tzvetan Todorov in *The Fantastic: A Structural Approach to a Literary Genre,* trans. Richard Howard (Ithaca, N.Y.: Cornell University Press, 1973), 3. Dostoevsky's observations on the fantastic in his 1861 preface to three stories of Edgar Allan Poe, which appeared in translation in *Time* (see chapter 4, note 8 above), exhibit his own canny apprehension that the mood of the fantastic is most effectively conveyed when it is enmeshed in occurrences that otherwise conform to the laws of everyday reality. See F. M. Dostoevsky, *Polnoe sobranie sochinenii v tridtsati tomakh,* 19:88.

7. See "The Kroneberg Case," trans. Ralph E. Matlaw, *BK,* 770–774. Dostoevsky polemicized with Spasovich over his defense arguments in the article excerpted here by Matlaw from *Diary of a Writer* (February 1876).

Selected Bibliography

Primary Works

The authoritative source for all of Dostoevsky's work is the *Polnoe sobranie sochinenii v tridtsati tomakh* (Leningrad: Nauka, 1972–   ). The general editors for this edition are V. G. Bazanov and G. M. Fridlender. *The Brothers Karamazov* appears in volumes 14 and 15. Volume 15 also contains variants to the text, notebooks for the novel, and an invaluable commentary with critical notes. This edition offers similar material for all of Dostoevsky's work and, for the reader able to read Russian, provides an astounding wealth of material. Another fine work is the collection of Dostoevsky's letters, *Pis'ma* (Letters), 4 vols., edited by A. S. Dolinin (Moscow and Leningrad: Gosizdat, 1928–59).

Primary works in Translation

I have listed the translations that I consider to be the best. The following list appears in a general chronological order, although shorter works published in collections are grouped together. Please refer to the chronology at the beginning of this book for a listing of Dostoevsky's works in the precise order in which he wrote them.

Poor Folk and Other Stories. Translated by David McDuff. New York: Viking Penguin, 1988. Contains *Poor Folk* (1846), "The Landlady" (1847), "Mr. Prokharchin" (1846), and "Polzunkov" (1847).

Great Short Works of Fyodor Dostoevsky. Introduction by Ronald Hingley. New York: Harper & Row, 1968. Includes *The Double* (1846), translated by George Bird; *White Nights* (1848), translated by David Magarshack; "A Disgraceful Affair" (1862), translated by Constance Garnett; *The Eternal Husband* (1870), translated by Constance Garnett; "A Gentle Creature" (1876), translated by David Magarshack; "The Dream of a Ridiculous Man" (1877), translated by David Magarshack.

Netochka Nezvanova (1849). Translated by Jane Kentish. New York: Viking Penguin, 1986.

"Uncle's Dream" (1859). In *The Short Novels of Dostoevsky*. Translated by Constance Garnett. New York: Dial Press, 1945.

The Village of Stepanchikovo and Its Inhabitants (1859). Translated by Ignat Avsey. London: Angel Classics, 1983.

Memoirs from the House of the Dead (1860–62). Translated by Jessie Coulson. Oxford: Oxford University Press, 1983.

The Insulted and Injured (1861). Translated by Constance Garnett. Westport, Conn.: Greenwood Press, 1975.

Winter Notes on Summer Impressions (1863). Translated by David Patterson. Evanston, Ill.: Northwestern University Press, 1988.

The Gambler (1866), with *"The Diary of Polina Suslova."* Translated by Victor Terras. Chicago: University of Chicago Press, 1972.

Crime and Punishment: Backgrounds and Sources, Essays in Criticism (1866). Edited by George Gibian. Translated by Jessie Coulson. New York: W. W. Norton, 1989.

The Idiot (1868). Translated by Olga and Henry Carlyle. New York: New American Library, 1969.

The Devils (often translated as *The Possessed*) (1871). Translated by David Magarshack. Middlesex, Eng.: Penguin, 1954.

A Raw Youth (sometimes translated as *The Adolescent*) (1875). Translated by Constance Garnett. New York: Dial Press, 1947.

The Diary of a Writer (1873–81). Translated by Boris Brasol. Introduction by Joseph Frank. Santa Barbara, Calif.: P. Smith, 1979. The *Diary* contains, in addition to a large mass of Dostoevsky's journalistic essays, numerous short stories, including "The Boy at Christ's Christmas Tree" (1876) and "The Peasant Marei" (1876).

The Brothers Karamazov: A Norton Critical Edition, with backgrounds, sources, and essays in criticism. Translated by Constance Garnett. Revised and edited by Ralph E. Matlaw. New York: W. W. Norton, 1976.

The Brothers Karamazov: A Novel in Four Parts with Epilogue. Translated and annotated by Richard Pevear and Larissa Volokhonsky. San Francisco: North Point Press, 1990.

Selected Bibliography

Notebooks and Occasional Writings

The Unpublished Dostoevsky: Diaries and Notebooks, 1860–81. 3 vols. Edited by Carl R. Proffer. Introduction by Robert L. Belknap. Translated by T. S. Berczynski, Barbara Heldt Monter, Arline Boyer, and Ellendea Proffer. Ann Arbor, Mich.: Ardis, 1973–76.

Dostoevsky's Occasional Writings. Translated by David Magarshack. New York: Random House, 1963. Contains four essays from the *Petersburg News* (1847), five articles from *Time* (1860–62), and other useful sketches and manifestos.

The Notebooks for "Crime and Punishment." Edited and translated by Edward Wasiolek. Chicago: University of Chicago Press, 1967.

The Notebooks for "The Idiot." Edited by Edward Wasiolek. Translated by Katharine Strelsky. Chicago: University of Chicago Press, 1967.

The Notebooks for "The Possessed." Edited by Edward Wasiolek. Translated by Victor Terras. Chicago: University of Chicago Press, 1968.

The Notebooks for "A Raw Youth." Edited by Edward Wasiolek. Translated by Victor Terras. Chicago: University of Chicago Press, 1969.

The Notebooks for "The Brothers Karamazov." Edited and translated by Edward Wasiolek. Chicago: University of Chicago Press, 1971.

Letters

Dostoevsky: A Self Portrait. Edited by Jessie Coulson. Westport, Conn.: Greenwood Press, 1962.

Selected Letters of Fyodor Dostoevsky. Edited by Joseph Frank and David I. Goldstein. Translated by Andrew R. MacAndrew. New Brunswick, N.J.: Rutgers University Press, 1987.

Fyodor Dostoevsky: Complete Letters. 2 vols. (other volumes forthcoming). Edited and translated by David Lowe and Ronald Meyer. Ann Arbor, Mich.: Ardis, 1988–89.

Bibliographies

There are several bibliographies that offer invaluable help in tracking down works by and about Dostoevsky. I have listed the most useful and accessible ones. See also the *Bulletin of the International Dostoevsky Society,* volumes 1–9 (1972–79), and the ongoing listings in *Dostoevsky Studies.*

F. M. Dostoevskii: Bibliografia proizvedenii F. M. Dostoevskogo i literatury o nem 1917–1965 (a bibliography of Dostoevsky's works and of works about him). Edited by A. A. Belkin, A. S. Dolinin, V. V. Kozhinov, and S. V. Belov. Moscow: Kniga, 1968.

Fedor Dostoevsky: A Reference Guide. Edited by W. J. Leatherbarrow. Boston: G. K. Hall, 1990. This is a superb guide.

Fyodor Mikhailovich Dostoevsky: A Bibliography of Non-Slavic Criticism about Him: 1900–1980. Edited by Martin P. Rice. Knoxville: University of Tennessee Press, 1984.

Seduro, Vladimir. *Dostoevski's Image in Russia Today.* Belmont, Mass.: Nordland Press, 1975.

———. *Dostoyevski in Russian Literary Criticism.* New York: Columbia University Press, 1957.

Secondary Works

These works are the most rewarding and useful for the general reader of Dostoevsky and *The Brothers Karamazov* to pursue. The titles are, for the most part, self-explanatory. I have included a few essential titles in Russian.

Books

Anderson, Roger. *Dostoevsky: Myths of Duality.* Gainesville: University of Florida Press, 1986.

Bakhtin, Mikhail. *Problems of Dostoevsky's Poetics.* Edited and translated by Caryl Emerson. Introduction by Wayne C. Booth. Minneapolis: University of Minnesota Press, 1984.

Belknap, Robert L. *The Genesis of "The Brothers Karamazov."* Evanston, Ill.: Northwestern University Press, 1991.

———. *The Structure of "The Brothers Karamazov."* The Hague: Mouton, 1967; reprint, Evanston, Ill.: Northwestern University Press, 1989.

Berdyaev, Nicholas. *Dostoevsky.* Translated by Donald Attwater. New York: New American Library, 1974.

Camus, Albert. *The Rebel: An Essay on Man in Revolt.* Translated by Anthony Bower. New York: Vintage, 1956.

Catteau, Jacques. *Dostoyevsky and the Process of Literary Creation.* Translated by Audrey Littlewood. Cambridge Studies in Russian Literature. Cambridge, Eng.: Cambridge University Press, 1989.

Selected Bibliography

Chances, Ellen. *Conformity's Children: An Approach to the Superfluous Man in Russian Literature*. Columbus, Ohio: Slavica, 1978.

Chapple, Richard. *A Dostoevsky Dictionary*. Ann Arbor, Mich.: Ardis, 1983.

Cox, Roger L. *Between Earth and Heaven: Shakespeare, Dostoevsky, and the Meaning of Christian Tragedy*. New York: Holt, Rinehart & Winston, 1969.

Dostoyevsky, Aimée. *Fyodor Dostoyevsky: A Study*. London: Heinemann, 1921. A largely unreliable account of her father's life. An important source for Freud.

Dostoevsky, Anna. *Dostoevsky: Reminiscences*. Translated by Beatrice Stillman. New York: Liveright, 1975.

Dunlop, John B. *Staretz Amvrosy: Model for Dostoevsky's Staretz Zossima*. Belmont, Mass.: Nordland, 1972.

Fanger, Donald. *Dostoevsky and Romantic Realism: A Study of Dostoevsky in Relation to Balzac, Dickens, and Gogol*. Cambridge, Mass.: Harvard University Press, 1965.

Frank, Joseph. *Dostoevsky: The Seeds of Revolt, 1821–1849*. Princeton, N.J.: Princeton University Press, 1976.

———. *Dostoevsky: The Years of Ordeal, 1850–1860*. Princeton, N.J.: Princeton University Press, 1983.

———. *Dostoevsky: The Stir of Liberation, 1860–1865*. Princeton, N.J.: Princeton University Press, 1986.

Gide, André. *Dostoevsky*. Translated by Arnold Bennett. Norfolk, Conn.: New Directions Books, 1961.

Girard, René. *Deceit, Desire, and the Novel: Self and Other in Literary Structure*. Translated by Y. Freccero. Baltimore: Johns Hopkins University Press, 1965.

Goldstein, David I. *Dostoevsky and the Jews*. Austin: University of Texas Press, 1981.

Grossman, Leonid. *Balzac and Dostoevsky*. Translated by Lena Karpov. Ann Arbor, Mich.: Ardis, 1973.

———. *Biblioteka Dostoevskogo po neizdannym materialam. S prilozheniem kataloga biblioteki Dostoevskogo* (Dostoevsky's library). Odessa: Ivasenko, 1919. Catalogs Dostoevsky's personal library.

———. *Dostoevsky: His Life and Works*. Translated by Mary Mackler. Indianapolis: Bobbs-Merrill, 1975.

———. *Put' Dostoevskogo* (The [creative] path of Dostoevsky). Leningrad: N.p., 1924. Analyzes Dostoevsky's intellectual development and the influence of romanticism and utopian socialist thought upon him.

Holquist, James Michael. *Dostoevsky and the Novel.* Princeton, N.J.: Princeton University Press, 1977.

Ivanov, Vyacheslav I. *Freedom and the Tragic Life: A Study in Dostoevsky.* Translated by Norman Cameron. New introduction by Robert Louis Jackson. Wolfeboro, N.H.: Longwood Academic, 1989.

Jackson, Robert Louis. *The Art of Dostoevsky: Deliriums and Nocturnes.* Princeton, N.J.: Princeton University Press, 1981.

——, ed. *Dostoevsky: New Perspectives.* Englewood Cliffs, N.J.: Prentice-Hall, 1984.

——. *Dostoevsky's Quest for Form: A Study of His Philosophy of Art.* Bloomington, Ind.: Physsardt, 1978.

Jones, John. *Dostoevsky.* Oxford: Clarendon Press, 1983.

Jones, Malcolm V. *Dostoevsky after Bakhtin: Readings in Dostoevsky's Fantastic Realism.* Cambridge, Eng.: Cambridge University Press, 1990.

——. *Dostoevsky: The Novel of Discord.* New York: Barnes & Noble, 1976.

——and Terry Garth, eds. *New Essays on Dostoyevsky.* Cambridge, Eng.: Cambridge University Press, 1983.

Kjetsaa, Geir. *Dostoevsky and His New Testament.* Atlantic Highlands, N.Y.: Humanities Press, 1984.

——. *Fyodor Dostoevsky: A Writer's Life.* London and New York: Macmillan Press, 1988.

Linner, Sven. *Dostoevskij on Realism.* Stockholm: Almqvist and Wiksell, 1962.

——. *Starets Zosima in "The Brothers Karamazov": A Study of the Mimesis of Virtue.* Stockholm: Almqvist and Wiksell, 1975.

Lord, Robert. *Dostoevsky: Essays and Perspectives.* London: Chatto & Windus, 1970.

Matlaw, Ralph E. *"The Brothers Karamazov": Novelistic Technique.* The Hague: Mouton, 1957.

Mikhailovsky, Nikolai. *Dostoevsky: A Cruel Talent.* Translated by Spencer Cadmus. Ann Arbor, Mich.: Ardis, 1978.

Miller, Robin Feuer, ed. *Critical Essays on Dostoevsky.* Boston: G. K. Hall, 1986.

——. *Dostoevsky and "The Idiot": Author, Narrator, and Reader.* Cambridge, Mass.: Harvard University Press, 1981.

Mochulsky, Konstantin. *Dostoevsky: His Life and Work.* Translated by Michael Minihan. Princeton, N.J.: Princeton University Press, 1967.

Morson, Gary Saul. *The Boundaries of Genre: Dostoevsky's "Diary of a*

Selected Bibliography

Writer" and the Traditions of Literary Utopia. Austin: University of Texas Press, 1981.

Peace, Richard. *Dostoyevsky: An Examination of the Major Novels.* Cambridge, Eng.: Cambridge University Press, 1971.

Perlina, Nina. *Varieties of Poetic Utterance: Quotation in "The Brothers Karamazov."* Lanham, N.Y.: University Press of America, 1985.

Rice, James L. *Dostoevsky and the Healing Art: An Essay in Literary and Medical History.* Ann Arbor, Mich.: Ardis, 1985.

Rozanov, V. *Dostoevsky and the Grand Inquisitor.* Translated by Spencer I. Roberts. Ithaca, N.Y.: Cornell University Press, 1972.

Sandoz, Ellis. *Political Apocalypse: A Study of Dostoevsky's Grand Inquisitor.* Baton Rouge: Louisiana State University Press, 1971.

Shestov, Lev. *Dostoevsky, Tolstoy, and Nietzsche.* Translated by Spencer I. Roberts. Athens: Ohio University Press, 1969.

Simmons, Ernest J. *Dostoevsky: The Making of a Novelist.* New York: Random House/Vintage Books, 1940.

Steiner, George. *Tolstoy or Dostoevsky?: An Essay in the Old Criticism.* New York: Vintage Books, 1959.

Terras, Victor. *A Karamazov Companion: Commentary on the Genesis, Language, and Style of Dostoevsky's Novel.* Madison: University of Wisconsin Press, 1981.

Thompson, Diane E. Oenning. *"The Brothers Karamazov" and the Poetics of Memory.* Cambridge, Eng.: Cambridge University Press, forthcoming.

Tynianov, Iu. N. *Dostoevsky and Gogol.* Part 1. Edited and translated by Priscilla Meyer and Stephen Rudy. Ann Arbor, Mich.: Ardis, 1979.

———. *Dostoevsky and Gogol.* Part II. Edited and translated by Priscilla Meyer and Stephen Rudy. In *Twentieth-Century Russian Literary Criticism.* Edited by Victor Erlich. New Haven, Conn.: Yale University Press, 1975.

Volgin, I. L. *Poslednii god Dostoevskogo: Istoricheskie zapiski* (Dostoevsky's Last year: Historical notes). Moscow: Sovetskii pisatel, 1986. A historical and novelistic re-creation of the last year of Dostoevsky's life.

Ward, Bruce K. *Dostoyevsky's Critique of the West: The Quest for the Earthly Paradise.* Waterloo, Ont.: Wilfried Laurier University Press, 1988.

Wasiolek, Edward. *Dostoevsky: The Major Fiction.* Cambridge, Mass.: MIT Press, 1964.

———, ed. *"The Brothers Karamazov" and the Critics.* Belmont, Calif.: Wadsworth Publishing Co., 1967.

Wellek, René, ed. *Dostoevsky: A Collection of Critical Essays.* Englewood Cliffs, N.J.: Prentice-Hall, 1962.

Zakharov, V. N. *Sistema zhanrov Dostoevskogo: Tipologiia i poetika* (Dostoevsky's system of genres: Typology and poetics). Leningrad: Leningradskogo universiteta, 1985. The classification of Dostoevsky's novels by genre, his creation of new genres, and new hybrids of genres.

Zander, L. A. *Dostoevsky*. London: SCM Press, 1948.

Articles and Parts of Books

Belknap, Robert L. "Dostoevsky's Nationalist Ideology and Rhetoric." *Review of National Literatures* 3, no. 1 (Spring 1972): 89–100.

————. "The Origins of Alesa Karamazov." *American Contributions to the Sixth International Congress of Slavists, Prague, 7–13 August 1968*, vol. 2. In *Literary Contributions*, edited by William Harkins, 7–28. The Hague: Mouton, 1968.

————. "The Rhetoric of an Ideological Novel." In *Literature and Society in Imperial Russia 1800–1914*, edited by William Mills Todd III, 173–201. Stanford, Calif.: Stanford University Press, 1978.

————. "The Sources of Mitja Karamazov." *American Contributions to the Seventh International Congress of Slavists. Warsaw, 21–27 August 1973*, vol. 2. In *Literature and Folklore*, edited by Victor Terras, 39–51. The Hague: Mouton, 1973.

Berlin, Isaiah. "The Hedghog and the Fox." In *Russian Thinkers*, 22–81. New York: Viking, 1978.

Catteau, Jacques. "The Paradox of the Legend of the Grand Inquisitor," translated by Françoise Rosset. In *Dostoevsky: New Perspectives*, edited by Robert Louis Jackson, 243–54. Englewood Cliffs, N.J.: Prentice-Hall, 1984.

Chances, Ellen. "Literary Criticism and the Ideology of 'Pochvennichestvo' in Dostoevsky's Thick Journals *Vremia* and *Epokha*." *Russian Review* 34 (1975): 151–64.

Freud, Sigmund. "Dostoevsky and Parricide." In *Dostoevsky: A Collection of Critical Essays*, edited by René Wellek, 98–111. Englewood Cliffs, N.J.: Prentice-Hall, 1962.

Hackel, Sergei. "The Religious Dimension: Vision or Evasion: Zosima's Discourse in *The Brothers Karamazov*." In *New Essays on Dostoevsky*, edited by Malcolm Jones and Garth Terry, 139–68. Cambridge, Eng.: Cambridge University Press, 1983.

Jones, Malcolm V. "Dostoyevsky: Driving the Reader Crazy." *Essays in Poetics* 12, no. 1 (1987):57–80.

Selected Bibliography

————. "The Legend of the Grand Inquisitor: The Suppression of the Second Temptation and the Dialogue with God." *Dostoevsky Studies* 7 (1986): 123–34.

Kelly, Aileen. "Dostoevsky and the Divided Conscience." *Slavic Review* 47 (1988): 239–60.

Knapp, Liza. "The Fourth Dimension of the Non-Euclidean Mind: Time in *The Brothers Karamazov* or Why Ivan Karamazov's Devil Does Not Carry a Watch." *Dostoevsky Studies* 8 (1988): 105–120.

Likhachov, D. S. "Predislovnyi rasskaz' Dostoevskogo" (Dostoevsky's 'Prefatory Narrative'). In *Poetika i stilistika russkoi literatury: Pamiati akademika V. V. Vinogradova* (Poetics and stylistics of Russian literature): 189–94. Leningrad: Nauka, 1971. An analysis of Dostoevsky's prefatory remarks.

Meijer, J. M. "Situation Rhyme in a Novel of Dostoevsky." *Dutch Contributions to the Fourth International Congress of Slavists, September 1958*, Slavistic Printings and Reprintings no. 20, 115–29. The Hague: Mouton, 1958.

Miller, Robin Feuer. "Dostoevsky and the Tale of Terror." In *The Russian Novel from Pushkin to Pasternak*, edited by John G. Garrard, 103–21. New Haven, Conn.: Yale University Press, 1983.

————. "The Metaphysical Novel and the Evocation of Anxiety: *Melmoth the Wanderer* and *The Brothers Karamazov*, A Case Study." In *Russianness: Studies on a Nation's Identity. In Honor of Rufus Mathewson, 1918–1978*, 94–112. Studies of the Harriman Institute. Ann Arbor, Mich.: Ardis, 1990.

Milosz, Czeslaw. "Dostoevsky and Swedenborg." In *Emperor of the Earth: Modes of Eccentric Vision*, 120–44. Berkeley: University of California Press, 1977.

Morson, Gary Saul. "Verbal Pollution in *The Brothers Karamazov*." In *Critical Essays on Dostoevsky*, edited by Robin Feuer Miller, 234–43. Boston: G. K. Hall, 1986.

Moser, Charles A. "*The Brothers Karamazov* as a Novel of the 1860s." *Dostoevsky Studies* 7 (1986): 73–80.

Natov, Nadine. "The Ethical and Structural Significance of the Three Temptations in *The Brothers Karamazov*." *Dostoevsky Studies* 8 (1987): 3–44.

Rosen, Nathan. "Style and Structure in *The Brothers Karamazov*: The Grand Inquisitor and the Russian Monk." *Russian Literature Triquarterly* 1 (1971): 352–65.

————. "Why Dmitri Karamazov Did Not Kill His Father." *Canadian American Slavic Studies* 6 (1972): 209–24.

Smyth, Sarah. "The 'Lukovka' Legend in *The Brothers Karamazov*." *Irish Slavonic Studies* 7 (1986): 41–53.

Terras, Victor. "The Art of Fiction as a Theme in *The Brothers Karamazov.*" In *Dostoevsky: New Perspectives,* edited by Robert Louis Jackson, 193–206. Englewood Cliffs, N.J.: Prentice-Hall, 1984.

———. "On the Nature of Evil in *The Brothers Karamazov.*" In *Text and Context: Essays to Honor Nils Ake Nilsson. Stockholm Studies in Russian Literature* 23 (1987): 58–64.

Thompson, Diane E. Oenning. "Poetic Transformations of Scientific Facts in *Brat'ia Karamazovy.*" *Dostoevsky Studies* 8 (1987): 73–91.

Todd, William Mills, III. "*The Brothers Karamazov* and the Poetics of Serial Publication." *Dostoevsky Studies* 7 (1986): 87–97.

Vetlovskaia, V. E. "Alyosha Karamazov and the Hagiographic Hero," translated by Nancy Pollack and Susanne Fusso. In *Dostoevsky: New Perspectives,* edited by Robert Louis Jackson, 206–26. Englewood Cliffs, N.J.: Prentice-Hall, 1984.

———. "Rhetoric and Poetics: The Affirmation and Refutation of Opinions in Dostoevsky's *The Brothers Karamazov,*" translated by Diana L. Burgin. In *Critical Essays on Dostoevsky,* edited by Robin Feuer Miller, 223–34. Boston: G. K. Hall, 1986.

Woolf, Virginia. "More Dostoevsky." *Times Literary Supplement* (22 February 1917). Reprinted in *Books and Portraits: Some Further Selections from the Literary and Biographical Writings of Virginia Woolf,* edited by Mary Lyon, 116–19. New York: Harcourt Brace Jovanovich, 1981.

———. "The Russian Point of View." In *The Common Reader,* 219–31. London: Hogarth Press, 1925.

Index

Index

Index

Index

The Author

Robin Feuer Miller is professor of Russian and comparative literature at Brandeis University. She has also been affiliated for the past 13 years with the Harvard Russian Research Center. She is the author of *Dostoevsky and "The Idiot": Author, Narrator, and Reader* (1981) and the editor of *Critical Essays on Dostoevsky* (1986). She is currently at work on *Dostoevsky: Transformations and Conversions*. Her other scholarly work has had a comparative focus. She lives in Massachusetts with her husband and their three daughters.